RUPERT'S LAND
A Cultural Tapestry

Edited by
Richard C. Davis

Essays by

Richard I. Ruggles

Olive P. Dickason

John L. Allen

Clive Holland

Sylvia Van Kirk

James G.E. Smith

Robert Stacey

Irene M. Spry

Fred Crabb

Edward Cavell

R. Douglas Francis

Robert H. Cockburn

Published by Wilfrid Laurier University Press
for The Calgary Institute for the Humanities

Canadian Cataloguing in Publication Data

Main entry under title:

Rupert's Land : a cultural tapestry

Revised versions of papers presented at a
conference held at the University of Calgary,
Jan. 30-Feb. 2, 1986.
Includes bibliographical references and index.
ISBN 0-88920-976-6

1. Rupert's Land — Congresses.   2. Northwest,
Canadian — History — Congresses.   3. Northwest,
Canadian — Description and travel — Congresses.
I. Davis, Richard Clarke, 1946- . II. Ruggles,
Richard I., 1923- . III. Calgary Institute
for the Humanities.

FC3206.R86 1988   971.2'01   C88-094424-2
F1060.R86 1988

61,117

Copyright © 1988
Wilfrid Laurier University Press
Waterloo, Ontario, Canada
N2L 3C5
88 89 90 91 4 3 2 1

Cover design by *Rachelle Longtin*

Printed in Canada

Rupert's Land: A Cultural Tapestry has been produced from a manuscript
supplied in camera-ready form by The Calgary Institute for the Humanities.

Cover: George Back, *Panoramic View 8 Miles from Fort Franklin* . . . 1826,
watercolour in pencil. PAC 93036. Courtesy Public Archives of Canada.
Back cover insets: Eskimo at Little Whale River; Rupert's House salt
store and forge; Long Dog and George Wells; Sir John Ross, *Passage
through the Ice*; perimeter of Rupert's Land (cartographer R. Hough)

TABLE OF CONTENTS

Foreword v

Preface vii

About the Authors ix

Introduction 1

1. Beyond the "Furious Over Fall": Map Images of
   Rupert's Land and the Northwest 13

   Richard I. Ruggles, Queen's University,
   Kingston, Ontario

2. Three Worlds, One Focus: Europeans Meet Inuit and
   Amerindians in the Far North 51

   Olive Patricia Dickason, University of Alberta,
   Edmonton, Alberta

3. To Unite the Discoveries: The American Response
   to the Early Exploration of Rupert's Land 79

   John L. Allen, University of Connecticut,
   Storrs, Connecticut

4. John Franklin and the Fur Trade, 1819-22 97

   Clive Holland, Scott Polar Research Institute,
   University of Cambridge, Cambridge, England

5. "This Rascally & Ungrateful Country": George Nelson's
   Response to Rupert's Land 113

   Sylvia Van Kirk, University of Toronto,
   Toronto, Ontario

6. Chipewyan and Fur Trader Views of Rupert's Land 131

   James G.E. Smith, Museum of the American Indian,
   New York

7. From "Icy Picture" to "Extensive Prospect": The
   Panorama of Rupert's Land and the Far North in the Artist's
   Eye, 1770-1830 147

   Robert Stacey, Toronto, Ontario

iii

8. The Palliser Expedition 195

    Irene M. Spry, Professor Emeritus, University of Ottawa,
    Ottawa, Ontario

9. The Church in the North 213

    Fred Crabb, Former Bishop of Rupert's Land,
    Calgary, Alberta

10. Image of Transition: Photography in Rupert's Land 227

    Edward Cavell, Peter Whyte Foundation,
    Banff, Alberta

11. The Ideal and the Real: The Image of the Canadian West
    in the Settlement Period 253

    R. Douglas Francis, University of Calgary,
    Calgary, Alberta

12. After-Images of Rupert's Land from The Journals of Ernest
    Oberholtzer (1912) and P.G. Downes (1939) 275

    Robert H. Cockburn, University of New Brunswick,
    Fredericton, New Brunswick

Index 298

FOREWORD

Established in 1976, the Calgary Institute for the Humanities has as its aim the fostering of advanced study and research in all areas of the humanities. Apart from supporting work in the traditional "arts" disciplines such as philosophy, history, ancient and modern languages and literatures, it also promotes research into the philosophical and historical aspects of the sciences, social sciences, fine arts, and the various "professional" disciplines.

The Institute's main *raison d'être* is to provide scholars, both established academics and post-doctoral fellows, with time to carry out their research. It also sponsors gatherings of persons who share common academic and intellectual interests, with a view to promoting discussion and disseminating ideas.

The Rupert's Land conference, held at the University of Calgary from January 30 to February 2, 1986, was such a gathering. The conference brought together a distinguished collection of scholars from Canada, the United States, and Great Britain and representing a variety of academic disciplines — history, literature, geography, art history, anthropology and religious studies. During the conference the scholars succeeded in constructing a cultural tapestry of the initial responses to Rupert's Land during the period of its control by the Hudson's Bay Company. These responses lay bare the roots of many of today's societal attitudes in Canada. The Institute is very pleased to publish here revised versions of the conference papers as a contribution to our understanding of the role played by Rupert's Land in Canada's cultural development.

We wish to record here our gratitude to The University of Calgary, and to the Social Sciences and Humanities Research Council of Canada for the grants which made the conference possible, and also to the Departments of English, History, Geography, the Faculties of Humanities and Social Sciences, University of Calgary, for their support. Publication has been made possible, in part, by a grant from the Endowment Fund of The University of Calgary. Thanks are due also, of course, to the editor of the volume, Richard Davis. We thank Jennifer Bailey for typing the volume.

Harold G. Coward, Director
The Calgary Institute for the Humanities

PREFACE BY THE EDITOR

The papers in this volume arise from an international conference entitled "Rupert's Land: A Cultural Tapestry" that was held from January 30 to February 2, 1986, at the University of Calgary. The conference, sponsored by the Calgary Institute for the Humanities, presented the same papers published here, although they have been revised by the authors to accommodate the insight and knowledge they gained from participating in this interdisciplinary meeting.

In addition to the much welcomed financial support acknowledged in Dr. Coward's Foreword, many individuals deserve a word of thanks. They include Don Smith, Wayne Davies, and Constance Martin for assisting with the conference, and Barbara Belyea for her important role in its initial conception. Harold Coward's close direction on how to turn an idea into a reality warrants a special expression of gratitude, as does the careful handling of details by Gerry Dyer. Jennifer Bailey has patiently and painstakingly prepared the camera-ready copy for this volume.

Richard C. Davis
The University of Calgary

ABOUT THE AUTHORS

John L. Allen is Professor of Geography at the University of Connecticut, where he has taught for the past twenty years. His interests in historical geography and the exploration of the American West have resulted in dozens of journal articles and book chapters. Of special relevance to his work here is *Passage Through the Garden: Lewis and Clark and the Image of the American Northwest*, which he published in 1975.

Edward J.R. Cavell has been the Curator of Photography at the Whyte Museum of the Canadian Rockies in Banff since 1977. The recipient of numerous awards and grants, Cavell is the author of *Sometimes a Great Nation: A Photo Album of Canada 1850-1925* (1984) and *Journeys to the Far West* (1979), to name but two of his books.

Robert H. Cockburn, who served for ten years as Head of his Department, is Professor of English at The University of New Brunswick. In addition to his considerable publications on Canadian poetry and fiction, Cockburn has written extensively on P.G. Downes for such journals as *Arctic*, *The Beaver*, and *Fram*. He is preparing for publication both a new edition of Downes's *Sleeping Island* and Oberholtzer's journal of his 1912 voyage.

Frederick Hugh Wright Crabb, now retired and living in Calgary, has served in many Anglican Church positions in England, the Sudan, and Canada. He was Principal, College of Emmanuel and St. Chad in Saskatoon between 1957 and 1967. After a number of years in Alberta, he was elected Metropolitan of Rupert's Land, with the title Archbishop of Athabasca in 1977, an office he held until his retirement in 1983.

Olive Patricia Dickason is Professor of History at the University of Alberta. Her books *Indian Arts in Canada* (1972) and *The Myth of the Savage and the Beginnings of French Colonialism in the Americas* (1984), as well as her many articles on relationships between Indians and European explorers and traders, have established her solid reputation in the field.

R. Douglas Francis, Associate Professor of History at the University of Calgary, is the author of the recently published *Frank H. Underhill: A Biography* (1986). His interests in the perception of the Canadian West have led to many publications, notably *The Prairie West: Historical Readings* (1985).

Clive A. Holland, former Archivist and Assistant Librarian at the Scott Polar Research Institute in Cambridge, England, is presently a Leverhulme Trust Fellow. He co-authored *The Exploration of Northern Canada, 500 to 1920; a chronology* (1978) with Alan Cooke and is collaborating with Richard C. Davis on an edition of John Franklin's journals and correspondence from his two land expeditions.

Richard I. Ruggles, Professor of Geography, founded the Department of Geography at Queen's University in 1960, and served as its Head for many years. A historical cartographer and geographer, Ruggles has numerous articles on the geography of Rupert's Land to his credit, and his book *Hudson's Bay Company Maps 1670-1870* has just been completed.

James G.E. Smith has been Curator of North American Ethnology at the Museum of the American Indian, Heye Foundation, in New York for the past decade. He is also Research Associate in Ethnology at the Royal Ontario Museum. He was previously on the staff of the National Museum of Man in Ottawa. His interests as a social anthropologist have included extensive fieldwork with Chipewyan, Cree, and Ojibwa, and have resulted in numerous publications on the structure, cultural ecology, and interethnic relations of the Canadian subarctic.

Irene M. Spry, Professor Emeritus of Economics at the University of Ottawa, has published extensively on matters related to the development of the Canadian prairies. Her interests in the expedition of John Palliser provide the core for many of these articles, and her reputation as Canada's foremost Palliser scholar is soundly based on her books *The Palliser Expedition* (1964) and *The Papers of the Palliser Expedition, 1857-1860* (1968).

Robert Stacey is a Toronto-based freelance writer, exhibition curator, and editor. Of relevance to this volume are his *"Western Sunlight:" C.W. Jefferys on the Canadian Prairies* (1985), and the forthcoming editions of George Back's 1825-27 and Lieut. Owen Stanley's 1836-37 illustrated arctic expeditionary journals that he is preparing for the Archives of Canadian Art imprint.

Sylvia Van Kirk is Associate Professor of History at the University of Toronto, where she teaches Canadian history and women's studies. Well known in fur-trade circles, she studied under Glyndwr Williams at the University of London, is the former General Editor for the Champlain Society, and is author of *"Many Tender Ties": Women in Fur Trade Society in Western Canada, 1670-1870* (1980).

INTRODUCTION

Richard Davis

Between 1670 and 1869, the Hudson's Bay Company held an exclusive trading charter over all lands drained into Hudson Bay. For nearly two centuries, the Company exported hundreds of thousands of pelts and left in exchange a wealth of European trade goods, a commerce that dramatically influenced the economic and historical development of the vast region known as Rupert's Land.

An influence less widely recognized, though of perhaps even greater relevance to twentieth-century Canada, rests in the intangible produce stimulated by that material trade. The fur industry drew Europeans to an alien land totally unknown to them, and these new arrivals in turn provided those who remained in Europe with tales and accounts of this foreign land and its people. The industry's lines of communication opened pathways that explorers, traders, clergymen, settlers, and travellers alike followed into the primordial silences. The seemingly endless tract of forest, tundra, and prairie of Rupert's Land evoked from these people a diversity of responses that, in many ways, reflects the diversity of modern Canadian culture. In fact, this intricate and multi-patterned image of Rupert's Land serves as an early profile of this country's cultural sensibility, so that when the young nation purchased Rupert's Land for £300,000 shortly after Confederation, it was only asserting full possession of its own national psyche. Today, nearly 120 years after that titular transfer, the origins of many current attitudes and values in Canada can be traced to some of those early responses to Rupert's Land.

The following papers reconstruct the salient images of the land and its people, images left by explorers, traders, Amerindians, landscape artists, settlers, travellers, and many others. Taken collectively, these diverse responses to Rupert's Land constitute a cultural tapestry that records the development of a budding Canadian identity, an identity that has evolved since the first meetings between Europeans and the New World Inuit and that continues to evolve today. An important realization made in this volume is that it is not only the land itself that gives shape and texture to the image. The image is instead more a complex of how the viewer adapts his own expectations to the reality of Rupert's Land. Cultural preconceptions, professional objectives, personal ambitions – all must be reconciled with the experience at hand.

With the advantage of hindsight, we can clearly define the geographical and historical limits of Rupert's Land. However, when Charles II granted the charter to the Hudson's Bay Company's first governor, Prince Rupert, no one had any idea of its extent. Nor did the Company of Adventurers care a great deal whether the lands in which they traded drained into Hudson Bay, as the extensive activity beyond the Methye Portage and to the north of Fort Edmonton readily attests. The cultural tapestry of Rupert's Land, then, extends beyond the historian's time or the geographer's space, and in their effort to reconstruct that tapestry, the authors of these papers shake free unnecessary temporal and spatial constraints. Events that occurred as early as the eleventh and as late as the twentieth centuries become integral parts of this tapestry, as do those that transpired well outside the Hudson Bay drainage.

The essays have been arranged here in an order that is roughly chronological, rather than geographical or thematic, although the temptation to make both geographical and thematic comparisons is considerable. Notwithstanding, a chronological arrangement has been used because it lends a sense of continuous evolution in the responses articulated toward the region, serving to remind the reader that the influence continues into our own lives, and did not end with the legal transfer of a deed of land in the past century.

Historical documents provide much of the detailed information on which these papers build, but the approach is not limited to the discipline of history alone. The papers represent an interdisciplinary study involving anthropology, history, art, geography, and numerous other fields. Such a multidisciplinary approach is essential to comprehend the richness of a tapestry woven by native people, explorers, fur traders, clergymen, settlers, photographers, and adventurers. Even this list demonstrates the inaccuracy of specialized parameters and categories, for the terms "explorer" and "fur trader" are clearly not mutually exclusive. That unwieldy and amorphous — but essential — concept we know as "culture" must provide the frame of these papers as they constantly cross disciplinary boundaries to reconstruct the tapestry of Canada's cultural prehistory.

The first paper, "Beyond the 'Furious Over Fall': Map Images of Rupert's Land and the Northwest," is by Richard I. Ruggles. Given the first position in this series because it establishes a sense of place, a geographic locale on which all other papers can focus, "Beyond the 'Furious Overfall'" does far more than delineate a finite region of the New World. Rather, this paper shows the extent to which the cartographer's two-dimensional image of physical space is a creation of the mapmaker and his culture. The historical map images of Rupert's Land have often been the product of economic and political ambitions, bearing little relevance to the physical configuration of an empirically measurable land. Ruggles breaks down the development of cartographic images of the region into three stages, leading us from the sixteenth-century imaginative renderings based largely on geographical theory and promotion of individual projects to the later realistic images based on observed phenomena. The transition between these two extremes is at the core of this paper, as it traces the centuries-old process that ultimately fills the unknown void with topographical features. During this transition, such illusory concepts as the inland Sea of the West, the River of the West, and the overland Northwest Passage persisted in Europe's maps of Rupert's Land, reappearing in the work of major cartographers as a testimony to what Europeans wanted to see—not what they saw—in the New World. Only by the mid-nineteenth century did maps of Rupert's Land and the Northwest—principally in Aaron Arrowsmith's 1858 map—depict an image of geographical place that was relatively free of mystery. From that time on, cartographic work reflected the observations of such scientific expeditions as Henry Youle Hind's and John Palliser's, thrusting the history of cartographic images of Rupert's Land into a thematic stage that concentrated on vegetation, geology, fauna, and similar matters, instead of the configuration of the land and its waterways.

The next essay in this volume, "Three Worlds, One Focus: Europeans, Amerindians, and Inuit Meet in the Far North," is by Olive Dickason, well known for her work on the Amerindian, especially as he was perceived during the early French colonial period. Here, she examines the first contacts that Europeans established with the specific cultures of Inuit and Amerindians, beginning with the Norse perceptions of Inuit when they first established contact. Freely stretching the geographic boundaries of Rupert's Land as well as its temporal limits, she examines subsequent contacts between such British naval figures as John Davis and Martin Frobisher and the inhabitants of Baffin Island. Although the earliest contacts were between Europeans and Inuit, European links with Amerindians were the more substantial, and this paper generally focuses on those more substantial first contacts established between 1500 and 1850. After a careful and well-informed probing, Dickason concludes that in spite of more than 800 years of contact—from the eleventh-century Norse meetings with Inuit to the mid-nineteenth-century first contacts between Europeans and Copper and Netsilik Inuit—the three cultures have remained distinct, never developing any significant sense of a multicultural community. Each culture seems to have allowed a cautiously tolerant cooperation with the other, a relationship that would permit trade but would not allow a true sense of fellowship or mutual respect to evolve. An understanding of this long-lived separateness between these three Canadian cultures has special relevance to such modern issues as native self-government and cultural autonomy.

John L. Allen, author of the third paper, turns the focus back to the geographical image of Rupert's Land, as did Richard Ruggles. But his concern is not with the transition from imaginative to realistic cartographic renderings of Rupert's Land, but with the dynamic influence that solid knowledge of Rupert's Land exerted on the conceptualization and discovery of the vast region that lay to its south. "To Unite the Discoveries: The American Response to the Early Exploration of Rupert's Land" clearly spells out the extent that exploratory work in Rupert's Land both served as a catalyst to the exploration of what would become the western United States and helped forge an image of it. Not only did Alexander Mackenzie's continental crossing to the Pacific coast spur U.S. President Thomas Jefferson to action, but the Arrowsmith maps of British North America — themselves compilations of work by such men as Mackenzie, Samuel Hearne, Peter Fidler, and David Thompson — gave Jefferson a solid cartographic image on which to construct his theoretical notions of symmetrical geography and a pyramidal height of land. The result of this combination of the geographical reality of Rupert's Land and geographical theory was a projected image of the western half of the continent south of the 49th parallel. When Jefferson sent out Meriwether Lewis and William Clark to test his hypothetical model of the Missouri River and the Rocky Mountains, Lewis and Clark in turn relied on the Arrowsmith charts of Rupert's Land to make critical decisions about their route, even though it lay far to the south of Mackenzie's crossing. The early geographical image of Rupert's Land, then, as this paper so lucidly illustrates, bears special relevance not only to the vast regions drained into Hudson Bay, but to a more southerly region of nearly equal proportions as well.

Clive Holland's essay "John Franklin and the Fur Trade, 1819-22" draws largely on extant correspondence between Franklin and numerous fur-trade figures during the Admiralty's first land expedition to the Arctic coast. Several excerpts from letters by Franklin and one of his midshipmen, George Back, record responses to the experience, especially concerning the difficulties of travelling across the heart of Rupert's Land before beginning actual exploratory work beyond Great

Slave Lake. But the real value of Holland's paper is that it seriously questions one of the popular explanations for the failure of the 1819-22 expedition. The prevailing notion is that the fur companies interfered with essential supplies intended for Franklin's party because they did not want exploratory activity in the region. Such activity — so the argument goes — would have appeared dangerous to a fur industry zealously seeking to maintain a profitable control over the native inhabitants. Yet Holland's scrutiny of the relevant correspondence presents evidence that the London headquarters of both the Hudson's Bay Company and the North West Company were eager to assist the Admiralty and that only an unexpected and unavoidable shortage of trade goods and manpower — brought about by struggles within the industry — led to the disastrous situation in which Franklin soon found himself. The argument, then, demands a reconsideration of the fur trade's attitude toward Rupert's Land and its responsibilities toward it. Although it has commonly been assumed that the fur companies were intentionally uncooperative with and hostile toward the Admiralty expedition because they were excessively protective of a domain they considered their sole property, this essay offers a totally new perspective on how the trading companies dealt with forces from the outside.

    "'This Rascally & Ungrateful Country:' George Nelson's Response to Rupert's Land" also deals with the fur trade's attitude toward its domain, but the focus is narrowed to the response of an individual clerk in the trade. Nelson, a clerk in the trade, commented profusely upon the land in which he worked and the Indians with whom he traded, and Sylvia Van Kirk demonstrates how frequently his response changed — not because of a shift in the season or the specific locale, but because the lenses through which Nelson viewed Rupert's Land had changed. Thus, the very authenticity of these historical documents is questioned, insisting that one recognizes the multiple filters of human consciousness through which Nelson's response must pass before it takes form as a verbal image. No doubt, Van Kirk still agrees with the notion that fur traders were the most accurate European commentators on Rupert's Land because they knew it best, but she points out that what they said must be considered in light of the special biases and conditions through which they were recorded. Those special conditions are myriad, and Van Kirk explores such shaping forces as the differences between journal-keeping practices in the Hudson's Bay Company and the North West Company, the influences of contemporary literary conventions, and the attractions of publishing a commercially successful account. But of equal influence are perceptual blinders or coloured filters that are entirely personal. For example, Nelson records substantially different attitudes toward the region in different accounts, some recorded immediately after a particular event, others years later through the haze of a selective memory and the eyes of an older observer. Nelson is an excellent subject here, for many of his early field journals (some in secret code, broken by Van Kirk) are extant, as are reminiscences written much later and fragments of a narrative he began toward the end of his life. He makes harsh remarks about the trade itself, but as Van Kirk reminds us, they were made by a man who never managed to advance in the service. His upbringing in the home of a clergyman, followed by later reading in contemporary philosophy, especially Rousseau, might well explain Nelson's remarkably changed attitude toward Indians that evolves through the early journal and the later reminiscences and narrative. Van Kirk's approach to Nelson's response is, in many ways, at the very core of this entire collection of papers, because the exploration and understanding of cultural antecedents—to which these essays are devoted—can only evolve out of our comprehending the expectations and preconceptions of the many individuals who encountered the physical land and forged an image of it that we call Rupert's Land.

The next paper shifts the focus to rest on how a cultural group of Amerindians perceived the land in which they had lived for many generations before Charles II bestowed its riches upon his own countrymen. In "Chipewyan and Fur Trader Views of Rupert's Land," James G.E. Smith, curator of the Museum of the American Indian, suggests that the essence of the Caribou Eater Chipewyans' response to the taiga-tundra region in which they lived was embodied in the relationship they shared with the caribou. Not only did *la foule*—the herds of migrating caribou—determine the nomadic life, the gender roles, and the basic social structures of the Chipewyan, but it was the object of a moral commitment that manifested itself in the religious and oral traditions of the Caribou Eaters. Smith, however, considers the total dependence on the caribou as a source of immense freedom for the Chipewyan, as this single species met the necessities of food, shelter, and clothing. With the appearance of trade goods of European manufacture, the perceived needs of the Chipewyan began slowly to expand beyond what the caribou could supply, a cultural change Smith views as an early erosion of Chipewyan values that, to the author's thinking, has resulted today in a welfare state. When the paper's focus turns briefly to the fur traders' view of the region, it remains on the intimate relationship between Chipewyan and caribou. The traders recognized, Smith argues, that so long as the caribou were at hand, it was difficult to encourage the

Chipewyan to leave off hunting in order to trap furs, and so long as caribou were killed, there was initially little need for the trade goods that fur could purchase. The successful trader, then, had to work at altering the traditional Caribou Eater Chipewyan way of life and their very relationship to Rupert's Land.

"From 'Icy Picture' to 'Extensive Prospect:' The Panorama of Rupert's Land and the Far North in the Artist's Eye, 1770-1870" offers Robert Stacey's comprehension of Rupert's Land and its environs as it was recorded in paint and pencil. After noting the paucity of truly fine landscapes of the region, he explores a number of the factors that contributed to this situation. Some of these reasons are intimately linked to the objectives of such institutions as the British Admiralty and the HBC; others have more to do with European tastes in landscape art. Stacey briefly introduces the aesthetic philosophies of the picturesque and the sublime, then demonstrates that the real landscape of Rupert's Land and the Far North fell into neither of these popular European moulds; when artists tried to force a fit, they produced an image that neither depicted the region accurately nor satisfied the aesthetic demands of Europe. Amid a wealth of detail both about expeditionary art and about popular nineteenth-century developments in visual presentation, Stacey builds the notion that European artists were not truly able to see the northern latitudes they painted, but instead could only see what was not there; the conditioning of European art had blinded the painter to this new land. As Ruggles shows to be true of the cartographic images of Rupert's Land, Stacey demonstrates that landscapes of the region were often pastiches of other visual images, with firsthand observation of the land playing a surprisingly small role. Nevertheless, while the imaginative successes inspired by the region were few, Stacey identifies the germ of an aesthetic vision, particularly in the work of George Back, that reaches maturity in the Canadian landscape art of this century.

"The Palliser Expedition," Irene Spry's welcome contribution to this volume, is concerned with a more pragmatic response to Rupert's Land—the findings of a scientific expedition sent out explicitly to assess the prairie region. The paper summarizes the various routes followed by Palliser's party, as well as the official results of the survey, but of special interest are the many perceptive observations Palliser makes about the less tangible dimensions of the country. Allen shows that Mackenzie's work north of the 49th parallel spurred the Lewis and Clark explorations to the south; Spry shows that Palliser's journey from Red River to the western slopes of the Rockies was also partially motivated by an external force: Britain wished to protect from America and Russia the region south of the North Saskatchewan River that it claimed but knew little about. The official report provided a map of the region, an understanding of its major features, such as the river systems and three prairie levels, an estimation of mineral wealth, and information about temperature and precipitation. In response to their instructions to assess the possibilities for agriculture and settlement, Palliser described a fertile belt running to the north of an arid region that held little promise for agriculture — the famous Palliser's Triangle. Having been requested also to appraise the possibility of linking the prairie region with the Pacific coast and with the present colony of Canada, Palliser reported skeptically: connections through the United States would be far less expensive. But aside from these pragmatic issues, Palliser makes especially astute remarks about the residents of Rupert's Land, including the Indians, the Métis, and the isolated freemen, and Spry draws these out of the official reports for better viewing.

Fred Crabb's "The Church in the North" examines the role that the Church has played in Rupert's Land, determining that individuals — not institutions — have been responsible for whatever successes have been made. The paper emphasizes the effect that various denominations have had on the native inhabitants of the region, and points out that much of the continuing work of the church in this century has been carried on by native and mixed-blood residents of Rupert's Land. After briefly surveying the historical growth of the Church in Rupert's Land, the focus shifts to examine the role of the residential school, the tool most commonly used by missionaries to bring about the cultural adaptation of the Amerindian. Sharply aware of modern criticism of the residential school system, Crabb acts as apologist as he explains the historical reasons for having first established the schools. Reflecting the missionaries' desire to bring their "pagan" charges to Christ, the schools were set up to assist the secular adjustment to the European world and values that the clergy considered would be the inevitable course of events. Crabb points out that many of the schools included such practical subjects as agriculture in their curricula. Significantly, some of these early schools have developed into leading educational institutions in modern Western Canada. But at the heart of Crabb's contribution is his grappling with the ultimate value of the Church in the North. Crabb readily admits that early missionaries often robbed the Amerindians of their own world and values, but he also forces us to consider the options that would have appeared open to clergymen in the nineteenth century. Viewed from such a perspective, but tempered with the recognition that the clergy's actions of the past have often been overly eager and strongly imperialistic, the Church of today has come to a better understanding of how to help the people they had sincerely tried to help in the past.

"Image of Transition: Photography in Rupert's Land" documents a time of major change in the perception of Rupert's Land, linking that period of change to technical developments in the photographic process. Change came rapidly to Rupert's Land during the second half of the nineteenth century, the result of a shifting economy, new political autonomy for Canada, and transport developments. But it was also a time of immense growth for the art of photography, and Edward Cavell wonderfully illustrates that the camera did not merely capture a two-dimensional image of an altered Rupert's Land, but that the camera itself brought about much of that change. After explaining in lay terms the essentials of the photographic process as it had developed by the middle of the nineteenth century, Cavell explains how the considerable technical limits were tailored to fit the prevailing European expectations, both about the wild domain of Rupert's Land and about general landscape aesthetics. As technical changes in the photographer's art made the process more portable and rapid, the landscapes of Rupert's Land gave way to photographs of the region's native peoples, thus creating an interest in social conditions of the area. The documentary photograph began to replace the romanticized and picturesque landscapes that had projected Rupert's Land in an image easily understood and appreciated by European audiences. "Image of Transition" makes us keenly aware that the view of Rupert's Land has been created by factors that have little bearing on the geographical and historical entity we term "Rupert's Land."

The paper that follows provides another look at the response to Rupert's Land during a period of major transition — here, the transition from fur trade to agriculture. The time frame — from the middle to the late nineteenth century — smoothly parallels that of Cavell's paper. In "The Ideal and the Real: The Image of the Canadian West in the Settlement Period," R. Douglas Francis concentrates on the methods by which the Government of Canada and numerous authors and painters created a new and attractive image of Rupert's Land that was designed to promote agricultural settlement in the prairie regions. Previous to 1869-70 and the Dominion's purchase of Rupert's Land, the region was perceived as a cold, barely habitable wilderness, heavily forested in the north and swept by an arid desert in the south. After purchasing what had for years been a fur-trade preserve, the Government of Canada consciously set about altering that perception. Augmenting thousands of Government pamphlets extolling the riches to be won through agriculture were novels and paintings that projected a secure, successful, and highly romanticized view of life. One readily sees parallels with the similar period of photography in Rupert's Land to which Cavell points, although Cavell emphasizes other factors as bringing about the shift in perception. Authors such as Robert Stead, Emily Murphy, and Ralph Connor created a mythical West that was egalitarian, optimistic, and heroic—not specifically with the intent of deceiving the innocent, but because the authors believed the myth they created. The pamphlets, books, and paintings were immensely successful, luring hundreds of thousands of immigrants to the West in only a few decades; there, they faced the reality of the land, not the idealized image that had drawn them to it. Using firsthand immigrant accounts and drawing on statistics of settlement, Francis concludes that a significant portion of those newly arrived settlers were severely disappointed by what they encountered, and Francis goes on to speculate that this major disillusionment lies at the heart of many forms of Western alienation familiar today. Not only does he suggest that the agrarian reform movement of this century and the Winnipeg bust of 1883 grew out of this failure of the reality to meet the idealized image, but Francis argues that the development of realism in Canadian literature was also a natural and inevitable outgrowth of this immense disillusionment. The image of Rupert's Land, ironically, returns full circle to one that is hostile to the civilized aspirations of cultured society, much as it had been before government pamphlets and popular Canadian fiction began reshaping the image.

The essay chosen to complete this reconstruction of the cultural tapestry that is Rupert's Land in Robert H. Cockburn's "After-Images of Rupert's Land." This paper neatly parallels the journals of two twentieth-century adventurers who travel to remote areas of the Barrens in order to participate in a way of life as old as the land itself. On a quest for ties with the past—with an older and slower way of life—these travellers seek out a world far from the reaches of modern civilization. The lucid 1912 journal left by Ernest Oberholtzer illuminates the "traditional and enduring" features of Rupert's Land, a region that Oberholtzer finds had changed little over the more than four decades since its transfer to the Dominion of Canada. The sense of isolation at the posts, the timeless rhythms of the people, the signs of caribou and their seasonal slaughter for food, York boats—these are but a few of the images Oberholtzer captures in 1912 that launch him into an earlier time. In 1939, Prentice Downes followed the same route that Oberholtzer had navigated down the Kazan River and through to Nueltin Lake, although Downes knew nothing of Oberholtzer's journey. Significantly, Downes's journal reflects that many of the traditions and lasting characteristics linking Oberholtzer with the past were still present in 1939, but he also realized that he would be the last to see the world of Rupert's Land, for the harbingers of change were everywhere – in the bush plane and the outboard motor, in commercial mines and fisheries, and in the spreading tentacles of government bureaucracy. As Downes reached his destination on Nueltin Lake, he witnessed – perhaps one of the last white men to do so – the migration of the Caribou Eater Chipewyan, those same people, the subject of James Smith's paper earlier in this volume, whose culture has been so enormously changed by the appearance of outside values.

Rupert's Land may have ceased to exist as a political entity in 1869, and, as the final paper attests, the traditions and even the physical face of the region may have undergone fundamental change, but the distinctive mark of Rupert's Land remains on Canada. Some authors represented here explicitly trace that influence into modern times, as do Francis, Smith, Dickason, and Crabb, suggesting direct links between the individual foci of their papers and developments in twentieth-century politics and society. Where Francis and Smith assign a causal relationship, Dickason and Crabb stress the importance of bearing in mind the past as we move into the future.

Other authors concentrate exclusively on reconstructing a detail of the tapestry, leading to a better appreciation of the response to Rupert's Land in the past; the actual process of carrying forward this new insight into an improved comprehension of Canada's cultural values today is left to the reader. The papers by Ruggles and Allen point to a pervasive external effect on the image of Rupert's Land, whereby prior images of the region do more to shape subsequent responses than does the land itself. In other cases, authors explore the perceptual limits imposed by the cultural baggage brought on the journey to Rupert's Land, as when Stacey probes into the depiction of a New World landscape through an aesthetic forged in the Old World. Cavell does much the same, but he adds another external limitation to the perception of this region: the technical limits of the photographic art. Those limiting forces, however, are not always external, as Van Kirk makes quite clear. Many of those biases that give shape to the image are products of the viewer's own state of mind, of his relationship to his audience and his material, and of his professional objectives.

In a multitude of ways, then, the images of Rupert's Land collected here truly reflect the cultural backgrounds of some of Canada's first viewers. It is not the geographical and historical entity of Rupert's Land that makes this tapestry significant to modern Canadian culture, but the perception of it through the multiple distortions that have worked together to make up the national psyche. As an image — rather than as a place — Rupert's Land constitutes a tapestry in which many of the values that concern Canada as a culturally sovereign nation are recorded.

As with any stimulating collection of papers, especially those crossing disciplinary boundaries, these essays raise more questions than they answer. Such is the nature of cultural introspection. But taken collectively, they provide a starting point from which to begin a much-needed rethinking of the origins of Canada's cultural psyche.

Chapter 1

BEYOND THE "FURIOUS OVER FALL": MAP IMAGES OF RUPERT'S LAND AND THE NORTHWEST

Richard I. Ruggles

On his final momentous voyage in search of a northwest Passage in 1587 Captain John Davis tracked south along the Baffin Island coast from the great northern embayment which he had reached, but not entered,[1] and sailed past the beginning of a very great inlet, "where to...his great admiration...he saw the sea falling down into the gulfe with a mighty overfal, and roring, and with divers circular motions like whirlepools, in such sort as forcible streams pass through the arches of bridges."[2] This "furious over fall," incipient Hudson Strait, lying south of Baffin Island and north of Terra de Labrador, was marked on a number of maps, first by Davis after his return to England, and then by others[3] (Fig. 1). Clearly, exclaimed Captain Luke Foxe later in his account of his own journey beyond the furious overfall, "Davis...did...light Hudson into his streights."[4]

Voyaging westward toward the Sea of China through such a beckoning channel proved not as "easie to be performed"[5] as Martin Frobisher had nonchalantly ventured would be the case. Many other seamen could attest to this. Waymouth[6] advanced along this passage; then Hudson, Munk, Button, Bylot, Foxe, and James in turn followed, and sailed off into a vast sea, only to discover that it was constrained to the west by an unwelcome coast. Cartographers limned in these confining shores, although enticing openings to the north on maps long sustained the hope of discovery of the sought-after waterway.

By 1670 the northern New World mystery[7] had been breached in a three-pronged manner—through the Strait of John Davis into Baffin Bay; through the gulf, estuary, and river of Jacques Cartier; and through the Strait of Henry Hudson into the heart of that charter territory granted by Charles II to his well-beloved cousin Prince Rupert and his fellow adventurers of England trading into Hudson Bay.[8] This charter was an eagerly-sought act of royal largesse, by which these "true and absolute Lords and Proprietors" were bestowed a domain of unknown size and extent in which to engage in sole trade and commerce. The proprietors had Captain James's map[9] and several coastal charts[10] available to instruct them on the geography of Rupert's Land. But these did not depict more than a narrow littoral. All else inland was unknown.

How far did the Charter's "Seas, Streights, Bays, Rivers, Lakes, Creekes and Sounds, in whatsoever Latitude" they should be "that lie within the entrance of...Hudsons Streight," extend? How much "Land, Countryes and Territories upon the Coasts and confines of the Seas" and other waters aforesaid existed? Where did the watershed boundary lie around the Rupert's Land perimeter? The general configuration and rough magnitude of the Labrador peninsula and the intervening strip of land between James Bay and the Great Lakes could be comprehended at that time. But to the west was Parte Incognita of indeterminate breadth. And to the north beyond Southampton and Foxe's discovered channel, was it largely water, or enclosing land? Almost two centuries of exploration were involved before these queries were completely answered, and the chartered precinct of Rupert's Land had been disclosed and mapped (Fig. 2).

The map of Canada at the time of surrender of Rupert's Land in 1870, as indeed of our nation today, evolved through the sketching and mapping of native people, explorers, traders, military officers, public servants, scientists, commercial cartographers, and others, and it took form especially as a result of increasingly precise astronomical observation and topographical surveying. Between these later realistic images and the earlier imaginative renditions of the map makers of this new land, hundreds of seemingly disparate map images of our North and West have intervened.

The history of the cartography of this immense region has involved the gradual merger of new configurations with older information. In this long transition, the continuing thread has been the replacement in symbols of imaginary speculations with observed phenomena. But this process has not been immediate and direct. Geographical myths have waxed and waned, and certain of them have persisted well into the nineteenth century. As the continent was enlarged in size and gained a more credible shape on maps, and as exploration stripped away hypothetical rivers, lakes, seas, and straits, large vacant spaces were left on maps. Mapmakers of the seventeenth through the nineteenth centuries resisted the medieval cartographic dictum "where in doubt, place terrors," or at least refrained from placing "o'er unhabitable Downs,...Elephants for want of Towns," as Swift accused mappers of the African wilderness.[11] These spatial vacuums were unembellished borderlands between the known and the unknown; they were great lacunae that cartographers gradually filled with contemporary outlines.

It has been said that map evidence is derived through geographical theorizing, is promoted to support a personal project, or is draughted from hard-won field experience. These are often entangled on the same map, or intertangled on maps of the same period, region, or national origin. A framework has been prepared into which these varying graphic perceptions of theory, promotion, and fact may be integrated. Up to 1870, mapping of this spacious region evolved through three phases. The first period commenced in 1500 when the first extensive map of newly discovered lands out in the western ocean was draughted by the Spaniard Juan de la Cosa, ship owner and navigator on the first Columbian expedition.[12] It ended in 1612 with the issuing of a coastal chart by the Dutch plattmaker, Hessel Gerritsz,[13] of the initial discovery of the great sea which lay beyond the furious over fall, that of Henry Hudson. In this region, and over this century, the maps were all imagery — all were perceptions of theory and of promotion; there were no observed facts here. Widely-held theories and arguments held sway upon the maps of various European nations, with delineations of open seas and epicontinental straits, of archipelagos, lakes and rivers, mountain uplands and broad lowlands, many with fanciful titles, and with supposed towns dotted across the landscape. These may be said to have been the first generation of hypothetical images.

The second period, which extended to the mid-nineteenth century, rapidly displaced the first in the seventeenth century as Rupert's Land was entered by the British and its marine heart was disclosed, as the French ranged into the upper Great Lakes, and as Indian information was incorporated into maps of the interior. One might say that the slate was gradually wiped clean of the distorted images of the past, as over the years the large, remaining voids were filled in with newly discovered features, which the mapmakers attempted to reconcile with older topographical forms. This long second period witnessed the preparation of hundreds of both manuscript and printed maps, which illustrated and aided in the transformation of this colonial trade area into the territory of a new nation. Many geographers and cartographers advanced new theories as to the disposition of riverways, lakes, and sea passages beyond the known frontiers, each of which gained credence in its time, and many of these men draughted their own versions of reality. Especially in the eighteenth century, a second generation of apocryphal images appeared on maps, which were in their turn deleted under the impress of the exploratory and mapping contributions of such as Turnor, Fidler, Thompson, Mackenzie, Cook, Vancouver, Clouston,[14] and many others. Up until the mid-nineteenth century, the purpose of maps was almost completely that of "way-showing"; they were general purpose maps upon which were plotted the trend of sea coasts, the complexity of lake shores, and the interconnections of riverways. Portages, waterfalls, and rapids were the specialized symbols used, since they were of such consequence for inland travel. Knowledge of the physical environment was scant and fragmentary, since scientific investigations had not been extended to any degree into the region. Some cartographers inserted a few hills or mountains, or spotted vegetation symbols somewhat indiscriminately on the maps. This was not a period of thematic mapping.

In the third period, the only change in the character of the many maps prepared in the several decades before 1870 was the preparation of a few special purpose or thematic maps. On the whole, these were geological or geomorphological in nature, or were demarcations of the major natural regions of the plains, such as the grasslands, the parkbelt, and the northern forest, issued by the first scientific expeditions onto the plains, of Palliser,[15] Hind,[16] and associates. Otherwise, exploration, which was concentrated along the channels among the arctic islands, along the continental coast, across the Barren Grounds, in the Mackenzie and Yukon river basins, and in the mountainous labyrinth of northern British Columbia, continued to provide a myriad of topographical images of these frontier regions.

In 1500, Juan de la Cosa prepared the first colourfully graphic map image of the rediscovery of America by Europeans, and thereby initiated the cartographic history of Rupert's Land. This image made manifest the theory that Columbus and Cabot had touched upon offshore islands and the eastern mainland of Asia. Behind the English flag-bedecked coast, probably of Newfoundland and possibly of Cape Breton, stretched a vast interior region, in a sense the progenitor of Rupert's Land, although a network of boundary lines was entirely spurious. This was the first of a number of maps that perpetuated such beliefs as an earth of shorter than actual circumference, a narrower than actual intervening ocean, and direct and uninterrupted crossings to the supposed east Asian littoral. There was no need of a Northwest Passage in this view of the northern hemisphere. In effect, the territory lying in the continental interior behind the New Found Land of Cabot and of Portuguese explorers was integrated in geographical discussions, and on some maps, into the confusing puzzle of northern Cathay and northeast Asia.[17] This approach did not last long as a viable theory in the sixteenth century.

It was followed by and co-existed with much more truthful and yet less inhibited assessments of the new transoceanic discoveries. A new world was emerging, first presented in 1507 by Martin Waldseemüller, who also first named this new continent, America. At first, New Found Land was not part of it. It lay, detached and insular, far northeast in the ocean, as depicted on Waldseemüller's 1513 map.[18] And yet, the question had not been decided, as the indefinite, unbounded, western side of this first defined part of Canada will attest. Rupert's Land was immersed in an expansive ocean. Over some years of coastal exploration, it was realized that this was indeed a New World obstacle, though it was not known whether it was a continuous body or an amalgamation of several disjointed fragments. How large it was, how long or how wide its extent, these could not be specified. There were two basic expectations: one, that the Western Ocean was not far distant, and two, that the narrow landmass would have either one or more passages through it or an easy access around its northernmost promontory. It would be merely a matter of finding the proper channel through, or of feeling one's way around the northern cape.

This problem of the New World barrier and how to pass it to reach the distant oriental lands was the fundamental motive for searching appraisals of the coastline north from Florida. The Spanish under Gomez and Ayllon,[19] and the French under Verrazzano,[20] first traced in the Atlantic strand, firmly establishing the general location, connection, and orientation of this seashore. In 1524, Verrazzano, persuaded that he saw the great sea across a narrow isthmus, likely the Carolina Outer Banks, inaugurated the Gibson Girl waist on a suite of maps; and this Sea of Verrazzano lasted for many decades, as on the well-known promotional map of 1582 by the Englishman Michael Lok, who was supportive of the Frobisher expeditions to the Northwest[21] (Fig. 3). This map combines much of the theorizing, wishful thinking, boosterism, knowledge, and indeed vanity of the Elizabethan Age. It repeats the Verrazzanian Sea, indicates Cartier's discoveries and those of Frobisher, but it converts the northeast of the continent into a virtual archipelago, including his own island of Lok (that is, Baffin Island). Moreover, it supports the idea of ease of access to a now definite Northwest Passage, past Queen Elizabeth's Land, the Land of Cortereal, Canada and Saguenay—in fact, leading into the heart of the future Rupert's Land.

But the flesh of Rupert's Land had long since been made real by cosmographers and cartographers; that is, the north part of this continent had burgeoned on maps. It had been widened to major proportions. Yet it had also been cabined with a mythical western coast, cribbed by a separating Strait of Anian from Asia, and confined by a northern shore, flanked by a sea passage. This expanse of land, anterior to the discovery and chartering of the Hudson's Bay Company's trade territory, was illustrated in what was a common cartographic style for some time. Most of the maps displayed fanciful landscapes, with mountain ranges, wooded plains, and meandering rivers; some had native inhabitants and several species of game. The Desceliers map of 1550 typifies the mixing of symbols evocative of European fauna and flora with those having some local authenticity, such as deer, bear, etc.[22] The surrounding waters were often garnished with enlarged, recognizable, but still somewhat fearsome sea creatures, although the era of sea monsters and abnormal bestiary on the land had passed. Often included were cartouche-bordered insets of the native economy, such as whaling, and beautifully-drawn engravings of current ship designs.

Two broad groupings of such essentially hypothetical maps may be discerned during this first period of cartographic images. On one hand, there were earlier maps whereon, for example, in the interior west of Labrador and north of New France, lay "parts unknown."[23] Or they were essentially Terrae Incognitae, unknown lands, and basically unnamed regions, beyond the St. Lawrence Gulf and River, where were located Canada, New France, and Arcadia.[24]

On the other hand, a second group of an equal if not larger number of maps appeared in the latter half of the century, which introduced for the first time into the northern interior a regional title, populated places, a roster of new toponyms, and a novel arrangement of lakes, rivers, and ocean embayments. The region of Conibas made its debut on the map of Canada, taking its place with other apocryphal geographical regions, such as Bergi Regio and Annian Regnum. Conibas Regio was the immediate precursor of Rupert's Land. The Lake of Conibas or Conibaz appeared as early as 1575 on André Thevet's map,[25] which lake drained north into a large gulf of the northern sea. In 1587 Conibaz remained as a regional name only, without an accompanying lake,[26] and it became a full-fledged region in 1597 when Cornelis van Wytfliet, in a separate small atlas of the Americas, draughted the first separate map of a region of the northern interior of Canada, naming it Conibas Regio with its local inhabitants, with towered towns, and highly amusing place names.[27]

There has been a suggestion that the large northern indentation was Hudson Bay, and a reflection of that shown peeping south of the north map border by Ortelius in his famous first modern atlas of 1570[28] and later by Mercator in 1595.[29] Were Hudson and James bays visited before Hudson, or were they heard about from reports to the French in the St. Lawrence basin? No evidence for either supposition is available. It has also been proposed that Lake Conibas may be an early rendition of Lake Ontario, or even all the Great Lakes, shown first in partial form on Mercator's world map of great repute of 1569,[30] with the unusual names being primordial tribal names of that area. Cornelis de Jode's map of 1593 is a good example of the repetition of this congeries of features, which were placed on some maps even as late as the 1770s (Fig. 4). Vaugondy's map of 1772 exemplifies a common trait followed by past cartographers, where some vestigial forms are maintained, but have been shifted west into an exploratory void before the advance of known geographic locations.[31]

By the time British seamen began to reappear in Hudson Bay toward 1670, there had been a lapse of some thirty years in maritime activity along this great strait and sea. The noteworthy voyages of Captains Foxe and James in 1631 and 1632 had concluded an epoch of British discovery, which had commenced with Frobisher and Davis in the icy northern waters of Davis Strait and Frobisher Bay. The next re-entrant that was essayed lay beyond the furious over fall, and in 1602 Waymouth merely breached the entrance to this channel, but did not pass into the Bay. This was the privilege of the ill-fated Hudson expedition of 1610-11, which examined only the easterly and most southerly parts of the sea, the details of which were published by Gerritsz in 1612. As a result there was every hope that there was not a closed western shore. The very disappointing truth was gained as successive navigators drew in this western coast, and this promising lead of a sea-passage ended essentially as a cul-de-sac.

During the six decades after Hudson's inaugural journey, the perception of this region, gained from the study of map images, owes much to only a handful of European mapmakers. Gerritsz, Foxe,[32] and James produced maps that were straightforward graphic assessments of exploration chronicles. They concentrated upon coastal outlines, with almost no concern for interior detail, for imaginary forms, or for decoration. Quickly, almost surgically, the previously displayed conjectural features were cleared away, and large open spaces remained. A map of 1625 by the English mathematician Briggs displays this candour clearly.[33] Other cartographers have depended upon the data provided from these mapmakers to a great degree.

In contrast, the French, who were not involved in exploration beyond the Hudson Bay watershed, maintained their interest in conceptual images of the North. Two cartographers were germinal during this period: Samuel de Champlain, explorer, geographer, cartographer, and administrator; and Nicolas Sanson, premier *géographe du roi de France*. Champlain, who gathered all of his material in the New World, drew the fundamental mother map, his final one of 1632.[34] On it are certain forms that are exactly reproduced or appear with variations on many later maps. Sanson, in 1650, draughted one of the most influential maps of the mid-to-later century, but for the Rupert's Land area it is based on Champlain.[35] For Hudson Bay, of course, Champlain depended upon Gerritsz. But Sanson has added British information on the west shore of the Bay, although he left a tantalizing, wide water gap, which fades southwest into the Mer Glaciale. This curious large bay-channel is an attempt to merge the actual results of voyaging into Champlain's version of a great bay and a northern frozen sea to the west. Both cartographers have added river and lake systems inland, although Champlain has been more generous with his topographical information. It is noticeable that, having been active in the difficult voyages in the

North, the English have shown the actual results of their quest for openings into a Northwest Passage on their maps, while the French have continued to compile maps with fanciful arctic routeways, similar in general nature to those of the previous century.

For over fifty years after the commencement of operations of the Hudson's Bay Company in 1670, the map images of Rupert's Land, inland from the Bay coast and beyond the Great Lakes watershed, were basically conjectural and imaginative in character. The representations were incipient or were spurious. The Bay shore was an exception, as necessary coastal charts had been draughted for the Company in the early years. However, the 1709 map by Samuel Thornton indicates how scanty was real knowledge of the country.[36] It depicts a supposed line of demarcation between French and British, running through a gigantic and misshapen Lake Mistassini, and this map was used in high-level discussions between the Company and government officials. A further example may be seen in a French map of 1733,[37] where the cartographer has differentiated by density and character of map symbol the difference in knowledge of the St. Lawrence River basin, south of Lake Mistassini, and the generalized pattern applied to the wilderness of Rupert's Land.

The Company had engaged in only a modicum of inland exploration during this time, as its trading required its customers to move down to the factories at the Bay shore. There was also still a belief that a water passage would be found out from the northern end of the basin, and it therefore supported marine exploration. Stories of mineral resources in the northern reaches of the continent – probably along the Northwest Passage – also encouraged this approach. Another factor was that for about thirty years the Company was engaged in a struggle with the French for control of the very shores of the Bay. However, three extensive inland journeys were taken by Company servants: Henry Kelsey from 1690 to 1692 to the Saskatchewan prairies;[38] William Stewart in 1715-16, in all probability into the Great Slave Lake region;[39] and from 1717 on for about three years, Richard Norton was in the Barren Grounds west of the Churchill River mouth.[40] These expeditions were not taken for a geographic purpose primarily, but rather to encourage customers to travel to the Factories, and to engender peaceful relations between groups.

Certainly, surveying and cartographic purposes were not involved either, for in none of these cases did any map, or even a sketch, result. Up to the end of this second period – that is, about 1731 – the Company had not developed support to any great extent for surveying and mapping, which characterized its later history. There was little in the way of map images, based on new information from interior Rupert's Land, available to English commercial cartographers.

Over this span of years, the French dominated the cartography of the region, although their concern lay mainly with New France. There were, among many, three significant cartographers for northern mapping: Hubert Jaillot, Guillaume Del'isle, and Jean-Baptiste Franquelin. In the area of concern, they did not alter the outlines of Hudson and James bays to any degree, which were based on English forms, but instead they functioned as the creators and arrangers of interior features. In their several maps, they established particular delineations that gained a surprising hold upon later cartographers, internationally. These features are usually imaginative representations of the geographic data available to them. They had to base their compilations on the reports of Indians and itinerant traders, as re-interpreted by other authors or *rapporteurs*. Such reports did not usually lack veracity, but instead only accuracy and exact location. Thus, the same statement might be interpreted in several ways by various mapmakers, which gave birth to divergent representations.

Jaillot's map of 1685 affords the opportunity to observe this process of image production in force.[41] On this map he displays five "trade-marks," which were picked up in whole or in part by others. Lac des Poux, ramrod-stiff north of Port Nelson, may have been the Churchill River and its widening in the form of Southern Indian Lake. To the south, possibly the Nelson River projected rigidly across the interior could be draining through Split and Sipiwesk lakes on the normal trading route, or even more engaging, could be a transcribed Indian version of the dicotyledonous outline of Lake Winnipeg. Thirdly, there is undoubtedly Hayes River and Knee or Oxford Lake, with the tributary Foxe River. Fourthly, there is apparently the Lake Abitibi-Frederick House Lake-Abitibi River complex, rotated about ninety degrees, but bearing overall its proper relationship to the Ottawa River and Lake Nipissing. And finally there is island-studded Alemenipigon, one of several antecedents of its final form, Lake Nipigon.

Del'isle, at the apex of French cartographic and geographic circles, provided in 1703 the summation of the academic understanding of the geography of the North of America.[42] Its clarity of expression is excellent. The artistry and design of the cartouche, which illustrates local fauna and flora, and the relationship between priest and native person, is augmented by the unusual backdrop of a waterfall.

The most creative cartographer was Franquelin, who alone of the three lived for some time in New France — as professor of hydrography, as well as compiler of geographic materials and of maps for the French government.[43] His personal contributions were never published under his own name, but often under the rubric of others. Franquelin introduced startling alterations to the iconography of Rupert's Land in the form of three large, interconnected lakes—Assinibouels, Christinaux, and Alemipigon. The latter is easily understood. Christinaux is most likely to be Split Lake, an important junction along the Nelson (Bourbon) River. Lac des Assinibouels (that is, of the Assiniboines) had a complicated history of development, but it has become identified as being the inflated ancestor of Lake Winnipeg, or even of the three major lakes of Manitoba together. The lake appeared with differing shapes and names on a variety of maps, but it was Franquelin who provided the main profiles, as for example his map of 1700[44] (Fig. 5). The surprisingly large lake to the south is, in fact, Milles Lacs in Minnesota, draining into the Mississippi, but which is attached in the normal fashion of the times both to that great river and also northward across the watershed to the lake of the Assiniboine Indians. Another modification that bears upon Rupert's Land is the obvious extension of the Mississippi far into the interior of Canada, a displacement to the north of fifty-five degrees into Alberta, over seven hundred miles from the true position of its source in the woodlands of Minnesota.

The mapping of Rupert's Land for the half century after the 1720s became much more voluminous. Both British and French had become engaged in trading sorties. The Hudson's Bay Company dispatched sloop parties north along the Bay's west coast to contact customers and to search for any possibility of there being an entrance to a strait. In 1754, beginning with Anthony Henday[45] and for twenty years more, servants were sent to renew the inland wintering system, into the Saskatchewan basin and northern grasslands particularly. In 1772, on the same type of programme, Samuel Hearne reached the mouth of the Coppermine River at the arctic coast, the first sighting by Europeans of this ocean shore.

In all, some forty-six maps[46] were drawn by Company employees during this time. But these were commercial documents, and not seen by either competitors or the public. The exception was Hearne's sketch, which was used later to illustrate his printed narrative.[47] Being secreted in Company files, their specific detail and more accurate outlines were not transferred to the compilations of European cartographers. Their maps were singularly bare, or repeated out-of-date forms. For example, Thomas Bowen, a leading London mapmaker, was able in 1778 to use only French features from the late seventeenth and early eighteenth centuries, along with La Vérendrye's outlines of the larger Manitoba lakes.[48] If the Company files had been opened earlier, as they were after 1790,[49] cartographers would have received the finer points of detail of Richmond Gulf on the Eastmain by Captain Coats, of 1749;[50] the character of the Nelson-Saskatchewan-Lake Winnipeg region, with tribal areas defined, by Andrew Graham in 1774;[51] or Samuel Hearne's complex of waterways from York Factory to Cumberland House when he returned in 1775 from opening this first inland Company post.[52] The images of Rupert's Land gained by the interested map reader were in a sense ones of malnutrition and of deprivation.

The French, oriented largely to the basin of the Great Lakes and the Mississippi watershed, had pressed across the continental divide into Rupert's Land along the whole northern perimeter to contest for the trade with the English. More significantly, they gained ascendency over the HBC in its charter territory for almost three decades, in the Pays d'en Haut (Upper Country), the Red and Assiniboine valleys, Manitoba lakes area, and the Saskatchewan River country. More than any of its precursors or immediate successors, members of the family of La Vérendrye were the pioneer delineators of this sector of the western interior. Moreover, French cartography took on the role—which interested and intrigued learned society—of presenting various versions of probable, possible, hypothetical, and fanciful passages, channels, seas, lakes, and other useful routeways across the northwest of the continent. These were descendants of, and therefore part of, the historic search for a passage to the Orient.

By the early decades of the eighteenth century, the true character of the St. Lawrence-Great Lakes region was well established. A Great Water[53] beyond the lakes had become a Great River,[54] the Mississippi, a discovery diverting the search for an easy water route south to the Gulf of Mexico. The belief was that an alternate route would be found, either up the Mississippi and the Missouri, or from the west side of Lake Superior, leading toward a height of land of unknown length and breadth. From this mountainous country, a river could hopefully be found to be followed west or southwest to the western ocean shore. As well, there was a strongly favoured theory that there was somewhere to the west a large inland sea—the Sea of the West[55]—extending far east into the plains, which would ease the burden of passage to the distant ocean.

The La Vérendrye family epoch lasted from 1728 to 1750, from this trader's first arrival at Lake Superior. He was given command of the Postes du Nord (Michipicoten, Nipigon, and Kaministikwia) just one year after his arrival and, in fact, just two years after he had almost decided to leave New France for the old country to try to make a better life for his young family. In his short time he had garnered reports on the probable character of the Upper Country from Indians and *coureurs-de-bois* who ranged its forests. He also received sketches on birch bark from several Cree Indians, and these were combined into a map by La Vérendrye, who also sent all materials to Quebec. There, and in France, these were transcribed.[56] The primary feature is the purported River of the West, having its source in waterways west of the Lake Superior watershed. The river was reported to flow straight toward the setting sun, and along its length was a double-chambered enlargement, Lac Ouinipigon. There were also, among many lakes, two larger ones — Lac du Bois (Lake of the Woods) and Lac Tacamamiouen (Rainy Lake). From Superior to Ouinipigon the country was wooded, and once beyond the source watershed, the land was level and without mountains. The River of the West continued for some ten days' journey to the west, and there near the ocean the ebb and flow of the tide could be seen. Near this river was a mountain of shining stones, which did not impede passage of the river.

Such a river, which the Indians' information and its interpretation promised to be a relatively open road to the sea, was a potent image, both for the colonial administration, which desired a project that could be completed quickly and with least expense possible, and for the leader himself, who apparently had been handed a graphic plan of action. Both made a serious error of interpretation of the materials. La Vérendrye's error grew out of his naiveté in such matters: he was unaware of the pitfalls of evaluating native information, of the levels of certainty of their knowledge, of their differing approaches to distance and direction estimation and spatial portrayal, and of the alterations occurring in the compilation process. It is becoming evident in recent research[57] that the details depicted all refer to features in the eastern prairies and not to the far distant cordillera and ocean shore.

The exploratory results of the French occupation of this part of Rupert's Land were transformed into a number of maps that reached Quebec, and eventually France. The details were copied or combined on the maps of European cartographers, usually without credit to the originators. The first evidence of this translation into the map pipe-line is a worksheet showing a pasted insert over an earlier published base map.[58] Nicolas Bellin, the chief cartographer for the office of the Marine, published the first map showing this La Vérendrye sketch, and he indicates that the river led to one of the hypothetical passages opening on the Pacific coast.[59] La Vérendrye's other maps[60] portray the gradual increase in detailed knowledge and in their assessment of shape and connections of Lakes Winnipeg and Manitoba, the courses of the Red and Assiniboine rivers, the crossing of the plains to the Mandan Indian area on the Missouri River, the first depiction of the hill regions of Riding and Moose mountains and associated features to the west, and the location of the newly built French trading posts. They also show the merging of the known with the expected but unknown, of the measured paths through the lakes with the reported, highly shortened river roads leading to Hudson Bay. La Vérendryean images of the West were reflected in scores of map adaptations over the years.[61] By the time of French withdrawal from Rupert's Land, the cartographic Terrae

Incognitae and Semi-incognitae matched reasonably the pattern of French and Company exploration by that date.

A number of illusory concepts of the West and Northwest were disseminated on maps and in books; were discussed and critically examined by the leading geographers, cartographers, and travellers of the time; and became part of the literature read by the fascinated public. These concepts fell into four categories: those concerned with rivers leading to the western ocean, being the cartographic forerunners of the Columbia, Fraser, Skeena, and other rivers; those illuminating the inland Sea of the West; those complicated straits and waterbodies that united the Atlantic and Pacific Oceans across the northwest of the continent; and finally those concepts that dealt with the configuration and character of the Pacific shoreline.

On the west coast, the earliest signs of the resplendent imaginative cartography to come were the openings to straits claimed to have been found and entered by several navigators, such as Juan de Fuca[62] and Martin D'Aigular,[63] as far back as 1592 and 1602. Depending upon the cartographer, these openings either led into the Sea of the West or into one of the cross-continental straits, or they lay at the mouth of the River of the West. An inland sea appeared on maps as early as 1705, but it was gradually shifted westward before the advancing front of exploration. On Philippe Buache's well-known map of 1754, the sea lay just beyond the lakes and the hill country of Manitoba, these outlines copied from a later map of the La Vérendrye enterprise[64] (Fig. 6).

Other involved configurations of the West came from Father Castel, a French priest and cosmographer, who corresponded with one of the missionaries in the Pays d'en Haut in 1750 and 1751.[65] Castel's geography brought, not the Sea of the West, but the western ocean itself just west of the Manitoba lakes and the Riding Mountain-Moose Mountain uplands. He also interconnected all waterways, believing not only in the unity of water courses, but also that Lake Superior's water level was as high or even higher than the local levels in the Alps or Pyrenees.

The apocryphal journey that offered the largest fund of dubious features to mappers was that of one Admiral de Fonte.[66] A letter, published in an English magazine in 1708 and purported to be written by him, described a trip north of the fiftieth parallel on the northwest coast of the Pacific. In it, he claimed to have found a complex of passages, lakes, and straits through which he sailed east, until he met a Boston merchantman coming west. J.N. Del'isle[67] and Buache, among others, took up the admiral's cause, publishing maps and writing books in support of his perception of the continental Northwest. The story was also publicized by Arthur Dobbs[68] in his battle with the Hudson's Bay

Company over its monopoly of trade, although he also supported a simpler solution as shown by the map of a French-Canadian Indian, Joseph La France.[69] The repercussions of this interest in and promotion of the theory were felt into the nineteenth century. A 1768 map by Thomas Jeffreys, reprinted later in the French *Encyclopédie*, is a good example of the images then in force.[70] Although by the later decades of the century almost all of these controversial patterns had been erased—either replaced with verified details or large areas were left blank by the draughtsmen—several maps still were printed as late as 1816 with quite grotesque forms of at least antiquarian interest.[71] The theory of a passage through northern Rupert's Land and the Northwest received two essentially fatal blows in the 1770s. The first was Hearne's oblique transect from Churchill to the Coppermine mouth at the Arctic shore, which negated any chance of a strait crossing his line of travel. The second was the reconnaissance by Captain Cook of the west coast, which put to rest most of the claims of an entrance there, although it required closer examination later by Vancouver to verify this conclusion.

Most people are surprised to learn that the urge to find a shorter and easier route between water bodies was not confined to the Northwest Passage. There was long interest in avoiding the difficult waters beyond the furious over fall in Hudson Strait by finding a passage out of a Labrador fiord, or from the south side of Ungava Bay across the Hudson Bay, usually with Richmond Gulf as terminus. A map printed in 1718 illustrates this[72] (Fig. 7). By 1825, as a result of exploration by the Hudson's Bay Company, this theory had been abandoned, the large peninsula of eastern Rupert's Land had been cleared, and newly surveyed topographic features draughted in place[73] (Fig. 8).

This map also introduces a far different map image of Rupert's Land and the Northwest, as well as all of Canada. There are many reasons for this, but most significant are the following. In the late 1770s the Hudson's Bay Company hired Philip Turnor as its first professional surveyor and mapmaker, whose basic task it was to observe for the precise locations of the major known waterways, and thereby to establish a new map base for the use of the Company.[74] This base was built upon through the following century. Also, it had begun its programme of inland exploration and trade development around the building of trading posts, and it encouraged the surveying and mapping of these areas by young men already trained in Britain, such as David Thompson and John Hodgson,[75] by giving lessons on the job to bright young men, such as Peter Fidler[76] and James Clouston, and by urging others to observe and sketch whenever possible[77] (Fig. 9). After 1790 the Company reversed its position on secrecy and allowed access to its files to several leading persons—Alexander Dalrymple for one, Aaron Arrowsmith, a rising star in the cartographic world, for another.[78] From this time until the mid-nineteenth century, the Arrowsmith firm became the unofficial cartographers of the Company, recording each gain of topographical information and producing a series of maps every several years. One turned to their maps for the most recent information on the north part of America. Also, the North West Company and other private traders added to the stock of maps, which were used by the commercial cartographers for compilation data. The Company allowed several authors, including Samuel Hearne, to search its files when writing their books.[79]

Thus, the maps of the North and West began to shed both illusory and, as well, antiquated configurations; large map voids were cleared, into which blocks of new shapes and forms were added over the years, as witness, for example, a 1786 map that welded new features from Hearne on to the long-repeated forms seen to the south[80] (Fig. 10). Arrowsmith's map of 1795 (1796) reflects the accumulated experience of the Hudson's Bay Company inland, and also the true position and conformation of the Northwest Pacific coast, surveyed by the Vancouver expedition just before 1795[81] (Fig. 11).

Through the first half of the nineteenth century, the mapped patterns of Rupert's Land and the Northwest altered through the efforts of a myriad of men, engaged mainly in the fur trade. Map images changed in a kaleidoscopic manner, largely through the addition of detail, river valley by river basin, mountain range after range, along the arctic shore and amid the arctic island channels. Spatial vacua dwindled as the frontiers were breached. By 1858, Arrowsmith could publish a map having few major mysteries, albeit that of the Northwest Passage had not been solved. The complexity of local topography awaited further exploration[82] (Fig. 12).

Mapping of the physical geographic complexity of this immense region did not begin in earnest until the 1850s, when two major scientific exploring expeditions entered the prairie portion of Rupert's Land to carry out what were, basically, geographical field investigations. There had been sporadic scientific studies earlier, commencing with the geological examination of areas near Lake Winnipeg by the Franklin expedition.[83] Richardson had gathered climatic data for many places in the Northwest,[84] and there were also pioneer climatic maps by Blodget and Devine.[85] However, the geological, physiographic, and land classification mapping of the British group led by John Palliser and the Canadian expedition of H.Y. Hind laid the foundation for all later thematic mapping of the region. Mention of two maps only will suffice to indicate the changes occurring in the map images of Rupert's Land. The first is the small-scale geological map of southern Manitoba by Hind, printed in his two-volume report on the expedition[86] (Fig. 13). The second map, by Hector, the geologist of the Palliser party, introduces his concept of prairie levels.[87] But perhaps the most significant element of both reports and maps was the introduction of the first definition and delineation of the fertile belt and the dry grasslands, and thereby the introduction of natural and economic regional mapping into the West and Northwest[88] (Fig. 14).

Soon after 1870, old Rupert's Land, merging into the new West and Northwest, sustained the imprint of the land surveyor, the impress of settlers, the inquisitive hammer of the government geologist, the classifying gleaning of the geobotanist, and the instrumental recording of topographer and climatologist. A new tide of map images was at hand.

Notes

1. Baffin Bay.

2. John Davys, *The Voyages and Works of John Davis, the Navigator* (London: Hakluyt Society, 1880), 56.

3. John Davis aided Emery Molyneux to portray this feature on his globe of 1593. Petrus Plancius and Cornelis Claesz used the detail on this inset on their map *Nova Francia, alio nomine dicta Terra nova ...*, drawn about 1593.

4. Luke Foxe, *North-West Fox; or, Fox from the North-west passage* (London, 1635), in Miller Christy, *The Voyages of Captain Luke Foxe of Hull and Captain Thomas James of Bristol, in search of a North-West Passage, in 1631-32*, (London: Hakluyt Society, 1894), 85. Foxe included George Waymouth in this statement also.

5. Coolie Verner and Basil Stuart-Stubbs, *The North Part of America* (Toronto: Academic Press Canada Limited, 1979), 16.

6. George Waymouth, for the East India Company, voyaged possibly 300 miles into Hudson Strait in 1602. He had been preceded in 1578 by Frobisher, who ventured a short distance into the passage.

7. The "problem" of the New World barrier was analyzed by Francis B. Steck, *The Jolliet-Marquette Expedition, 1673* (Quincy, Ill.: Franciscan Fathers, 1928), and the idea of three phases — southern, western, and northern — was included therein.

8. The royal charter of 1670 was granted to eighteen subscribers incorporated as the "Governor and Company of Adventurers of England trading into Hudsons Bay."

9. Thomas James, *The Platt of Sayling for the discoverye of a Passage into the South Sea. 1631 1632*, in James, *The strange and dangerous voyage of Captain Thomas James* (London, 1633). A chart maker, Norwood, was paid £2 in May, 1669, by the group for having drawn a "Map of Hudsons bay according to Capt. James's Descriptions." A14/1, fo.108, HBC Archives.

10. John Thornton, a leading London chart maker, draughted eleven charts of all or part of Hudson Bay for the Company from 1680 to 1702, which no longer exist in the Archives.

11. Jonathan Swift, "On Poetry: A Rhapsody," in *Swift: Poetical Works*, ed. Herbert Davis (London: Oxford University Press, 1967), 574.

12. Although there is contention, it is attributed to la Cosa, owner and mate of the *Santa Maria*, and the date as 1500; in the Museo Naval, Madrid.

13. *Tabula Nautica*, in Hessel Gerritsz, *Descriptio ac Delineatio Geographica Detectionis* (Amsterdam, 1612).

14. James Clouston, HBC schoolmaster, Eastmain, Hudson Bay, 1811; trader after 1814, and until 1825 main explorer-mapper of interior Quebec.

15. Captain John Palliser, chief of British scientific exploring expedition, 1857-59, from Lake Superior to Rocky Mountains, and beyond to Columbia River.

16. Henry Y. Hind, professor of chemistry and geology, Trinity College, Toronto, led the Canadian scientific exploring expedition of 1857-58 to the Canadian prairies.

17. The new discoveries were normally attached to the eastern shore of a major peninsula projecting eastward from mainland Asia, as depicted for example by the world maps of Contarini, 1506; Ruysch, 1507; and Bertelli, 1565, among others.

18. Martin Waldseemüller, *Orbis Typus Universalis*, or the Admiral's Map, in the "Supplement" of contemporary maps in the Strasbourg edition of Ptolemy's Geography, 1513.

19. Estevan Gomez, Portuguese navigator sent by Spain, 1524-25, to explore North American east coast from Florida north past Nova Scotia. Lucas Vasquez de Ayllon had supported exploration along Atlantic coast from 1521, until he led settlers in 1526 in an unsuccessful project to the Carolina coast.

20. Giovanni da Verrazzano, Florentine, undertook the first French exploration of American coast, searching for route to Cathay, 1524. His brother Girolamo draughted a world map in 1529 on which the isthmus and nearby western sea were portrayed.

21. Michael Lok of London had this woodcut map printed in Hakluyt's *Divers Voyages Touching the Discouerie of America and the Islands Adjacent* (London, 1582).

22. Pierre Desceliers of Dieppe, part of manuscript world map, Add. Ms. 24065, 1550, British Museum, London.

23. As, for example, Giacomo Gastaldi, *La Nuova Francia* in Giovanni Battista Ramusio, *Navigationi et viaggi* (Venice, 1556).

24. Such as Bolognino Zaltieri, *Il Disegno del discoperto della noua Franza*, included in Lafreri Atlas (Rome, 1566).

25. André Thevet, *Quarte Partie du Monde*, 1575.

26. On map *Novus Orbis* (Paris, 1587).

27. Cornelis van Wytfliet, *Conibas Regio Cum Vicinis Gentibus,* in *Descriptionis Ptolemaicae augmentum* (Louvain, 1597).

28. Abraham Ortelius, *Americae Sive Novi Orbis, Nova Descriptio,* in his *Theatrum Orbis Terrarum* (Antwerp, 1570).

29. A bay, or small sea, extending south from an American north coast appeared on Gerard Mercator's world map of 1569, and was also included on the 1595 map published in Mercator's atlas by his son Rumold after his father's death.

30. Gerard Mercator, *Nova et avcta orbis terrae descriptio ad vsvm nauigantium emendate accommodata*, 1569.

31. Robert Didier de Vaugondy, *Carte des parties nord et ouest de L'Amerique dressée d'après les relations les plus authentiques par M en 1764. Nouvelle édition réduite par M. de Vaugondy en 1772.*

32. Luke Foxe, *Polar Map or Card*, in *North-West Fox* (London, 1635).

33. Henry Briggs's, *The North part of America*, in Samuel Purchas, *Purchas his Pilgrimes*, to accompany Brigg's text *A Treatise of the North-West Passage to the South Sea, Through the Continent of Virginia, and by Fretum Hudson* (London, 1625).

34. Samuel de Champlain, *Carte de la Nouvelle France*, in his *Voyages de la Nouvelle France Occidentale* (Paris, 1632).

35. Nicolas Sanson, *Amerique Septentrionale* (Paris, 1650).

36. Samuel Thornton, a map of Hudson Bay and Strait, made "at the Signe of the Platt in the Minories" (London, 1709).

37. Father Laure, Jesuit priest, *Carte du Domaine Du Roy en Canada*, 1733.

38. Henry Kelsey, teen-age Company employee, was sent north of the Churchill River about 210 miles in 1689, a prelude to the first

inland journey of a European to the interior grasslands from 1690 to 1692.

39. William Stewart's task was to act as a peace intermediary between the Chipewyan Indians and their neighbours, and to encourage them to come to trade at Churchill Factory.

40. Richard Norton was sent inland to give notice to the Indians between Lake Athabasca and the Slave River area, and the lower Churchill, of the opening of the new factory, and to urge them to come to trade.

41. Alexis-Hubert Jaillot, *Partie De La Nouvelle France*, (Paris, 1685).

42. Guillaume Del'isle, *Carte du Canada ou de la Nouvelle France* (Paris, 1703).

43. Jean-Baptiste-Louis Franquelin introduced a network of mighty rivers and spacious lakes to the maps of the Northwest, which were based partly on Indian and on fur trader-explorer information.

44. *Partie De L'Amerique Septentrionale Contenant La Nle France...*, 1700.

45. First HBC servant inland in new program; total of fifty-four persons sent to plains over two decades, or nineteen different individuals.

46. Based on author's study of HBC map and text records.

47. Samuel Hearne, A *Map of part of the Inland Country to the Nh Wt, of Prince of Wale's Fort Hs; By, ...*, 1772. G 2/10, HBC Archives.

48. Thomas Bowen, *A New & Accurate Map of North America; Drawn from the most Authentic Modern Maps and Charts*, in Middleton's *Complete System of Geography* (London, 1778).

49. See Richard I. Ruggles, "Governor Samuel Wegg 'Winds of Change,'" *The Beaver* 307 (Autumn 1976): 10-20.

50. William Coats, *To the Honourable Governour The Deputy Governour and Committee of the Hudsons Bay company this chart of Artiwinipeck is humbly dedicated and Presented...*, 1749. G1/18, HBC Archives.

51.   [Andrew Graham], *A Plan Of Part Of Hudson's-Bay, & Rivers, Communicating with York Fort & Severn*, [1774]. G 2/17, HBC Archives.

52.   Samuel Hearne, *A Map of some of the principal Lakes River's &c leading from YF to Basquiaw*; ..., [1775]. G 1/20, HBC Archives.

53.   Cartier had proved the St. Lawrence to be a great river, not a strait, and had heard of a large water-body west of Hochelaga. By 1632 it had been shown that this was a chain of lakes and not a sea. There was a strong possibility that the Great Water lay just beyond Lake Huron.

54.   The large sea became equated with a "great river" based on reports from Nicolet, Radisson and Groseilliers, and Jesuit missionaries.

55.   Related to the riverine commentaries with a transmutation to a Sea of the West theory, which in the eighteenth century was either the western sea lying just beyond the lakes of Manitoba or a large gulf of the sea extending into the plains.

56.   The sketches were combined into one sketch by La Vérendrye, which became the basis for printed maps in France, and also for manuscript transcriptions.

57.   Malcolm G. Lewis, *Euroamerican Misinterpretation of Amerindian Maps*, unpublished paper, 11th. International Conference on the History of Cartography, Ottawa, 1985, 17 pages.

58.   A worksheet prepared by using Guillaume Del'isle's printed base.

59.   Nicolas J. Bellin, *Carte De L'Amerique Septentrionale Pour servir a l'Histoire de la Nouvelle France*, 1743.

60.   At least twelve maps were prepared by the La Vérendrye group or, at their behest, by Indians, which were sent to the colonial government.

61.   For example: Samuel Dunn, *A Map of the British Empire in North America* (London, 1776); J. Carver, *A New Map of North America, From the Latest Discoveries*, 1778; and Thomas Kitchin, *North America Drawn from the latest and best authorities*, [1808].

62.   A Greek pilot who alleged discovery in 1592 of a large inlet on the Pacific coast between 47°N and 48°N latitudes.

63. A member of the Spanish Vizcaino expedition of 1602-03, who reported seeing the opening of a great river on the Pacific coast at 41°N latitude.

64. Philippe Buache, *Carte Physique des Terreines les plus élevés de la Partie Occidentale du Canada*, (Paris, 1754).

65. He obtained much of his information from Father Coquart. He prepared several versions of the continent's geography, and also elaborated plans for French occupation of the West.

66. This letter appeared in *Monthly Miscellany, or Memoires for the Curious*, April and June, 1708. The water routes includedRivière and Lac Bernarda, Rivière de Los Reyes and de Haro, and Lac de Fonte, and he described a complex of islands, Archipelago St. Lazare, north of the 50th parallel on the Pacific coast.

67. Joseph-Nicolas Del'isle, younger brother of Guillaume, draughted a number of maps, the best known being *Carte Generale Des Découvertes de l'Amiral de Fonte et autres Navigateurs...pour la recherche du Passage a la Mer du Sud* (Paris, 1752).

68. In his book, *An Account of the Countries adjoining to Hudson's Bay* (London, 1744).

69. *A New Map of Part of North America...as described by Jospeh La France ...*, printed in Dobbs, *An Account of...Hudson's Bay*.

70. Thomas Jeffreys, *Carte Générale des Découvertes De L'Amiral De Fonte representant la grande probabilité d'un Passage Au Nord Ouest*, 1768, reproduced in the famed *Encyclopédie* of France.

71. William Goldson, *Chart on Mercators Projection, exhibiting the Tracks of Maldonado and de Fonte, in 1598 and 1640; Compared with The Modern Discoveries* (London, 1793).

72. Nicolas De Fer, *La France occidentale dans l'Amerique septentrional ou le cours de la riviere de St. Laurens aux environs de la quelle se trouvent le Canada...* (Paris, 1718).

73. James Clouston's final map of 1825 had become available. Its details appeared on Arrowsmith's publications and also on a map by Sidney Hall, *British North America* (London 1829).

74. Turnor prepared eleven manuscript maps, one of which was at large scale in fourteen sheets. Only eight maps are still located in the HBC Archives.

75.   Details of the early training of these young apprentices is given in Richard I. Ruggles, "Hospital Boys of the Bay," *The Beaver* 308 (Autumn 1977): 4-11.

76.   Turnor chose Fidler to accompany him across to the Athabasca to replace Thompson, who had broken his leg. He trained Fidler in surveying techniques.

77.   This map was undoubtedly drawn by Edward Jarvis, with Donald McKay; *A Map of Hudsons Bay and interior Westerly particularly above Albany*, 1791, G 1/13, HBC Archives. It illustrated their trading plan for the Company from the upper Albany across to the Red-Assiniboine valleys.

78.   Alexander Dalrymple was a friend of Governor Samuel Wegg of the HBC, and Fellow of the Royal Society with him. He used both map and text information to prepare papers on trade topics and maps of the northern regions.

79.   Samuel Hearne, *A Journey From Prince of Wales's Fort, in Hudson's Bay, To The Northern Ocean ...* (London, 1795). See Richard I. Ruggles, "Governor Samuel Wegg Intelligent Layman of the Royal Society 1753-1802," *Notes and Records of the Royal Society of London*, 32 (March 1978): 181-99.

80.   *The British Colonies in North America from the best Authorities*, 1786.

81.   Aaron Arrowsmith, *A Map Exhibiting all the New Discoveries in the Interior Parts of North America* (London, 1795 [1796]).

82.   John Arrowsmith, *Map of North America* (London, 1858).

83.   John Franklin, leading the British Arctic Land Expedition in 1819, spent October to January, 1820, at Cumberland House. He and his officers made observations in this general region during this time.

84.   From 1819 for over thirty years, John Richardson provided much scientific information on weather, climate, and agricultural possibilities of this region, based on his own field observations and reports from HBC officers and other sources.

85.   Lorin Blodget, *Climatology of the United States and of the Temperate Latitudes of the North American Continent* (Philadelphia, 1857); Thomas Devine, *Map of the Northwest Part of Canada, Hudson's Bay & Indian Territories* (Toronto, 1857).

86.   Henry Youle Hind, *Geological Map of a Part of Rupert's Land*, 1860, in H.Y. Hind, *Narrative of the Canadian Red River Exploring Expedition of 1857 and of the Assiniboine and Saskatchewan Exploring Expedition of 1858* (London: Longman, Green, Longman and Roberts, 1859 and 1860), vol. 2, facing page 239.

87.   James Hector, *Map of Winnipeg Lake Basin.   Shewing the distribution of the Superficial deposites*, in *Papers Relative to the Exploration of British North America by Captain Palliser* ... Sh. 8 (London, 1859 and 1860).

88.   Part of map by John Arrowsmith, *Country Between the Red River Settlement and the Rocky Mountains; Showing the Various Routes of the Expedition, under the Command of Captn. John Palliser. 1857 & 1858* (London, 1859), in *Papers Relative to the Exploration...by Captain Palliser.*

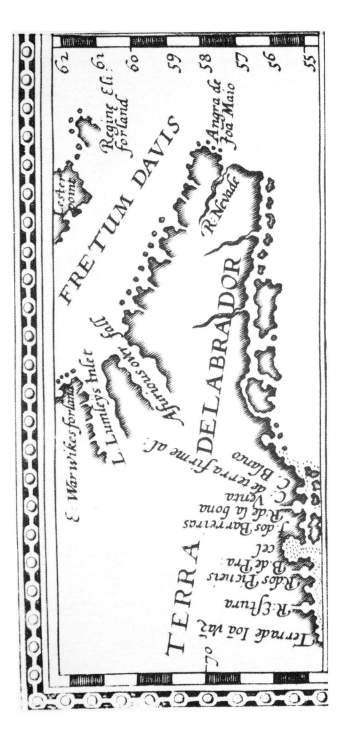

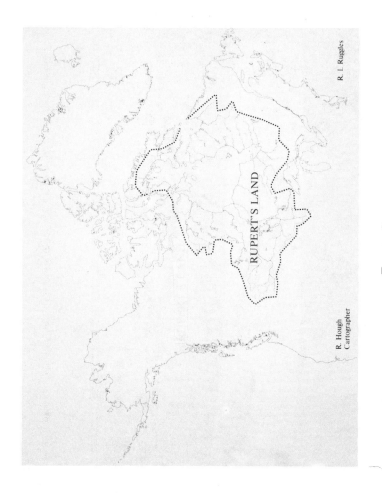

RUPERT'S LAND

R. Hough
Cartographer

R. I. Ruggles

FIGURE 2

The perimeter of Rupert's Land, as interpreted from the Hudson's Bay Company charter

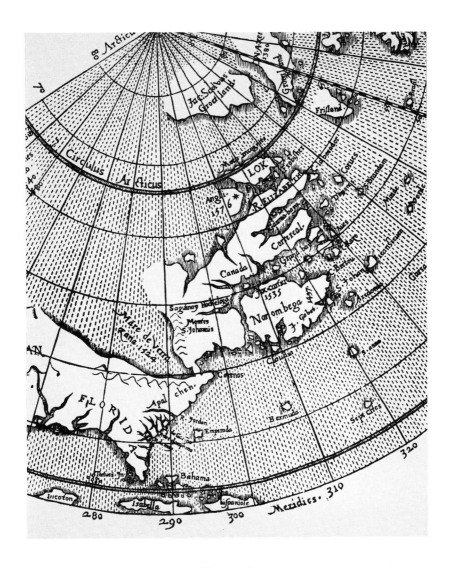

FIGURE 3

This map was draughted in 1582, showing North America
*Illustri Viro, Domino Philippo Sidnaeo Michael Lok Civis Londinensis Hanc
Chartram Dedicabat*

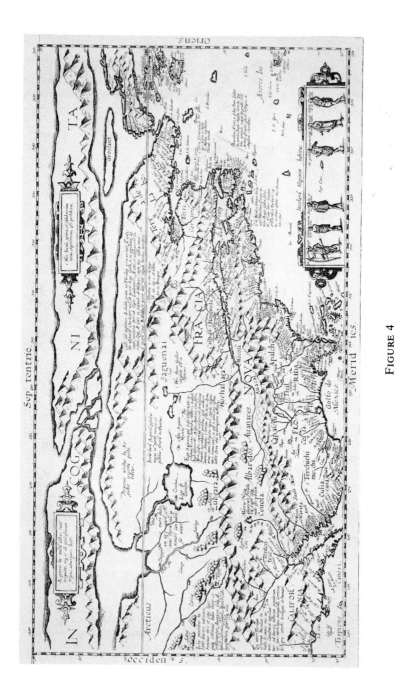

FIGURE 4

Cornelis de Jode, *Americae Pars Borealis, Florida, Baccalaos, Canada, Corterealis*
(Antwerp, 1593)

FIGURE 5

Jean-Baptiste-Louis Franquelin's manuscript map, *La N^{le} [Nouvelle] France*, draughted in 1700; this is the northwest part

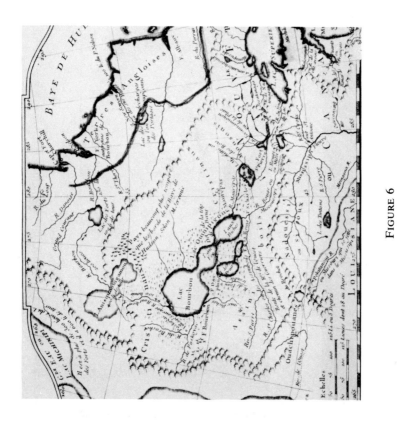

FIGURE 7

This is a map by H.A. Chatelain, *Carte de la Nouvelle France* (Paris, 1719), which is almost a direct copy of N. de Fer, 1718

FIGURE 8

Sidney Hall's map of 1828 is based largely on Hudson's Bay Company data, as transmitted through Arrowsmith published maps

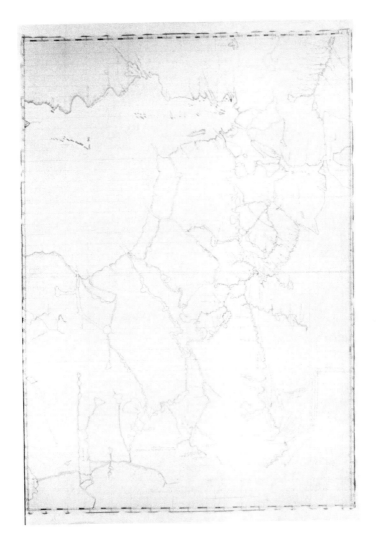

FIGURE 9

McKay-Jarvis manuscript map, courtesy of the Hudson's Bay Company Archives. It extends northwest to Great Slave Lake

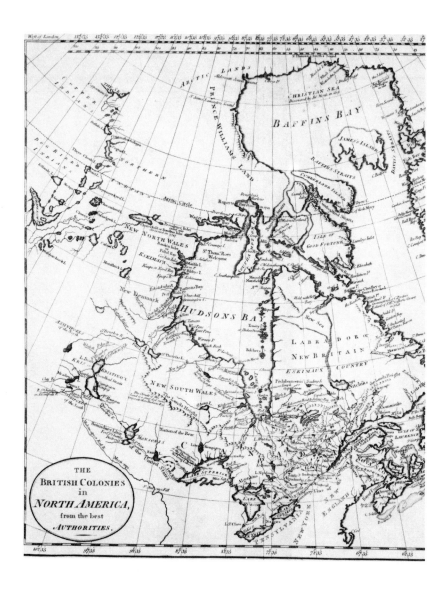

FIGURE 10

This printed map illustrates the dearth of detailed information west of Hudson
Bay, except for Hearne's information across to the Coppermine River

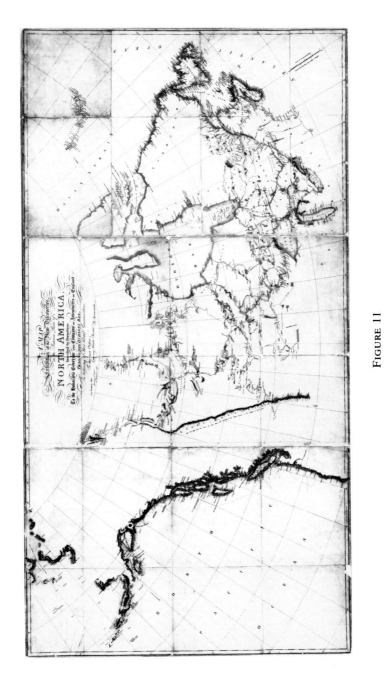

FIGURE 11

Aaron Arrowsmith Map of North America, 1795 (1796)

FIGURE 12

John Arrowsmith, *British North America* (London, 1858)

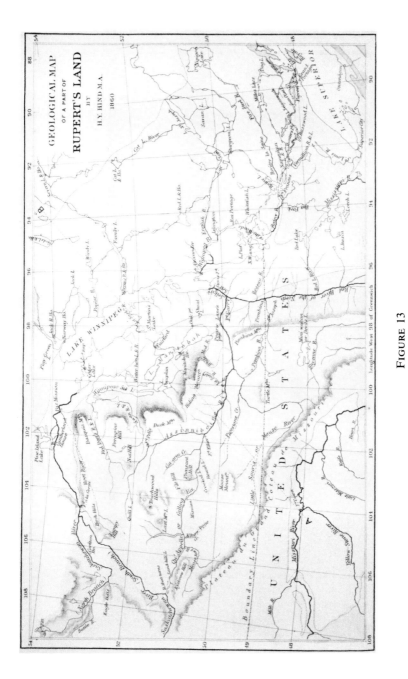

FIGURE 13

Hind's geological map of the eastern plains, from the 1857–1858 expedition, printed 1860

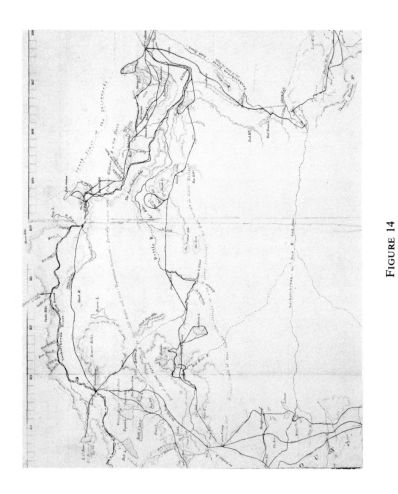

FIGURE 14

John Arrowsmith's printed version of Palliser's map showing the boundaries of the
natural regions across Saskatchewan and Alberta

Chapter 2

THREE WORLDS, ONE FOCUS: EUROPEANS MEET INUIT AND AMERINDIANS IN THE FAR NORTH

Olive Patricia Dickason

First contacts between white men and peoples of the New World occurred over a much longer period than is usually realized. Far from being confined to the dim and distant past, when Europeans were discovering that the world was larger and much more complex then they had imagined, first encounters have been continuing into the historical present in such inaccessible areas as the interior of Brazil, and in the near-historical present, in the icy fastness of the Arctic. As far as Canada is concerned, first meetings for which there is a reasonably acceptable record began with the Norse about A.D. 1000, and continued at least until mid-nineteenth century, when isolated bands of Copper and Netsilik Inuit were first met; even then, sustained contact with some of these people did not develop until the second decade of the twentieth century. In other words, first meetings occurred, off and on, over a period of more than eight hundred years. For Rupert's Land Amerindians, first contact appears to have been with Henry Hudson (fl. 1607-1611) in James Bay in 1611, more than a century after encounters had become sustained for those of the North Atlantic coast. Although Amerindians followed the Inuit in meeting Europeans, they established sustained contact much sooner. This paper will be largely concerned with first meetings in that part of the Canadian North referred to as Rupert's Land; however, since the boundaries of that huge region have never been clearly defined, I will take advantage of the situation to begin with the earliest known encounters, even though they occurred east and perhaps north of lands draining into Hudson Bay. The time period will range from A.D. 1000 to the beginnings of permanent European settlement in the Northwest during the first decades of the nineteenth century. It will be seen that despite the great length of time involved, only a limited and partial sense of community developed, under the specific conditions created by the fur trade and whaling. Eight hundred years later, the three worlds of Inuit, Amerindians, and Europeans were still essentially distinct, as each had responded to the impact of contact according to its own cultural ethos, and so had evolved in its own individual way.

The first recorded encounters in the New World took place in the Eastern Arctic, perhaps some of them on Baffin Island, and along the North Atlantic coast of what is now Canada. Two of the peoples most likely to have been involved have since disappeared. The Skraelings (from *Skraelingjar*, meaning small, withered), whom the Norsemen first met on friendly terms that soon turned hostile, were probably Dorset, but the term could have been used also for the Beothuck. When the Norse arrived, the Dorset, descendants of the Pre-Dorset who had been in the region since 4000 B.P., were giving way to the recently-appeared Thule Inuit.[1] Possible Norse encounters with the Beothuck of Newfoundland were even more ephemeral. Europeans who arrived later (mainly British) caused the Beothuck to retreat to the Exploits River region in the interior of their island habitat, where they survived in diminishing numbers until the last known of their peoples died in 1829.[2]

Norse references to Skraelings are not particularly informative, whether dealing with the aborigines of Greenland or with those of Canada. The comments that have been reported give the impression that the Norse thought of the Skraelings as beings apart, possibly placing them in a category similar to the folkloric creatures with which they had populated their Old World forests. For instance, during the period 1001-1005, Thorgills Orrabeinsfostri, travelling in East Greenland, reported seeing two "troll wives," which conjures up a picture that was reinforced by Ari a century later in his *Historia-Norvegiae*, when he wrote of Skraelings as "very little people," entirely lacking in iron, who "use whale teeth for arrowheads and sharp stones for knives."[3] The Skraelings encountered by Thorfinnr Karlsefni Thordarson and his band when attempting to colonize the mainland were described as "small ill-favoured men" who had "ugly hair on their heads. They had big eyes and were broad in the cheeks."[4]

The earliest illustration that we have of the Arctic's "little people" did not appear until centuries later, in 1539. It adorns the *carta marina* of Olaus Magnus, which shows one of them fighting a normal-sized European.[5] The small stature and full beard the artist has used to depict the Skraeling accords with a 1563 description of Greenlanders as "Pigmies" who were "hayrie to the outermost joynts of the finger; and that the males have beards down to the knees, but, although they have the shape of man, yet they have little sense or understanding, or distinct speech, but make shew of a kind of hissing, after the manner of Geese." The same report also tells of finding "a little man dead, with a long beard, with a little boat."[6] The term "Skraeling" was not used in this account, which postdates the disappearance of the Norse settlements by about a century. A 1572 edition of the *carta marina* shows the Skraeling without a beard and trimmer in physique, consequently appearing younger. Their reported short stature is a puzzle, as archaeological evidence has not supported the notion that the Dorset were smaller than the Inuit. The proportions lent by the style of their clothes possibly could have helped to create such an impression. Capturing the distinctive appearance of New World people would bedevil Old World artists for some time.[7]

Early English arctic voyage accounts seldom refer to the stature of the natives they met, perhaps because the Inuit, unlike the Dorset, presented nothing unusual to report. Of those explorers who did comment, John Davis (1550?-1605) in 1587 noted that their stature was "good," and James Hall (d.1612) in 1605 found it "reasonable," whereas John Knight (d.1606) the following year adjudged the natives to be "little people," with "little or no beard." One could speculate that Davis and Hall had seen Thule Inuit, and that Knight had encountered a remnant group of Dorset. In 1631, small size was again reported for arctic peoples, this time by Luke Foxe (1586-1635). On an island thought to be Silumiut lying north of the entrance to Chesterfield Inlet, Foxe's crew uncovered graves containing skeletons "not above 4 foot long."[8] Archaeology has confirmed that the burials were indeed Inuit, but it has not confirmed the small size; the remains could have been those of children. Foxe himself never encountered living Inuit to verify his observations.

Whether Dorset or Thule, the natives were willing to trade products of the hunt for weapons, but caution prevailed on the part of the Europeans, particularly the Norse who, on one reported occasion, would only offer milk in exchange for furs.[9] That trading did occur can be inferred by the presence of European artifacts at archaeological sites, especially burials, and, even more intriguing, by the discovery in Bergen, in what was apparently a thirteenth-century context, of a walrus figurine of Inuit workmanship. Bergen was the Norwegian port that dealt with Iceland and Greenland.[10]

That the men of bone and stone were capable of holding their own against the men of iron in pre-firearms days is evidenced by the short duration of Norse attempts to settle on northern Newfoundland and mainland coasts, as well as by the fate of the more enduring Greenland settlements.[11] The slim record that we have of these events indicates that hostilities preceded the abandonment of the colonies. In Greenland, other factors were likely more important, such as the deterioration of the climate, beginning in the thirteenth century and culminating in the Little Ice Age, c.1650-c.1850. The situation favoured the Inuit, who moved south as the climate became colder; at the time the settlements had been founded, there had been no Inuit in southern Greenland. When Sir Martin Frobisher (1539?-1594) visited Greenland in 1578, only Inuit were on the island, no Norse.[12]

The Inuit whom Frobisher encountered on his earlier voyages (1576, 1577) as well as in 1578 were obviously already familiar with Europeans and their ships. They possessed iron; during one of his several melees with them, Frobisher was struck by an arrow with an iron tip.[13] He amplified the brief Norse descriptions of these people: "They be like *Tartars*," he wrote in his account of his first voyage, 1576, "with long blacke haire, broad faces, flat nosed, and tawny Coloured, wearing Seale skinnes, and so doe the women, nothing differing; but the women in the Face hath blue stroakes downe the Cheekes, and about the eyes."[14] Frobisher's reference to Tartars reflects the identification between the Asiatic warrior-nomads and New World peoples that had been going on since the days of Columbus in various parts of the Western Hemisphere. It had the weight of classical authority behind it, as the Romans had described the Tartars in terms connotative of Amerindians and Inuit. The same was also true for the Scythians, with whom New World peoples were even more frequently compared.

A later English expedition visiting an Inuit camp that had been precipitously abandoned at their approach revealed that life could be bountiful for the natives in a land that appeared stark and inhospitable to Europeans. It was an observation that was corroborated in later reports.[15] The Inuit's dogs were frequently reported to be fat, in one case to the point that "they could scarce goe."[16] That the dogs were able to fend for themselves, even in competition with their owners, was attested to by later travellers.[17]

The habit of the Inuit of availing themselves without permission to useful items of European equipment did nothing to promote camaraderie. Inuit actions reflected the native idea, found among hunting and gathering peoples throughout the New World, that those who were so abundantly and so well equipped as the Europeans visiting them, were under an obligation to share with those who were less well off. Since Europeans showed little, if any, inclination to do this voluntarily, the Inuit took it upon themselves to show the way. As Frobisher reported, in "their Canoes of Leather, (they) had like to have stolne his Boate from him before he was aware."[18] Despite such mutual irritations, each sometimes went to considerable lengths to put the other at ease. Davis, on his first encounter with Inuit, ordered "his Musitians to

play, wherein they [the Inuit] tooke great delight, and fals a dauncing."
The Inuit became "familiar," to the point of selling "their cloaths from
their backs." On his second voyage, when Davis wanted to explore the
country, fifty Inuit in their kayaks turned up to act as his escort. On land,
the "people very carefully helpe him up and down the steepe Rockes."[19]
At times relations relaxed to the point where athletic competitions took
place. On one such occasion the English out-leaped the Inuit, but the
latter out-wrestled the best of the English to the ground. Some of the
natives climbed the ship's rigging "into the maine top."[20]

Still, forgetting precaution could lead to disaster, as when a group
of Inuit succeeded in capturing five of Frobisher's crew along with their
boat. Frobisher never did get his men back,[21] although he was able to
effect a spectacular retaliation by luring an incautious native close to his
ship, leaning over his ship's side, and lifting the man out of the water,
kayak and all. The Inuk in vexation was reported to have bitten his
tongue in two, but survived to become a great success in England.[22] He
was displayed as one of Frobisher's "tokens of possession," indisputable
proof that the explorer had found and claimed new lands for Her
Majesty.[23] The Inuit, for their part, maintained an oral tradition of the
time when they were visited by the *kodlunas* (today's *kabloonas*), which
was recorded, three centuries later, in 1861; as well, they had carefully
preserved "sundry odds and ends" from Frobisher's expeditions, such as
pieces of red brick and brass rings.[24]

Frobisher's captured Inuk did not live long to enjoy his new life in
England. This was the usual fate of New World individuals taken to the
Old World at this time; change of diet and living conditions, not to
mention unfamiliar diseases, usually quickly proved fatal. Europeans left
to stay in the New World appear, on the whole, to have enjoyed a
happier fate, so much so that it was not long before individuals were
choosing to stay over. For obvious reasons, the record of what happened
to them is even scantier than it is for New World people in Europe. The
persons selected for this service were convicts, perhaps condemned
criminals. If they were not simply being left for punishment, but were
being offered a chance to redeem themselves, their function was to learn
the language and way of life of the people among whom they were to live,
as well as something about their land. The idea was for these
"interpreters" to report back to officials of their mother country when
they were picked up several years later, if anyone remembered, or cared
enough, to do so. The Portuguese did this in Brazil, beginning with Pedro
Cabral in 1500 (the men he left behind were never seen by the
Portuguese again). The French were particularly successful with this

practice in Brazil, creating a cadre of on-the-scene "interpreters" who became key factors in the highly profitable French brazilwood trade of the sixteenth century. The Danes also did this in Greenland, as described by James Hall on his voyage of 1605: "He [the Danish Commander] sets on land one young man to be left in the Countrey, to his cruell fortune, this was done by expresse command of the *State-holder of Denmarke*, before his coming forth; they also in the Pinnace set another on land, both being malefactors, giving of them small necessaries. (*It may be those people lived a long time after, and may bee yet living, if the Salvages have not devoured them.*)"[25] Hall did not state what the Danish Stadtholder had expected to achieve by this action.

According to Oswalt, the English at this period did not consider the Inuit as being particularly different from themselves, referring to them as "countrie people" rather than as "savages."[26] The accounts of Frobisher, Davis, and Hall, as well as other explorers, indicate otherwise; the term "salvage" was generally used to refer to Inuit. Inuit were reported to "eate all their meate raw," and also to "eate grasse like bruit beasts, without table or stoole, and when their hands are inbrued in blood they lick them clean with their tongues."[27] The term "country people," while in itself neutral, could refer to "salvages" as is evident in the account of Davis's expedition in 1585. In that particular case, the "country people" were believed to be sun-worshippers. However, because they were "very tractable, voide of subtilety," the English judged them to be "easie to be brought to civility."[28] But on Davis's second voyage, 1587, Inuit were taken to be "Idolaters and witches,"[29] serious charges in an age when Europeans burned witches alive at the stake, and when Christians tended to consider non-Christians to be *ipso facto* enemies. Hall reflected this attitude when he referred to the Inuit's "wicked condition."[30] The English also appear to have shared with Europeans in general the belief that all New World peoples were cannibals, a too-readily accepted generalization from early reports of cannibalistic practices in the West Indies and Brazil. Davis's men shared this view, as had Frobisher's; John Knight, in 1606, wrote simply that they were "man-eaters."[31] Hall, noting that some "of our men conceived them to be Man-eaters," could not, on the basis of his own experience, justify such an assessment. But he cautiously warned, "let others take heed."[32] Later, reports became more colourful as they parted company from substantiation: to quote Nicolas Jérémie (1669-1732), "when they kill or capture any of their enemies, they eat them raw and drink their blood. They even make infants at the breast drink it, so as to instil in them the barbarian ardour of war from their tenderest years."[33]

That the English took the "savagery" of the Inuit for granted is evident in the royal instructions to Thomas Button (d. 1634) in 1612, when he was about to sail in search of the Northwest Passage: "You must be careful to prevent all Mutynie amongst yor people, and to preserve them as muche as maie be from the Treacherie and villanie of the SALUAGES, and other Easterne people."[34] Oddly enough, once the English took possession of Rupert's Land and became a permanent trading presence in the region, they did not, in all the voluminous documentation of the Hudson's Bay Company, call either Inuit or Amerindians "savages," although the term (as well as such adjectives as "wild," "brutish," "barbarous," and "heathenish") was sometimes used to describe their customs and way of life. This is all the more striking in view of the use of the term by earlier explorers, as well as by contemporary officials and settlers on the Atlantic seaboard and in the St. Lawrence Valley.

It was on Frobisher's second voyage, 1577, that the explorer conducted his well-known experiment to observe "savage" sexual behaviour. It had been widely reported that the sexual habits of New World peoples were chaotic, with no regard for consanguinity, and with indiscriminate mating on chance encounters.[35] Accordingly, when Frobisher and his crew captured, in separate incidents, an Inuit man, and later a woman with her child, the captors brought the prisoners together "to behold the manner of their meeting." The couple reacted with considerable formality, and although they were put into the same quarters to live together, "yet they did never use as man and wife, though the woman spared not to do all necessary things that appertaine to a good huswife...as in making cleane their Cabine, and in every other thing appertaining to his ease."[36]

The closest to sustained contact that developed between natives of the Eastern Arctic and Europeans during this period was through the medium of whaling. This began along the Labrador Coast and the Strait of Belle Isle, where Inuit whalers met with Basque whalers, and later with French. Initially, these encounters followed the pattern of trading and raiding. It is not known if this behaviour extended to the Davis Strait, where Dutch, Danish, and Norwegian whalers were operating irregularly off the Greenland coast, but by the first half of the eighteenth century, Inuit were occasionally working with European whalers in those waters as that enterprise both regularized and intensified.[37] It was a cooperation that would reach its fullest development during the nineteenth century, after the scene of operations had moved to northwestern Hudson Bay and Americans had become major participants. That would last until the first decade of the twentieth century.

Apart from the Norse encounters with Skraelings, almost all these early contacts appear to have been with Inuit. Since voyage chroniclers did not differentiate when writing about "salvages," this is a matter of inference, principally from the location of the contact but also from the skimpy ethnographic descriptions. When the English did meet an Amerindian, as Hudson did in James Bay, they went to some trouble to demonstrate friendliness. The Amerindian liked the knife, looking glass, and buttons that the crew had scrounged from their personal belongings for presentation to him. On a second visit, he came pulling a sled upon which were the skins of two deer and two beaver. He placed the crew's gifts on the beaver before presenting the pelts to Hudson in exchange. Upon Hudson's acceptance, the Amerindian put away the items the English had given him; that particular transaction was complete. When Hudson then offered a hatchet, the native reciprocated with one of the deer skins, but Hudson insisted on both. Accepting this, "although not willingly," the Amerindian indicated that he would return again, but never did.[38] Such behaviour suggests that the Amerindian had a clear idea of the exchange rate he expected in trade, which may have been in accord with that of the north/south native networks that even at that time operated as far north as James Bay. Or perhaps the episode simply illustrates the Amerindian distaste for haggling over individual items, a characteristic which the English would later learn to accommodate.[39] The Cree, for their part, have a startlingly different remembrance of their first trade with the English. They recall that the latter wanted their fur clothing, and persuaded them to trade the clothes off their backs in exchange for English garments, in an episode somewhat reminiscent of one of Davis's encounters,[40] as well as those of other explorers, including Jacques Cartier.

Hudson appears to have been more eager to meet with Amerindians than the latter were to meet the English following the trading encounter. His motives were simple, "for hee was perswaded that if he met with the Salvages, hee should have refreshing of fresh meat, and that good store." But he was disappointed, for "though the Inhabitants set the woods on fire before him, yet they would not come to him."[41]

The presence of white men in the Arctic may have had more effect upon the natives than the incidence of direct contact would suggest. From the time of their first appearance in the region, white men had frequently encountered disasters that had forced them to abandon supplies and equipment, and sometimes even their ships. For the Inuit, these provided the occasion for serendipity; for instance, when the Dane, Jens Munk (1579-1628) had to abandon his ship *Unicorn* after a disastrous wintering-over in the Churchill River area, 1619-20, the natives of Hudson Bay reaped the benefits from this source of highly-prized items such as iron. According to Jérémie, Amerindians were the first to exploit this treasure trove, but at a high cost: not being familiar with the properties of gunpowder, they set fire to a keg, blowing themselves up.[42] That did not deter other Amerindians from exploiting the site, as well as Inuit from across the Bay.[43] In 1631, Thomas James (1593-1635) found evidence of native use of a wreck on Danby Island. The effects of this availability of usually scarce goods upon the groups involved have not been assessed for this early period, but a recent study by Clifford G. Hickey of a similar situation arising from the abandonment in 1853 of the British Royal Navy's *Investigator* on northern Banks Island suggests that they could have been considerable, both socially and economically. Using the Banks Island experience as a model, one effect could have been intensification of kin relationships as well as their transformation into formal exchange partnerships in order to cope with the sudden access to wealth, resulting in clearer definition of social boundaries; economically, it could have led to an extension of the "foreclosure period" of reciprocal obligations, which in turn could alter the resource procurement patterns employed to meet those obligations.[44] These, of course, represent only one set of possible reactions and interactions that could be brought into play, depending upon the groups involved and the particular local situation. It sometimes happened that wrecks were not found; at least, when Europeans came across them, they showed no signs of having been used. This was apparently the case at Port Nelson, where Thomas Button had wintered over 1612-13 with a heavy loss of men, abandoning a ship and supplies when he sailed the following summer. Foxe came upon the apparently untouched site nearly twenty years later; a little more than forty years after that, in 1673, it was still reported to be undisturbed when Médard Chouart Des Groseilliers (1618-1696?) visited the location.[45]

Deserted campsites or cabins also could provide useful materials, although with nothing like the bounty of shipwrecks. Such cabins, of course, would have been found in the boreal forest rather than on the barren grounds. Peter Fidler (1769-1822) told of an occasion in Slave River country in which Canadians built a small log structure to protect a cache of furs and other supplies, which had been "protected or Guarded all winter by an Image set upon a painted red pole over the house about the size of a small child. Not an Indian would go up to the House to look at it...being thoroughly persuaded that if they even attempted to take anything away the Een coz zy as they called it would acquaint the Canadians of the offender."[46] It could also have been that so long as there was an indication of ownership, and that the owners intended to return, the cache would not have been touched. In that case, the "Een coz zy" would have been simply fulfilling that function. There are frequent references in early accounts to the scrupulousness with which both Inuit and Amerindians respected caches.

Intermittent interactions between visitors and natives of that "rich and plentiful Country, abounding in all kinds of animals,"[47] started to become continuous with the English trading expedition to James Bay in 1668, and the establishment two years later of the Hudson's Bay Company's Fort Charles on Rupert River at "the bottom of the Bay." It was the Cree, rather than the Inuit, who first became involved directly in this new relationship. Somewhat less intensively and more indirectly, relations were also established with a branch of the Cree, the Montagnais, who with their close relatives, the Naskapi, inhabited the Québec-Labrador peninsula, and with the Ojibway, between the James Bay Cree and Lake Superior. The people of the Hudson Bay region recently had come into contact with the French, who in 1663 had finally penetrated into the area, overland from Québec, after several unsuccessful attempts. The French found that the Cree and Montagnais/Naskapi had long been trading indirectly with Europeans through native networks linking them with the St. Lawrence, and were not anxious to disturb the *status quo*. In fact, they resisted the idea, influencing the French to turn back before reaching James Bay.[48] European goods had been filtering through these networks by four main routes: through Tadoussac via the Saguenay River since at least the middle of the sixteenth century; from Huronia since early in the seventeenth century via two systems, that of the Spanish and Mattagami rivers, and that of the Ottawa, Temiskaming, and Abitibi rivers; and from Trois-Rivières since mid-seventeenth century via the St. Maurice and Nottaway rivers. This probably does much to explain why Hudson's trading episode remained the only one with Amerindians at the time of English exploration of the Bay. It does nothing to explain, however, why the English during this period did not trade regularly with the Inuit. Although the latter were blocked from access to the St. Lawrence system because of uncertain relationships with the intervening Amerindians,[49] some trade goods appear to have been filtering through more northern systems from both east and west, and perhaps also from the south. When

Hearne's party killed a group of Inuit at the mouth of the Coppermine River, beads of a type not traded by HBC were found among their effects.[50] The Hudson's Bay Company did not begin to establish posts in the Arctic until 1908.

The quick acceptance of English trade once Fort Charles was established reflected fundamental changes in southern trading patterns and consequently in northern networks. The decline of Tadoussac at the mouth of the Saguenay after the establishment of Québec in 1608, and the French penetration into the Great Lakes region to establish direct contact with the Huron a few years later, meant that the focus for the northern trade also shifted west. The result was that the two routes from Huronia to James Bay rose in importance. Huronia remained the hub of the north/south networks for thirty years, until the Iroquois dispersed the Huron in 1649. The disruption at the southern termini was aggravated by the eruption of the Iroquois at the networks' far northern ends. Raiding parties reached as far as James Bay until the Iroquois were distracted by their invasion of Illinois in 1680, an event that rekindled their protracted war with New France. The northern trading networks that had operated so satisfactorily from distant prehistoric times were left in disarray, cut off as they now were from access to trading goods from the south. A more fortuitous time for the establishment of Fort Charles could hardly be imagined; its instant success resulted in the rapid spread of HBC forts around the Bay. By 1685 the English system was essentially in place, and the French had countered with some forts in the interior, but were relying principally upon the trading activities of their *coureurs-de-bois*. The Amerindians who had been invisible to British explorers hunting for the Northwest Passage now came willingly to trade, and almost overnight homeguard bands were an established feature of the posts, following a pattern of behaviour that had been already experienced by the French.[51]

This eagerness for trade did not mean that there was an instant overall acceptance of "superior" European items, but two items that appear to have been adopted very early were the metal axe and kettle. This the Europeans easily understood, as it fitted in with their notions of what was practical and useful. They soon assessed Amerindian preferences shrewdly enough to evolve the tomahawk, one of the first items developed by Europeans specifically for the Amerindian trade. Combining as it did the war axe and the peace pipe, it had connotations beyond the "practical," and accorded with the Amerindian concept of the duality of nature, the dichotomy of life and death. Another successful item was Brazil tobacco; smoking was ritually important, and northern Amerindians quickly learned to esteem tobacco of this grade. Europeans had more difficulty in understanding Amerindian preferences for other goods, such as mirrors, and beads of certain types and colours. These objects substituted for traditional shiny metals, crystals, quartzites, and certain types of shells – all believed to possess qualities relating to the fundamental nature of the universe in both its physical and spiritual aspects. The desire of Amerindians for these items related to their mystical view of the operation of the cosmos, which to them was just as practical as its material aspect. Beads had the added advantage of being in the form of berries, reputed to have extraordinary curative powers.[52] Whether or not Europeans understood this "other-worldly" aspect of the trade, they soon learned what types of goods would induce Amerindians to do business with them.

It was no accident that Canada's stereotypical fur trade developed in the northern forests. Apart from the basic fact of the availability of the highest quality furs, the generalized nature of the hunting demanded by boreal forest ecology was the most adaptable to the needs of the trade. More specialized hunters, such as those who harvested the bison herds of the plains or the caribou herds of the Arctic, had much less incentive to participate, because needs were already satisfactorily provided for, and because of the conflict between their type of hunting and that required for furs. The Loucheux of the Yukon, for example, were at first not interested in trade goods apart from beads. In the seventeenth and eighteenth centuries, the gun was of more use to the boreal forest hunter than it was to hunters of the plains bison or the barren grounds caribou. Much depended, however, upon particular circumstance and the quality of the guns and ammunition.[53] Hearne found Northern Amerindians using guns in combination with bows and arrows in communal deer hunts.[54] Even so, early acceptance of the gun was curtailed by its marked limitations: uncertain performance in damp or cold weather, an insecure supply of ammunition, and the difficulty of repair. Similarly, metal traps were not initially seen as particularly useful, as traditional hunting methods easily procured all that was needed. Both guns and metal traps had added handicaps – cost and foreign production. Still, the restricted herding or solitary habits of boreal forest big game favoured the use of the gun, particularly as the weapon itself was improved. Guns were adopted faster than steel traps, which Amerindians at first tended to acquire for the metal, which they could reshape into useful objects such as chisels and blades of various types.[55]

The Cree (Christino, Kristinaux), amongst whom the English found themselves, were already the largest single group among Canadian Amerindians and were destined to become even more numerous and widespread as they prospered through their fur trade connections. They already had a reputation as hunters, as Pierre Esprit Radisson (c.1640-1710) had reported: "They are the best huntsmen of all America and scorns [sic] to catch a castor in a trap....They kill not the young castors, but leave them in the water, being that they are sure that they will take them again, which no other nation doth."[56] Such observations may have influenced the English to find the Cree to be "of a humane Disposition," capable of soon becoming civilized.[57] Although "civilizing" Amerindians was not on the English programme, good relations were essential. The seriousness with which this was regarded is witnessed by the circumspection of the Hudson's Bay Company in avoiding direct references to natives as "savages."

The English sought to secure their position by entering into alliances or "agreements," the records of which have not survived, although there are references to them. Bostonian Zachariah Gillam (1636-1682), captain of the 1668 expedition, is reported to have negotiated the first of these "treaties," as they were called at the time.[58] In 1680, the bayside governor, John Nixon, was instructed "to take possession of those places as soon as may be," as well as to "contrive to make compact wth. the Captns. or chiefs of the respective Rivers & places, whereby it might be understood by them that you had purchased both the lands & rivers of them, and that they had transferred the absolute propriety to you, or at least the only freedome of trade."[59] Further, the governor was to confirm these agreements by whatever means the Amerindians considered the "most sacred & obligatory." That latter proviso probably reflects, at least in part, the influence of Des Groseilliers, one of the instigators of the venture of the English into the Bay, who was with Captain Gillam on the first voyage. Des Groseillier's advice would have reinforced what the English already knew of the highly successful French fur trade in New France, utilizing techniques which the French had first worked out trading for dyewood in Brazil. Measures that were the most "obligatory" for Amerindians were periodic renewals with appropriate ceremonies and gift exchanges; in the Amerindian view, no such arrangement could continue automatically without being encouraged in this way. But no matter how careful the attention to trading protocol, such an arrangement could never have involved the transfer to "absolute propriety," a concept that would have been incomprehensible to the northerners. At most, they would have been negotiating for friendship and fair dealing, without which trade would have been insecure. That some sort of agreement was reached can be inferred from the fact that Amerindians felt free to come to the posts, as well as from the impression, of one observer at least, that the Hudson's Bay Company was paying the Amerindians "rent."[60] Governor Nixon's instructions indicate how wide was the cultural gap between Amerindians and English, and how limited was the existing basis for the development of mutual understanding and respect.

The few English who manned the posts were not only outnumbered, they did not at first sufficiently possess the skills to survive in that northern region; the homeguards were their principal source of fresh food. The English at Eastmain House at one point sought to reduce this dependence by training the most promising of their men in the techniques of hunting and fishing "until they become good Artists therein," but were discouraged when the trainees did not develop a sufficient level of skill.[61] By way of contrast, bayside governor James Knight (1640?-1719/20) later recorded at Fort Churchill that Amerindian hunters brought back only a few "partridges" (ptarmigan), whereas Englishmen brought back thirty-two.[62] Eventually both Amerindians and Inuit would become dependent upon posts for food from time to time as fur trade cycles interfered with subsistence cycles, particularly after game became depleted. Such crises could result in violence, as at Hannah Bay in 1832.[63] They also modified Amerindian food-sharing customs, at least as far as Europeans were concerned.

Samuel Hearne (1745-1792) discovered this while on his epic journey to the Arctic, when Northern Amerindians (Chipewyans) in his group never offered "the least morsel of victuals, without asking something in exchange, which, in general, was three times the value of what they could have got for the same articles, had they carried them to the Factory, though several hundred miles distant." As Hearne himself realized only too clearly, a common bond of fellowship had not developed: "It showed plainly how little I had to expect if I should, by any accident, be reduced to the necessity of depending upon them for support."[64] Insult was added to injury when strange Amerindians from the north visited his encampment and insisted that he distribute those of his goods that he did not absolutely need, a procedure which Hearne described as "plundering." His guide, unable to prevent the enforced sharing, had "assumed a great air of generosity; but the fact was, he gave freely what it was not in his power to protect."[65] Despite the inconveniences, Hearne was not left destitute, and his worry about being left without support proved groundless. It appears likely that the Amerindians were making a point: "when in Rome, do as the Romans do." In other words, share and share alike.[66] Hearne was impressed with the fortitude with which the Amerindians bore hunger, a quality "much easier to admire than to imitate." At the end of three or four days of fasting, his companions would be "as merry and jocose on the subject, as if they had voluntarily imposed it on themselves." Hearne acknowledged the salutary effect of avoiding a display of fear of starvation, especially when the threat was only too real.[67]

Amerindians were apparently slow to take to the foods Europeans brought with them. According to Hearne, "these people, when I first knew them would not eat any of our provisions, sugar, raisins, figs, or even bread; for though some of them would put a bit of it into their mouths, they soon spit it out again with evident marks of dislike; so that they had no greater relish for our food than we had for theirs."[68] Some individuals used this reaction to demonstrate their cultural superiority. Esquawino (Esqua:wee:Noa in the journals), known to the English at Moose Fort as Snuff the Blanket, developed the effective technique "of holding his garment to his Nose when he enters ye Factory to avoid ye ill scent & from his refusing to eat any Victuals dressed in any Utensil of ours."[69] On the other side of the picture, Hearne learned to appreciate some (though not all) Amerindian dishes "that were it not for prejudice...might be eaten by those who have the nicest palates."[70] Meat dried and powdered by Chipewyans he found to be more palatable than that prepared by Cree homeguards.[71] Amerindians also eventually demonstrated dietary adaptability; they became so fond of prunes and raisins that they would "give a Beaver Skin for twelve of them to carry to their Children." But they continued to disdain cheese, "having taken up an Opinion that it is made of dead Mens Fat."[72] The persistent belief on the part of Europeans—that Amerindians of the Far North, like Inuit, were cannibals from force of circumstance—was categorically dismissed by Hearne.[73]

The slowness of the English penetration of the interior, so controversial during the eighteenth century, was at least partly due to their too-determined attempt to distance their rank and file from Amerindians. In the words of Joseph Robson (fl. 1733-1763), "To converse with an Indian is a great crime, but to trade with him for a skin is capital, and punished by a forfeiture of all wages."[74] Such a policy, concerned only with trade, had the side effect of restricting land travel for inexperienced company servants. Not until this policy was relaxed, at least tacitly, did exploration of the interior become feasible. The first to undertake an extended voyage, Henry Kelsey (c.1667-1724) had prepared for it by living with Amerindians to the extent of becoming "indianized," and by having undertaken a northward trip with Chipewyan lads the previous year.[75] In 1690-92, he was guided by his Amerindian family and their kin to the northeastern edge of the Great Plains, and there saw a northern fringe of the great bison herds of which the Spaniards had encountered southern stragglers in Mexico in 1519 and the French had reported from the Great Lakes in 1652.[76] Kelsey's feat was not to be repeated for another twenty years, but the point had been made. Adapting to Amerindian expertise was a major factor in the success of later voyages; Hearne, for example, encountered only failure until he accepted the advice of his Chipewyan guide Matonabbee (c.1737-1782) and travelled with him *en famille*, allowing the Amerindians to pursue their own way so long as the ultimate objective of the voyage, the attainment of the Coppermine River, was not lost sight of.[77] The man who was later acclaimed as the best surveyor of them all, David Thompson (1770-1857), began his wilderness travels at the age of fifteen, when he was sent overland from Churchill to York Factory with two Amerindian companions.[78] Sending youths to travel, or to live, with Amerindians was not an unqualified success, however; there were those who were more interested in escaping post discipline than they were in learning about their hosts or participating in their daily routines. Matthew Cocking (1743-1799) saw this as the reason why some did not succeed in getting along with the natives; Fidler, on the other hand, after wintering with the Chipewyans in 1792, reported that willingness to pitch in and help could lead to disrespect on the part of the natives, whereas a stiff refusal to take part in their activities could lead to courteous treatment and a generous share of provisions.[79]

Amerindians and English continued to be baffled by each other's ways, even as the trade brought prosperity to both sides. A particular area of difficulty was that of reciprocity and the obligations it entailed. Ignoring accepted standards of behaviour could cause resentment and lead to trouble, as happened at Henley House in 1754. When the postmaster did not honour the expected obligation for subsistence to relatives of women who were being kept in the post, the Amerindians turned on the English, killing them and looting the establishment.[80] Europeans, puzzled by native attitudes and behaviour with respect to prices and bargaining, concluded the New World peoples were not economically minded. Nothing could have been further from the truth, but there is also no doubt that economic assumptions differed substantially. Amerindians were just as interested as Europeans in striking a good bargain, but the goods they accumulated were for redistribution to satisfy social obligations and to acquire prestige, rather than for exclusive personal use. Further, Amerindians, seeing no great virtue in the work ethic as such, welcomed higher prices because then they could produce less to satisfy their needs.[81]   The English soon discovered that such attitudes were not to be confused with lack of entrepreneurial enterprise; Amerindian traders at first were as eager as anyone to set themselves up in business and to challenge English attempts at establishing a monopoly.   Capitalizing on English/French rivalry, they would persuade hunters on their way to bayside posts to part with their best furs, and then shop around for the best deal available. One such entrepreneur, Esquawino of Moose River, was described by James Duffield at Moose Fort as "ye grand politician of all being a free Agent travelling about, sometimes to ye French, at others to Albany & this Fort, never drinks but has allways his scences about him & makes ye best of his Markett at all places."[82]   That the Company did not regard Amerindian competition, actual or incipient, with a tolerant eye had already been made evident in 1724 when Richard Staunton, the master at Albany Fort, had been censured for teaching a native lad to read and write.   London complained: "The Company are very much displeas'd to hear that any Indian is taught to Write & Read or admitted into ye Trading Room to prye into ye Secrets of their affairs in any nature whatsoever without our order & charge you strickly not to continue that nor suffer any such Practices for ye future."[83]   One of the consequences of natives learning European entrepreneurial skills was later to be illustrated by George Atkinson, Jr., the Métis son of the chief trader at Eastmain, 1778-92.   The young man, sent to England for the year in 1790, apparently learned quickly; upon his return, he urged post hunters to ask higher prices for their furs.[84]

Eventually even the Inuit came within the orbit of European-controlled networks.   At Churchill, HBC developed this connection through the use of interpreters, whom the Company began to train during the second half of the eighteenth century.[85]   Its original purpose of developing the Chipewyan trade was soon extended to include that of the Inuit, so that besides English, three native languages were also involved—Chipewyan, Cree, and Inuktitut.   Old hostilities did not automatically die out, but their expression transformed as the European-controlled trade gained the upper hand.

The trade brought with it a new set of difficulties that were perhaps even more serious, as they struck at the very basis of life itself in the North.   The consequences of excessive exploitation were soon to become painfully evident, first of all in core areas that gradually fanned out to include the whole North.   Once steel traps were adopted, and used with castoreum as bait, the taking of beaver became so easy that Amerindians found themselves temporarily awash in an unaccustomed wealth of trade goods. "Every intelligent Man saw the poverty that would follow the destruction of the Beaver, but there were no Chiefs to control it; all was perfect liberty and equality."[86] What caused this shift in traditional attitudes in respect to production has been the subject of speculation rather than of systematic study. With it went the old self-reliance that had been so characteristic of Amerindians and Inuit in the days when they had been able to live well by means of their own resourcefulness.

The eight-hundred-year period of contact covered by this paper was not enough to build the sense of fellowship and mutual respect needed for the creation of a truly multicultural society. Although first contact was with the Inuit, first permanent relationships were with Amerindians; it would take another good two hundred years before the English began to establish permanent posts in the Arctic, a step never taken by the French because of the loss of their North American base in 1760. This situation was reflected in attitudes toward the natives: both English and French found Inuit more difficult to deal with than Amerindians, and judged them accordingly. But the difference was only relative, because in neither case were alliances based on a solid sense of community. The cooperation that did develop was due to the force of circumstances. In the words of Eric Ross, "It is melancholy to reflect that, with few exceptions,...desire for European goods on the part of the Indians and the Europeans' desire for the Indians' furs, forms the only basis of 'friendship' between the traders and the savages of the Northwest."[87] A similar observation can be made concerning Inuit participation with whites in arctic whaling; when the industry declined, so did the partnership. HBC factors and traders may not have referred to natives as "savages," but their sense of social distance is still evident in their journals and correspondence. For example, in reprimanding Governor Nixon "with to[o] much inhumanity and cruelty towards the Natives," London observed that not only were such actions unwise from the point of view of personal safety, but "Experience teaches that mild and Gentle Usage doth more obtaine upon the most Savage Nature than to[o] much severity."[88]

Nearly a thousand years after their first tenuous contact, the three worlds of the Inuit, Amerindian, and Euro-Canadian are as distinct as ever. But new avenues for interaction are opening up, a consequence of the post-Second-World-War invasion of modern technology into even the farthest corners of the Far North. If these developments have complicated the search for accommodation, they have also given it a new urgency, in which the "traditional" is demonstrating that the "modern" has no monopoly on flexibility. Assimilation, once thought to be the only answer, has appeared less viable since the perception that native cultures were disappearing from the face of the earth has proved to be exaggerated. Co-operation is taking its place, and traditional native self-reliance is re-emerging in the guise of demands for recognition and self-government, creating unforeseen situations. New problems call for new solutions, and the old resourcefulness and adaptability that created distinctive life-styles in the past are now being called upon to tackle challenges of a very different order. The partnership that was once restricted to fur trading and whaling is now being worked out on a much broader base.

Notes

The research and writing of this paper was made possible by a grant from the Social Sciences and Humanities Research Council of Canada.

1. Jean S. Aigner, "Early Arctic Settlements in North America," *Scientific American* 253 (1985): 160-69, speculates that the Thule prevailed because of greater flexibility and adaptability. Thule and Dorset artifacts are illustrated in Tryggvi J. Oleson, *Early Voyages and Northern Approaches 1000-1632* (Toronto: McClelland and Stewart, 1963), plates 4 and 5.

2. Frank G. Speck's speculations about the possibility of surviving remnants of the Beothuck being scattered as far south as Cape Cod have not been borne out. See his *Beothuck and Micmac* (New York: Museum of the American Indian, 1922).

3. Kaj Birket-Smith, *Eskimos* (Copenhagen: Rhodos, 1971), 13. An account of the first meeting of Greenland Skraelings with Norsemen is reproduced, ibid., 28-29. See also L.H. Neatby, "Exploration and History of the Canadian Arctic," in *Handbook of North American Indians*, volume ed. David Damas (Washington: Smithsonian Institution, 1984), 5:377-90.

4. Wendell H. Oswalt, *Eskimos and Explorers* (Novato, California: Chandler and Sharp, 1979), 11.

5. Edward Lynam, *The Carta marina of Olaus Magnus, Venice 1539 and Rome 1572* (Jenkintown, Pa.: Tall Tree Library, 1949); Olaus Magnus, *Carta Marina* (Uppsala: Bokgillet, 1964).

6. Miller Christy, *The Voyages of Captain Luke Foxe of Hull, and Captain Thomas James of Bristol, in search of a North-West Passage, in 1631-32* (London: Hakluyt Society, 1894), 1:104-05.

7. A 1566 woodcut on a handbill printed in Augsburg of a "small person" (actually, an Inuit woman and her child) who had been captured and brought to Europe by the French after killing her husband, is more successful in presenting the manner of dress (except for her boots) than physical characteristics. The accompanying text describes her and her husband as cannibals. (See W.C. Sturtevant, "The first Inuit depiction by Europeans," *Etudes/Inuit/Studies* 4 (1980): 47-49.) A painting of a West Greenland family dated 1654 hangs in The National Museum,

Copenhagen. It is reproduced in Birket-Smith, *Eskimos*, 37. The vagaries of perceptions are illustrated by the story of Thorvaldr, son of Eric the Red, killed by a uniped (one-legged man) while on an exploratory voyage that had taken him near the Land of the Unipeds.

8. Christy, *Voyages*, 2:319. For the English, the planks "coffining" the skeletons were a welcome find for firewood. Foxe's men later robbed another gravesite for the same purpose (ibid., 334).

9. Oleson, *Early Voyages*, 24-25.

10. Birket-Smith, *Eskimos*, 13-14.

11. A résumé of possible scenarios explaining the abandonment of the Greenland colonies is given by Thomas H. McGovern, "Thule-Norse Interaction in Southwest Greenland: a Speculative Model," in *Thule Eskimo Culture: An Anthropological Retrospective*, ed. Allen P. McCartney, National Museum of Man Mercury Series, Archaeological Survey of Canada no. 88, (Ottawa, 1979), 171-88.

12. Birket-Smith, *Eskimos*, 15.

13. Robert McGhee, *Canadian Arctic Prehistory* (Toronto: Van Nostrand Reinhold, 1978), 108.

14. Christy, *Voyages*, 1:42. Frobisher later described Inuit in more detail, particularly in his account of his second voyage. It has been speculated that in comparing Inuit with Tartars, Frobisher was laying the groundwork for the major effort of his third voyage, by convincing his backers that he had indeed reached the Asiatic continent. That third expedition, consisting of fifteen ships with one hundred colonists aboard, was the largest to sail into the Arctic until the Second World War.

15. For just one illustration, when scurvy appeared among the members of a nineteenth century expedition, the victims were advised that the best cure was to go and live with the Inuit, presumably to share their diet. See Charles Francis Hall, *Arctic Researches and Life Among the Esquimaux* (New York: Harper, 1865), 219.

16. Christy, *Voyages*, 1:77, 87, 100-101.

18.   Christy, *Voyages*, 1:39.

19.   Ibid., 1:62, 66.

20.   Ibid., 1:66, 68.

21.   On his second voyage, Frobisher was informed that three of the five men were still alive, and that they would be brought to him. But there is no further reference to them. (Ibid., 1:47.)

22.   Ibid., 1:39. Trading was the usual pretext for luring victims to their fate. This was how Henry Green, who had led the mutiny against Hudson in 1611, was himself killed by a group of ostensibly friendly Inuit. (Ibid., 1:153-55.)

23.   W.A. Kenyon, *Tokens of Possession* (Toronto: Royal Ontario Museum, 1975), 121. Other reasons quickly developed for taking New World natives to Europe. Among these were to provide information and to be trained as interpreters between Europeans and their own people in the Americas.

24.   Hall, *Arctic Researches*, 251, 290, and 385.

25.   Christy, *Voyages*, 1:90-91.

26.   Oswalt, *Eskimos and Explorers*, 35-36.

27.   Ibid., 1:50. As Inuit reactions to Europeans foods and eating habits appear not to have been recorded for this early period, a nineteenth-century account may provide some parallels: "The natives of Sekoselar were not partial to civilized food....We gave each of them a mug of coffee and sea-biscuit. They tasted it— spit it out—-tried it again and again, and finally the man contrived to 'worry' it down; but the woman gave it up, declaring, in her own Innuit way, that 'such *stuff* was not fit to eat'." (Hall, *Arctic Researches*, 297.)

28.   Christy, *Voyages*, 1:62.

29.   Ibid., 1:67.

30.   Ibid., 1:88.

31.   Ibid., 1:111.

31. Ibid., 1:111.

32. Ibid., 1:101.

33. Nicolas Jérémie, *Twenty Years of York Factory, 1694-1714* (Ottawa: Thorburn and Abbott, 1926), 16. Jérémie did not provide any supporting evidence for his claims.

34. Christy, *Voyages*, 2:638. The linking of the Inuit to easterners may refer to Europeans' early impression that New World peoples were either Tartars or related to them. See *supra*, 5.

35. Such reports had started with Vespucci. See, for example, Fracanzano da Montalboddo, *Sensuyt le nouveau monde & navigation faictes par Emeric Vespuce Florentin*, trans. by Mathurin Du Redouer (1515, facsimile, Princeton: Princeton University Press, 1916), 154.

36. Christy, *Voyages*, 1:46-47.

37. The lack of documentation for whaling in Davis Strait during the seventeenth century was pointed out by W. Gillies Ross, "The Annual Catch of Greenland (Bowhead) Whales in Waters North of Canada 1719-1915: A Preliminary Compilation," *Arctic* 32 (1979): 94.

38. Christy, *Voyages* 1:135-36.

39. Adaptation to bargaining apparently worked the other way in the Beringian trading network of Alaska and eastern Asia. There the Inuit, after exposure to the trading practices of Russians and other Europeans, developed into as hard bargainers as they. See Clifford G. Hickey, "The Historic Beringian Trade Network: Its Nature and Origins," in *Thule Eskimo Culture: An Anthropological Retrospective*, 422.

40. Toby Morantz, "Oral and Recorded History at James Bay," *Papers of the Fifteenth Algonquin Conference*, ed. William Cowan (Ottawa: Carlton University, 1984), 181-82. I am indebted to Dr. Jennifer S.H. Brown, University of Winnipeg, for this reference. See also *supra*, 6.

41. Christy, *Voyages*, 1:137.

42.   Jérémie, *Twenty Years*, 18-19. See also Brenda L. Clark, *The Development of Caribou Eskimo Culture*, National Museums of Canada Mercury Series (Ottawa, 1977), 10-11.

43.   James G.E. Smith, "Chipewyan, Cree, and Inuit Relations West of Hudson Bay 1715-1955," *Ethnohistory* 28 (1981): 136, 140.

44.   Clifford G. Hickey, "An Examination of Processes of Cultural Change among Nineteenth Century Copper Inuit," *Etudes/Inuit/Studies*, 8 (1984): 13-35.

45.   John Oldmixon, *The British Empire in America* (London: Printed for J. Brotherton, etc., 1741), 1: 549-50.

46.   J.B. Tyrrell, ed., *The Journals of Samuel Hearne and Philip Turnor* (Toronto: Champlain Society, 1934), 553-54.

47.   That was Angus Shaw's description in 1794 of the region around the confluence of the Sturgeon and North Saskatchewan rivers. It applies generally to the Far North, including the Arctic. (Morton, *History of the Canadian West,* 463.)

48.   Daniel Francis and Toby Morantz, *Partners in Furs: A History of the Fur Trade in Eastern James Bay 1600-1870* (Kingston and Montreal: McGill-Queen's University Press, 1983), 17. Bruce Trigger describes Huronia's establishment and growth as a trading centre in "The French Presence in Huronia: The Structure of Franco-Huron Relations in the First Half of the Seventeenth Century," *Canadian Historical Review* 49 (1968): 107-41.

49.   See Smith, "Chipewyan, Cree and Inuit Relations."

50.   Samuel Hearne, *A Journey to the Northern Ocean in the Years 1769, 1770, 1771, and 1772*, ed. J.B. Tyrrell (Toronto: Champlain Society, 1911), 330n. Hickey speculates that these beads could have been Russian (personal communication). Luke Foxe in 1631 had considered the possibility that Inuit were trading "by way of Canada" when he found worked copper in Inuit graves. See Christy, *Voyages*, 2:320.

51.   For a description of homeguard activities at Eastmain House and Rupert House, see Francis and Morantz, *Partners in Furs*, 82-86; for later developments, see ibid., 170-71.

52. Christopher L. Miller and George R. Hamell, "Trading in Metaphors: Toward a New Perspective on Indian-White Contact" (1985, mimeographed).

53. The company realized only too clearly the link between the quality of its guns and the trade: "Pray observe whenever any Guns prove defective," London instructed in 1724, "send them home to us, & if ye Indians complain of any send us word whose Guns they are that we may take notice of ye makers accordingly." HBC Official London Correspondence Book Outwards, 1679-1741, A.6/1: 86-86v, HBC Archives. See also Arthur J. Ray, *Indians in the Fur Trade* (Toronto: University of Toronto Press, 1974), 75-79.

54. Hearne, *Journey to the Northern Ocean*, 310.

55. Francis and Morantz, *Partners in Furs*, 61-63, 86, and 170.

56. Arthur T. Adams, ed., *The Explorations of Pierre Esprit Radisson* (Minneapolis: Ross & Haines, 1961), 147. Radisson and Des Groseilliers had visited Lake Superior and its environs, 1659-60, although how far north they got remains uncertain. Their reports were the major source of British information. Radisson's original manuscripts are in the Bodleian Library, Oxford; the Archives of the Hudson's Bay Company; and the British Museum.

57. Arthur Dobbs, *An Account of the Countries adjoining to Hudson's Bay* (1744; reprint, New York: Johnson, 1967), 59.

58. Peter A. Cumming and Neil H. Mickenberg, *Native Rights in Canada* (Toronto: General Publishing, 1972), 142.

59. HBC Official London Correspondence Book Outwards 1679-1741, A.6/1.6, HBC Archives; E.E. Rich, ed., *Letters Outward 1679-1694* (Toronto: Champlain Society, 1948), 9; Cumming and Mickenberg, *Native Rights in Canada*, 142, n.36; Francis and Morantz, *Partners in Furs*, 23. These instructions were repeated to Nixon's successor, Henry Sergeant, in 1683. See A.6/1:30v, HBC Archives.

60. Francis and Morantz, *Partners in Furs*, 23-24; Edwin Thompson Denig, *Five Indian Tribes of the Upper Missouri*, ed. John C. Ewers (Norman: University of Oklahoma Press, 1961), 112.

61. Francis and Morantz, *Partners in Furs*, 25-26, and 88. Henry Kelsey's journal gives a vivid picture of the bounty provided by

Amerindian hunters. See Arthur G. Doughty and Chester Martin, eds., *The Kelsey Papers* (Ottawa: Acland, 1929).

62. Entry for 23 September 1718, Fort Churchill Journal 1718-1721, B.42/a/1:24v-25, HBC Archives.

63. Francis and Morantz, *Partners in Furs*, 158-60. According to Morantz, Cree oral tradition supports the official HBC version of the affair, but gives additional details as to what happened to the families of those who were executed as a consequence. See Morantz, "Oral and Recorded History," 181-82.

64. Hearne, *Journey to the Northern Ocean*, 93-94.

65. Ibid., 97-98.

66. According to Birket-Smith, Amerindians had a compulsion to prove their superiority over European travelling companions, a characteristic he found to be happily lacking in the Inuit. (*Eskimos*, 60.)

67. Hearne, *Journey to the Northern Ocean*, 113-14.

68 Ibid., 185n. For a similar reaction on the part of Inuit, see *supra*, n.26.

69. Moose Fort Journal, 1742, B.135/a/11:67, HBC Archives; cited by Francis and Morantz, *Partners in Furs*, 58-59.

70. Hearne, *Journey to the Northern Ocean*, 306.

71. Ibid., 291.

72. Dobbs, *An Account*, 42.

73. Hearne, *Journey to the Northern Ocean*, 85-86n.

74. Robson, *An Account of Six Years Residence in Hudson's Bay, from 1733 to 1736, and 1744 to 1747* (London: Payne and Bouquet, 1752) 17.

75. Smith, "Chipewyan, Cree, and Inuit Relations," 137.

76. Actually, the French had encountered bison in the northeastern woodlands much earlier, as attested by an engraving of bison-

hunting in André Thevet's *La Cosmographie Universelle*, (Paris: Chaudiere, 1575).

77. Hearne, *Journey to the Northern Ocean*, 14.

78. J.B. Tyrrell, ed., *David Thompson's Narrative of his Explorations in Western America* (Toronto: Champlain Society, 1916), xxvi.

79. E.E. Rich, ed., *Cumberland House Journals 1775-82. First Series, 1775-79* (London: Hudson's Bay Record Society, 1951), 109-10; Tyrrell, *Journals of Hearne and Turnor*, 535, Peter Fidler's Journal. A first-rate study of the social consequences of this accommodation is by Jennifer S.H. Brown, *Strangers in Blood* (Vancouver: University of British Columbia Press, 1980).

80. Charles Bishop, "The Henley House Massacres," *The Beaver* 307 (Autumn 1976): 36-41. Sylvia Van Kirk, *Many Tender Ties* (Norman: University of Oklahoma Press, 1980) 43-44.

81. Bruce Trigger, *Natives and Newcomers* (Kingston and Montreal: McGill-Queen's University Press, 1985), 188-94. For the varying effects of the trade on native societies and economies, see Shepard Krech III, ed., *The Subarctic Fur Trade* (Vancouver: University of British Columbia Press, 1984).

82. B.135/a/11:69, HBC Archives; cited by Francis and Morantz, *Partners in Furs*, 59. Captain Snuff fell afoul of the Moose Fort postmaster in 1759, who accused him of trying to keep the Upland Amerindians from trading and of trying to stir rebellion among the homeguard. Captain Snuff was jailed at the fort, and hanged himself because of this loss of face. Moose Fort Journal 1758-1759, B.135/a/31:27v-29v, HBC Archives.

83. A.6/4:86v, HBC Archives; cited by Francis and Morantz, *Partners in Furs*, 91.

84. B.77/e/5:5, HBC Archives; cited by Morantz, "Oral and Recorded History," 183.

85. Eric Ross, *Beyond the River and the Bay* (Toronto: University of Toronto Press, 1970), 106.

86. Tyrrell, *David Thompson's Narrative*, 204-06.

87. Ibid., 42.

88.   Letter, 15 May 1682, HBC Official London Correspondence Book Outwards 1679-1741, A.6/1:16, HBC Archives.

Chapter 3

TO UNITE THE DISCOVERIES: THE AMERICAN RESPONSE TO THE EARLY EXPLORATION OF RUPERT'S LAND

John L. Allen

It was late in the year 1801, and Thomas Jefferson, third president of the United States, was worried. In London, a publishing event had just occurred that had stirred the imagination of the Western world and jolted Jefferson's thinking on the geography of the western interior of North America. This event was the publication of Alexander Mackenzie's *Voyages from Montreal...through the Continent of North America, to the Frozen and Pacific Ocean*.[1] Shortly after its London release, Mackenzie's book was circulating in both New York and Philadelphia, and Jefferson learned of it from a colleague in the American Philosophical Society of Philadelphia who wrote to inform the president that the book was available in that city.[2] Jefferson's correspondent, a physician, was most interested in Mackenzie's reports of attempts to vaccinate the northwestern tribes against the ravages of smallpox. But although the President himself had exerted efforts to diffuse the benefits of Mr. Jenner's happy discovery, he probably felt that his correspondent had missed the point. The phrase from *Voyages* that must have leaped out at Jefferson was that relating how the intrepid British explorer had inscribed on a rock near the shores of the great Pacific Ocean, using bear grease and vermilion powder, the words "Alexander Mackenzie, from Canada, by land, the twenty-second of July, one thousand seven hundred and ninety three."[3]

The race for domination of the western interior of North America, the clash of imperial ambitions for a transcontinental commercial route, was being won by the British, and given his own geopolitical aspirations, Jefferson was right to be concerned. Mackenzie's discovery of what might have been a commercially feasible route to the Pacific suggested the strong possibility of commercial control over the lucrative Indian and fur trade of the interior and, with it, control over the continent as far as the western ocean. The president quickly ordered a copy of Mackenzie's important book from a New York book dealer and, along with it, a copy of London cartographer Aaron Arrowsmith's latest map of North America, showing the observations of Mackenzie and other recent British explorers in the lands west of Hudson Bay.[4] Nor was this the president's only response: he began poring over the collection of books and maps on western North America that he had gathered while U.S. minister to France in the 1780s; he instructed his private secretary, Meriwether Lewis (a young Virginian he had selected for the post partially because of his "knolege of the western country"[5]) to begin making preparations for an American exploration to the Pacific; and he informed the Spanish, British, and French ministers to the United States of his intention to mount an expedition which would, as he put it, "unite the discoveries" of the explorers of Rupert's Land with those of an American party farther south.[6] The twin publication of Mackenzie's *Voyages* and Arrowsmith's seminal map had triggered the response that would result in the Lewis and Clark expedition, opening a new round of maneuvering in the conflict of colliding geopolitical ambitions for control of the American and British North American West.

That Thomas Jefferson's sponsorship of the Lewis and Clark expedition was based solely—as he would have liked the foreign ministers of Britain, France, and Spain to believe—on a desire for "the advancement of geography" was, of course, not true. In his December 1802 request to the U.S. Congress for funds with which to mount the expedition, Jefferson flew more accurate colours as he noted that an American exploration to the Pacific would consolidate the Indian trade and enhance the interests of commerce; that it should also, as Jefferson put to Congress, "incidentally advance the geographical knowledge of our own continent can not but be an additional gratification."[7] Some months later, when Jefferson provided Meriwether Lewis with instructions for his transcontinental trek, the president's ultimate goal became even more clear. "The object of your mission," he wrote to Lewis, was to locate "the most direct & practicable water communication across this continent for the purposes of commerce."[8] To Jefferson, the establishment of a commercial link between the Pacific and the United States implied territorial control over the areas that lay between—and herein lies his primary response to the early exploration of Rupert's Land.

An American Image of the Western Interior

Jefferson's interest in the link between commerce and geopolitics had begun to take shape long before Mackenzie's transcontinental crossing. Indeed, as a boy in the Virginia Piedmont, young Jefferson may well have become infected with the plans and ambitions of his father and a group of Virginia friends and relatives to expand that colony's territory into the Mississippi Valley and beyond by developing commercial links between the Atlantic and the great inland waterways.[9] During his early period of service to the new republic, between 1783 and 1793, Jefferson gathered materials on the geography of western North America—particularly those from British sources, generated largely by commercial exploration—and by the 1790s had developed what was probably the best single collection of published works in North America on the subject.[10] Also during this time, Jefferson was instrumental in suggesting and organizing three abortive attempts to have the potential commercial water route between the Atlantic and Pacific explored.[11] From all of this activity there had developed, in Jefferson's mind, an image of the essential features of western geography that was to become crucial to the inception, organization, and execution of the Lewis and Clark expedition. And critical to the formation of this image was the geographical information contributed by British exploration in the lands lying to the west of Hudson Bay.

As British explorers sought a route to the western sea by way of the Saskatchewan system and the Canadian Rockies, they made signally important contributions to the geographical lore that was translated into the American image of the interior at the time of Lewis and Clark. Much of this lore spoke enthusiastically about the cardinal elements of western geography—the mountains and river systems—as offering easy commercial accessibility for the interior portions of the continent and as facilitating the completion of transcontinental communication by water. Combined with this lore contributed by exploration was that produced through British theoretical geography, and the result for Americans such as Thomas Jefferson and Meriwether Lewis was an optimistic view of the feasibility of the Passage to India.

As early as the 1720s the combination of British theoretical geography and exploration had introduced the concept of symmetrical geography to the North American continent. It was known that the rivers flowing west from the Appalachian system into the Mississippi Basin had sources relatively close to the Atlantic Ocean where they interlocked with the source waters of streams heading east to the Atlantic. According to the tenets of symmetrical geography, the same set of conditions should apply on the western margins of the continent. This reasoning on symmetrical drainage divides soon resolved itself into definite views of the nature of western drainage divides, and it was buttressed by experience when Samuel Hearne, one of the earliest British explorers in the Canadian West, told of mountains in the western reaches of the continent beyond which all the rivers ran westward.[12] Hearne had postulated, without seeing it, the Continental Divide, and his notions on the dividing nature of the western ranges became fixed in British geographical lore during the eighteenth century. Peter Fidler, a surveyor for the Hudson's Bay Company, following instructions received from Indians during his travels in the western interior, depicted the nature of this divide in a sketch map of the Northwest.[13] On this sketch was shown a range of mountains labelled as "the Rocky Mountains" from which a series of rivers was shown running, some into the Missouri and some into the Saskatchewan system. On the western slopes of this same range of mountains were represented other rivers with sources adjacent to those of the Missouri and Saskatchewan drainages and with courses carrying them directly west to the Pacific. The implications for a potential commercial water route were clear, and they were made even more clear when Peter Pond, a Connecticut Yankee employed by the North West Company, produced a map based on his own sojourns in the Canadian West.[14] On Pond's map, the Rockies were shown as a single ridge of mountains positioned around the 113th meridian of longitude. Near the headwaters of the Missouri appeared the source region of a river Pond called the "Naberkistagon"; the origins of the name are uncertain but what was meant by it is not. It was the Oregon or River of the West, and the commercial route to the Pacific must have seemed obvious to those who viewed Pond's map. The cartographic representations of the western interior produced by Hearne, Fidler, and Pond became important source materials for British cartographers of the late eighteenth century and, subsequently, important source materials for the shaping of American images of the interior.

British geographical lore obtained during the exploration of Rupert's Land and adjacent territories contributed concepts other than that of symmetrical drainage systems to the American image of the western interior. The first of these was the concept of the pyramidal height of land, a theory related to the posited Continental Divide, but in which the sources of eastward and westward flowing streams were confined into a relatively small geographical area, rather than being strung out, fanlike, on Atlantic and Pacific sides of a long linear dividing ridge. The concept of a pyramidal height of land was a very old one in geographical theory[15] but was stimulated in the late eighteenth century by the travel accounts of Robert Rogers and Jonathan Carver,[16] both of whom envisaged, in the western interior, a core drainage area consisting of the highest land on the continent. From this core drainage region, the cardinal rivers of North America—the St. Lawrence, the Mississippi, the Nelson, and the Oregon or River of the West—flowed their respective courses to the eastern, western, and southern oceans and to Hudson Bay. In the British lore, the access to this core drainage area was either from the Saskatchewan system or the Missouri's upper reaches, and it was believed that once the core area was reached, it would be a simple task to locate the waters flowing west to the Pacific and, hence, to determine the location of the centuries-old dream of a water communication across North America.

Still another British contribution to the American image of the geography of the interior and of the Passage to India was, like the concept of the pyramidal height of land, related to the concept of the Continental Divide. This third contribution was that of the conceptual short portage between eastward- and westward-flowing streams, alluded to as early as 1673 by French explorers in the Mississippi Valley[17] but refined and stamped indelibly on the source materials for the American image by British exploration in Canada. Unlike other features of the conjectural geography of the western interior, the short portage had been proven by exploration when Alexander Mackenzie followed the Peace River to its source in the Canadian Rockies and there discovered "a beaten path leading over a low ridge of land eight hundred and seventeen paces in length"[18] and then dropping into the upper waters of the river which Mackenzie — and those, such as Thomas Jefferson, who read his travel volume — assumed was the Columbia, the real world version of the mythic Oregon or Great River of the West. Mackenzie's discovery of the short portage was impressed upon Jefferson's imagination, and the concept of the close proximity of navigable headwaters for Atlantic and Pacific streams was given a prominent place in American images of the interior. It was made even more relevant to Jefferson's visionary geopolitics when combined with Mackenzie's assertion that the Rocky Mountains, where he had crossed them near the 55th parallel, were approximately three thousand feet above sea level and that they ran to the south "with less elevation,"[19] continuing to serve as a range dividing the waters of the Atlantic from those of the Pacific. The critical phrase in Mackenzie's *Voyages* was "with less elevation" — since Mackenzie had crossed the Rockies and located a short portage via a low and barely discernible pass, the prospects for an even easier crossing to the south, near the Missouri's headwaters, seemed to Jefferson to be a virtual certainty. The idea received further impetus from another British explorer in Rupert's Land, the great David Thompson, who noted that the headwaters of the Missouri gave several passages across the mountains and that these mountains near the Missouri's westernmost reaches were comparatively low.[20]

All three of these concepts—the Continental Divide, the pyramidal height of land, and the short portage—appeared not only in the published journals of Canadian exploration available to Thomas Jefferson but also in published extracts of those journals in American geographies and gazetteers and, as has been noted, in cartographic representations of the North American continent. Of the cartographic source materials for Jefferson's image, Aaron Arrowsmith's maps of 1795 and 1802, based on data provided the cartographer by the Hudson's Bay Company, were considered by the president and others to be the best available and were, therefore, perhaps the single most important elements in the source materials for Jefferson's image of the interior.[21]

The Arrowsmith map of 1795 was striking in its lack of concrete geographical data for the areas south of the 50th parallel and in its failure to show Mackenzie's successful crossing of the Continental Divide in 1793. It did, however, incorporate data contributed by Mackenzie on the western reaches of the Saskatchewan system and by Hearne, Fidler, and Pond on the area between Hudson Bay and the Rockies. For Jefferson's purposes, perhaps the most significant portion of the Arrowsmith 1795 map was that showing the potential overland connections between the upper Missouri and the Saskatchewan. Such proximity was worrisome from the president's point of view because it suggested easy British entry into territory that was outside any national power's direct sphere of influence but that would, it was hoped, shortly become controlled by interests centred in the United States. The Arrowsmith 1795 map was also of interest in its failure to link the upper Missouri to either the "Stony Mountains" to the west or the Mississippi to the east. The Missouri was shown simply as a fragment of a stream upon which the Mandan villages, known to both British and American fur traders, were located. To the west of the Mandans appeared the Rockies or "Stony Mountains," with a legend inscribed along their eastern flanks that read "3520 Feet High above the Level of their Base and according to the Indian accounts is five Ridges in some parts." Some of the peaks in this range were named, apparently from Peter Fidler's reports obtained by the cartographer through the Hudson's Bay Company. The chief importance of this section of Arrowsmith's 1795 map was its indication that the Rocky Mountains may have been something other than the narrow, single ridge most of the British lore had suggested. Of more relevance for Jefferson's image were Arrowsmith's next productions, those of 1802, maps that reflected the latest in British intelligence on Rupert's Land.

The crucial Arrowsmith 1802 map was the second edition, which was essentially a copy of the 1795 map but with several highly important supplemental details, especially in the region of the upper Missouri and the Mandan villages. The Missouri River, in particular, was shown in much greater detail and no longer represented as a fragment; much of its course above the Mandan villages was elaborately presented, probably from Fidler data and that obtained from David Thompson of the North West Company. The upper Missouri drainage was shown as a huge fan or triangle with its broad base lying against the eastern front of the Rockies. From the mountains a number of rivers flowed east within this fanlike basin, joining their waters into two major streams that came together to form the Missouri proper just above the location of the Mandans in what is now central North Dakota. The northern of the two major branches was not labelled, but the southern bore the appellation "River Mississury" at its source in the mountains almost due west of the Mandan villages. The implication from this representation was important for Jefferson: the Missouri flowed almost a due west-to-east course from its source to the Mandans, and an American expedition following the Missouri could reach the Rockies and, hence, the passage to the Pacific, without crossing territory still, as Jefferson put it, "in a course of ascertainment"[22] by British travellers working for the Hudson's Bay and North West companies. Even more critical, perhaps, was the notation near the Missouri's southern reaches that "Hereabout the Mountains divide into several low ridges." No rivers were shown flowing to the Pacific from this region, but to someone such as Jefferson, well versed in British concepts of symmetrical drainages and the pyramidal height of land, the implication was clear that an exploring party might possibly locate a critical source region of several "low ridges" that would provide an easy access to the southern waters of the Columbia. This not only paved the potential way to the Pacific but, again, avoided the territories under investigation by the British to the north.

During the planning phase of the Lewis and Clark expedition, as Jefferson was collecting and analyzing data on the western interior, the geographical lore represented by the Arrowsmith maps, as well as that obtained from some other cartographic sources such as the map that accompanied Mackenzie's *Voyages* and a David Thompson map of the Mandan villages, was combined with data from French and Spanish sources to produce an American map that clearly illustrates the character of Jefferson's image of the West in 1803. This map, produced by the Washington draftsman and cartographer Nicholas King, was basically a copy of Arrowsmith's second 1802 production, illustrating the cardinal relevance of British lore for Jefferson's conceptions.[23] There were, however, two major departures from Arrowsmith's view of the western interior on the King map. In the first variance of Arrowsmith's second 1802 map, which showed a "Great Lake River" adjacent to the head of the Saskatchewan and west of the Rockies with the caption "The Indians say they sleep 8 nights in descending this River to the Sea," King moved the Great Lake River into a position much closer to the northern waters of the Missouri than to the southern waters of the Saskatchewan. His reasons for this variation are unknown, but the suggestion on the map is that the Missouri, as well as the Saskatchewan, provided access to a stream conjectured to flow a short course to the Pacific. In his jockeying for geopolitical position, Thomas Jefferson may have been looking for a way to cut off the British advance westward up the Saskatchewan by developing a route into the same Pacific waters from the Missouri and, therefore, from the Mississippi and American territory.

The second and much more important major departure made by King's map from Arrowsmith's 1802 map was in the American cartographer's representation of the Rocky Mountains and of the Missouri's southern reaches west of the Mandan villages. Where Arrowsmith had shown a range of mountains running from Canada all the way to New Mexico (albeit with the note that they divided into several low ridges south of latitude 50), King's Rockies had a southern terminus around the 46th or 47th parallel. Around the southern end of the mountains, King placed a great southern branch of the Columbia, runnning in an east-west direction from a source near the 106th meridian of longitude to join the Columbia or "River Oregan" near the Pacific. What sources of data were used to produce this conjectural southern stream is unknown, but it ran through an area in which Arrowsmith had drawn a major mountain range that served on his map, and in many contemporary geographical theories, as a continental divide.

A clue to this invented river may be found in the word "Conjectural," which appears scrawled across the map near this great southern branch of the Columbia. Wishing still to avoid, if possible, the British line of advance across the continent to the north and believing firmly in the British tenets of symmetrical geography, Thomas Jefferson may simply have invented a southern branch of the Columbia to provide geographical symmetry (most rivers, in his geographical understanding, had two major branches) and to suggest a southern approach to the Pacific via the headwaters of the Missouri and the as yet unnamed southern tributary of the Great River of the West. Such an invention was made critical by an event that had just transpired in Europe. In a series of diplomatic agreements unrelated (formally, at least) to the planning of the Lewis and Clark expedition, the United States had just purchased Louisiana Territory from France.[24] In his (and France's) definition of Louisiana, Jefferson included all the western drainage basin of the Mississippi River. Such a definition obviously incorporated the entire Missouri system into the newly purchased territory and made the location of any American discovery of a route to the Pacific much more valuable if it could be located within the Missouri system south of the 50th parallel. In any case, the great southern river on the King map seems to have provided Jefferson and, of course, Meriwether Lewis, with an alternative route to the Pacific not derived primarily from British lore. During the course of the expedition itself, this conjectural southern route would, particularly when combined with British geographical data, become the basis for key decisions made in the field by Lewis and his co-commander, William Clark.

There were components of the American image of the western interior at the time of the Lewis and Clark expedition that were not derived directly from British exploration in Rupert's Land: notions on the length and navigability of the Missouri and Columbia rivers, on the character of the Pacific coastal regions through which the Columbia was believed to flow, and on the land quality of the vast plains between the Rocky Mountains and the Mississippi. But of all the elements in the American image, those most critical for Jefferson's geopolitical designs — for his desired combination of territorial and commercial control over an immense portion of the North American continent — were the elements obtained from British exploratory lore and cartography. These elements — the nature of the Rocky Mountains as a dividing ridge between the Missouri system and the rivers of the Pacific, the concept of the core drainage area, and the notion of a short portage — were to prove critical to the field operations of Lewis and Clark. Indeed, in one of the most delightful historical ironies in the annals of North America, geographical lore emanating from British efforts to consolidate territorial control over the western portions of the continent became crucial to the success of an American exploratory venture attempting to counter that British challenge.

Testing Jefferson's Geography: The Lewis and Clark Expedition

When Lewis and Clark began their epic journey up the Missouri River in the spring of 1804, they carried with them a mental picture of the geography of the western interior that had been derived primarily from

British exploratory lore and filtered through the geographical imagination of Thomas Jefferson.[25] There were two significant features of this geography of hope. The first was the fanlike drainage system of the Missouri River with its base along the eastern flank of range of mountains where, between the 45th and 50th parallels, a number of small but navigable streams had their sources and then flowed eastward to form two major rivers that joined near the apex of the triangle at the Mandan villages. Of these two major rivers, the southernmost was the true Missouri, and from its sources it ran a west-to-east course to the Mandans. The second major component of the image was the configuration of the Rocky Mountain range as a narrow, single-ridged structure, extending from north to south and being extensive in neither height nor breadth. On the western slope of this range, opposite the heads of the Missouri and the rivers that fed into it, lay the source waters of the Columbia, streams also assumed to be navigable. The assumed navigability of the upper reaches of both Atlantic and Pacific drainages was coupled with the minimal size conception of the Rockies to create the core of misconception in the image: the Missouri was navigable to its source in a range of low mountains, and only a short and easy portage across that range would link the waters of the east with the waters of the west. With this linking, the ancient dream of the all-water commercial route across North America could become reality.

During the captains' first season of exploration, as they proceeded up the Missouri to the Mandan villages where they spent the winter of 1804-05, the image with which they had left St. Louis underwent modification as newer data obtained in the field from fur traders and Indians began to alter their British-derived geographical lore.[26] The first restructuring in their view of the farther West as shown on William Clark's map, drawn at the Mandan villages and representing the captains' image after the first full year in the field, related to the nature of the Missouri drainage system above the Mandan villages. Holding to the fanlike drainage arrangement as shown on the Arrowsmith map, Lewis and Clark used newly obtained information to increase their understanding of the finer details of that river system. The Missouri, as it had on the Arrowsmith 1802 map, ran a straight-line easterly course from the mountains to the Mandans. Now, however, it had three major branches instead of the two represented by Arrowsmith. The central branch was the Missouri proper, the southern branch was the Yellowstone, and the northern branch or the Milk River was the channel "through which," Clark wrote, "those small streams, on the E side of the Rocky mountins laid down by Mr. Fidler, pass to the Missouri."[27] This observation was to prove of great significance to the expedition during the summer of 1805.

The second major restructuring or refinement of the image represented by the King and Arrowsmith maps was in the course of the Missouri within the Rocky Mountains and of the configuration of the mountains themselves. The captains had learned during the winter of 1804-05 that the Missouri's sources were far to the south of their location on the King and Arrowsmith maps. From this southern source, the river flowed north between two narrow, parallel ridges of the Rockies before turning toward the east, cutting through a third ridge, and then following the west-to-east course laid down by King and Arrowsmith. This division of the Rockies into a series of parallel ridges was an important piece of information and, at least in part, verified the information presented on Arrowsmith's maps that the mountains "divided into several low ridges" south of Mackenzie's crossing. At the point where the Missouri cut through the third or easternmost ridge of the Rockies their new image placed the Great Falls, a landmark absent in their pre-exploratory lore but one that would prove essential to the expedition's eventual success.

Above the Great Falls, at about the point where the Missouri made its great bend to the south, the river was joined by another stream coming from the westernmost ridge of the Rockies and heading near the Great Lake River, a major northern tributary of the Columbia according to the data from both Mackenzie's *Voyages* and the Arrowsmith 1802 map. From these British sources, Lewis and Clark knew that the Great Lake River was unnavigable, and this shorter route to the Pacific was eschewed in favour of one the Indians at the Mandan villages had told them about. If they would follow the Missouri to the south, beyond the Great Falls and beyond the mouth of the stream coming from the west, they would find the river "navigable to the foot of a chain of high mountains being the ridge which divides the waters of the Atlantic from those of the Pacific Ocean" (*Original Journals* 6:55). Crossing this ridge, according to their Indian informants, would bring them to a large river that was navigable to the sea. The Indians further related that the crossing between the Missouri and this large western river could be accomplished in less than half a day's travel. The information from Mackenzie on the short portage was verified by Indian lore, and as the captains prepared to leave the Mandans in the spring of 1805, their belief in the prospects for the discovery of Jefferson's desideratum — the commercial route to the Pacific — was firm.

The Corps of Discovery commanded by Meriwether Lewis and William Clark departed the Mandan villages in April of 1805, bound for the Great Falls, the short portage, and — they hoped — glory. Passing the major southern tributary, the Yellowstone, and the major northern tributary, the Milk River, about where they had expected to find those streams, the captains continued upriver in the optimistic belief that their image of the rivers and mountains, shaped during the previous winter, matched closely with geographic reality.   Before they reached the confirming landmark of the Great Falls, however, they were presented with an obstacle barring their farther confident path westward. This was the completely unexpected Marias River, entering the Missouri River from the north and almost equaling it in size.[28] In the explorers' image, there was only one major northern tributary (the Milk), and they had passed the stream fitting that description several weeks earlier. What to be made of this second northern river? Or, if the northern branch were the true Missouri, what was to be made of the southern branch? Their information contained no account of a large tributary stream entering the Missouri from the south above the mouth of the Yellowstone. The true Missouri was the one that had been represented as heading near navigable Columbian waters, and correct determination as to which stream was the Missouri was, in the captains' view, critical to the continuation of their journey. Camp was made on the point of land formed by the junction of the Missouri and Marias, and here the decision that would determine the success or failure of Jefferson's grand design would be made:

> To mistake the stream at this period of the season, two months of the traveling season having now elapsed, and to ascend such stream to the rocky Mountain or perhaps much further before we could inform ourselves whether it did approach the Columbia or not, and then be obliged to return and take the other stream would not only loose us the whole of this season but would probably so dishearten the party that it might defeat the expedition altogether, convinced we were that the utmost circumspection and caution was necessary in deciding on the stream to be taken. (*Original Journals* 2:113)

This vital decision at the Marias was made by Lewis and Clark on the basis of field observation, good geographical logic, and reliance on the data acquired from the British exploration of the Canadian interior.

On June 3, 1805, Captains Lewis and Clark made a brief field reconnaissance of the two rivers — Missouri and Marias — near the junction.   On the basis of that investigation, coupled with their understanding of western geography from the King and Arrowsmith maps, they were prepared to make a decision as to which river should be followed. The southern branch (the Missouri proper) exhibited the characteristics of a mountain stream, with clear water and a gravelly bed. The northern branch, on the other hand, was obviously a plains stream with a muddy bed and roily, silt-laden water. The captains knew that the Missouri came directly from the mountains whereas the northern feeders of the Missouri—in Arrowsmith's fanlike drainage system—had to pass over a large extent of plains country before entering the main stream. Therefore, the southern branch, the river exhibiting the characteristics of a mountain rather than a plains stream, was most probably the true Missouri. The other members of the party, however, were equally convinced that the northern stream, precisely because it so resembled the Missouri they had been following for over two thousand miles, was the true course to the short portage. Wishing to avoid making a decision that would go against the majority opinion of their men, the captains determined to make further field observations, Clark to proceed with a small party up the southern branch and Lewis to pursue a course of exploration up the northern.

Clark's investigations carried him to a point from which the mountains were visible in a configuration that seemed to match the information received from Indians at the Mandan villages; this confirmed his belief that the southern branch was the correct route to be followed. Lewis, following the Marias to the northwest, journeyed much farther before the mountains came into sight—as was to be expected if the Arrowsmith data were reasonably accurate. When mountains, and particularly a high conical peak, were finally visible on the northwestern horizon, Lewis had become "well convinced that this branch of the Missouri had it's direction too much to the North for our route to the Pacific" (*Original Journals* 2:125), and returned to the base camp at the Missouri-Marias junction to rejoin Clark and the remainder of the party.

As the captains compared notes on their separate explorations, they became even more firm in their opinion that the proper Missouri was the southern branch. Attempting to explain their decision to their men, who, virtually to a man, still believed the northern river to be the correct one, the captains used their field copy of the Nicholas King map—derived from Arrowsmith's 1802 production. The Arrowsmith map, Lewis pointed out, provided a strong argument against the north branch as the true Missouri. Even if Arrowsmith's informant, Peter Fidler, had penetrated as far south as the 47th parallel and had seen only small streams running east rather than the large Missouri, then the presumption was, claimed Lewis, that "those little streams do not penetrate the rocky mountains to such distance as would afford rational grownds for a conjecture that they had their sources near any navigable branch of the Columbia" (*Original Journals* 2:134-35). This eliminated, in Lewis's mind, the Marias from consideration as the true Missouri or route to the Pacific. Moreover, Arrowsmith had "laid down a remarkable mountain in the chain of the Rocky mountains called the tooth" near the sources of the Missouri's northern branches, and it was this mountain that Lewis believed he had seen during his field reconnaissance. That the main stream of the Missouri "should take it's sources to the N.W. under those mountains the travels of Mr. Fidler forbid us to believe" (*Original Journals* 2:135-36).

The members of the Corps of Discovery, excepting their captains, still remained obdurate in their belief in the northern branch, and Lewis and Clark determined to make one more field test. With a small party, Lewis travelled up the southern branch until he came to the Great Falls, the landmark described by the Indians at the Mandan villages. With this discovery he, and the entire command, knew that the proper route lay to the south. Beyond the Great Falls lay the short portage to the westward-flowing streams that would bring them to the Columbia and the Pacific, and the entire party set its course southwest for the Falls and the Passage. What followed was a heartbreaking, months-long attempt to locate the fabled short portage. That the party eventually succeeded in reaching the Pacific, in spite of repeated disappointments arising from the disjunction between the geography of hope and the geography of reality, is in large measure attributable to the strength of the two captains and their men's willingness to accept and abide by their decisions. That willingness was enhanced beyond measure by the decision at the Marias—a decision made on the basis of lore obtained from British sources—and it would not be an exaggeration to claim that upon that decision rested the eventual success of America's exploratory epic.

It matters little that the success of Lewis and Clark was not in the discovery of the Passage to India—for, in the form envisioned by Jefferson and the British theorists and explorers of the late eighteenth and early nineteenth centuries, the Passage did not exist. It matters little that the image upon which Jefferson had founded his great geopolitical designs was a faulty one—for it was based on hope and not reality. What does matter is that the Corps of Discovery travelled to the Pacific and back and, through the exploration of the lands between the Mississippi and the great western ocean, gave the American people a West with which the mind could deal rather than a West of rumour and conjecture. It also matters, in view of the events that would encompass the first half of the 1800s, that Thomas Jefferson's response to the early exploration of Rupert's Land eventually achieved at least part of what he had hoped it would. For the traversing of the continent by Lewis and Clark, the uniting of their discoveries with those of the courageous employees of the North West and Hudson's Bay companies to the north, gave the United States a claim on the Pacific Northwest that would not be relinquished. And when "the Oregon Question"—who would control the bulk of the Columbian Basin—became an issue of international dispute in the 1840s, the eventual resolution of that question in favour of the United States can be attributed to a tall red-haired Virginian geopolitician who saw in Mackenzie's *Voyages* a great deal more than an adventure tale.

Notes

1. Alexander Mackenzie, *Voyages from Montreal through the Continent of North America to the Frozen and Pacific oceans in 1789 and 1793* (1801; reprint, Toronto: The Courier Press, 1911).

2. Jefferson's correspondent was Caspar Wistar, a Philadelphian who succeeded Jefferson as president of the American Philosophical Society. Wistar's letter is in the Jefferson Papers of the Library of Congress, Wistar to Jefferson, 8 January 1802.

3. Cited in Donald Jackson, *Thomas Jefferson and the Stony Mountains* (Urbana: University of Illinois Press, 1981), 124.

4. James Cheetham to Jefferson, 22 February 1802, Jefferson Papers, LC.

5. Jefferson to Lewis, 23 February 1801, Jefferson Papers, LC. This letter is also printed in Donald Jackson, *Letters of the Lewis and Clark Expedition with Related Documents, 1783-1854* (Urbana: University of Illinois Press, 1962), 2-3.

6. Letter of Carlos Martinez de Irujo, Spanish minister to the U.S., to Pedro Cevallos, Foreign Minister of Spain, 2 December 1802. Printed in Abraham P. Nasatir, ed., *Before Lewis and Clark: Documents Illustrating the History of the Missouri, 1785-1804* (St. Louis: St. Louis Historical Documents Foundation, 1952), 2:712-14.

7. Jefferson's message to Congress, 18 January 1803, Jefferson Papers, LC. Also printed in Jackson, *Letters*, 10-14.

8. Jefferson to Lewis, 20 June 1803, Jefferson Papers, LC. Also printed in Jackson, *Letters*, 61-66.

9. John Logan Allen, *Passage through the Garden: Lewis and Clark and the Image of the American Northwest* (Urbana: University of Illinois Press, 1975), 60-61.

10. Allen, *Passage*, 62-63.

11. In communications with George Rogers Clark, John Ledyard, and Andre Michaux, Jefferson had, between 1783 and 1793, made a

series of preliminary attempts at discovery of the water route to the Pacific. See Allen, *Passage*, 64-67.

12. Samuel Hearne, *A Journey from Prince of Wales's Fort in Hudson's Bay to the northern Ocean in the Years 1769, 1770, 1771, and 1772*, ed. J.B. Tyrrell (Toronto: Champlain Society, 1911).

13. A copy of Fidler's map is reproduced in Allen, *Passage*, 22.

14. A copy of Pond's map, drafted by St. John de Crevecoeur, was presented to the U.S. Congress in 1784. The map is reproduced in Allen, *Passage*, 24-25.

15. See John L. Allen, "Pyramidal Height-of-Land: A Persistent Myth in the Exploration of Western Anglo-America," *International Geography*, 1:394-95.

16. Allen, *Passage*, 23-26.

17. Father Jacques Marquette was apparently the first explorer to speculate on the possible connections between the Missouri and streams flowing to the Pacific. See "The Journal of Father Marquette" in Reuben Gold Thwaites, ed., *The Jesuit Relations and Allied Documents* (Cleveland: Burrows Bros., 1896-1901), 59:141-43.

18. Mackenzie, *Voyages*, 2:109.

19. Mackenzie, *Voyages*, 2:346.

20. J.B. Tyrrell, ed., *David Thompson's Narrative of His Exploration in Western America, 1784-1812* (Toronto: Champlain Society, 1916), 187.

21. Information on Arrowsmith maps and their role in shaping American attitudes toward the West may be found in various issues of *The Medical Repository*, edited by Samuel Latham Mitchell and one of the most respected periodicals published in the United States. Mitchell, an amateur geographer, frequently published items of geographical interest. See especially the material on Arrowsmith in vol. 5, lst hexade, 1802, 462.

22. Jackson, *Letters*, 63.

23.   The King map was discovered by the author in a collection of materials relating to the Lewis and Clark expedition in the Geography and Maps Division of the Library of Congress. Prior to this discovery, this important map was identified only as "Anonymous." A full discussion of the King map and a reproduction of it may be found in Allen, *Passage*, 97-103.

24.   The news of the Purchase was made public on July 4, 1803 (see *The National Intelligencer*, Washington, July 4, 1803: 1-2), although Jefferson had known of it for several months.

25.   Lewis and Clark had spent the winter of 1803-04 at the mouth of the Wood River (Illinois), across the Mississippi from the mouth of the Missouri, and here they had obtained geographic data from fur traders and others in St. Louis. But their view in the spring of 1804, when they departed for the West, was still basically a Jeffersonian image. See Allen, *Passage*, 160-80.

26.   For details on the modification in their image of the West, see Allen, *Passage*, 181-251.

27.   Reuben Gold Thwaites, ed., *The Original Journals of the Lewis and Clark Expedition* (New York: Dodd, Mead, 1904-05), 6:53.

28.   *Original Journals*, 2:109. The Marias is nowhere as large a stream as the Missouri under normal conditions of flow, but the captains encountered it during its flood stage and before peak run-off had begun to swell the Missouri.

Chapter 4

JOHN FRANKLIN AND THE FUR TRADE, 1819-22

Clive Holland

When, today, we consider Franklin's first Arctic Land Expedition of 1819-22, we tend to think of its final stages: the short coastal journey and the long despairing march back to Fort Enterprise, marred by starvation, murder, and cannibalism. On this occasion, however, I would like us to consider the earlier stages of that expedition: namely, Franklin's passage through Rupert's Land toward unknown territory and his dealings with the fur-trading companies during that journey.

To introduce this paper, it will be necessary to review briefly the conditions prevailing in 1819 from two separate angles: first, from the point of view of the British Admiralty and its newly adopted plans to explore the Northwest Passage, and second, with regard to the condition of the fur trade in northern Rupert's Land at what was, for both the Hudson's Bay and North West companies, a very critical period.

First, the Admiralty. They had begun their assault on the Northwest Passage with a voyage under Commander John Ross in 1818 which, as is well known, was disappointing in its results, achieving little more than the re-exploration of Baffin Bay and ending with a dispute between Ross and his second-in-command, William Edward Parry, about the possibility of pursuing a passage through Lancaster Sound. In 1819, therefore, the Admiralty attempted a different approach. First of all, Parry was sent back to Baffin Bay with instructions to settle the matter of the penetrability of Lancaster Sound. Second, in an entirely novel approach, Lieutenant John Franklin was sent on an overland journey to establish the whereabouts of the northern coastline of the North American continent in the hope of guiding the seaborne expedition towards its destination. This plan, as was realized at an early stage, placed Franklin very much in the hands of the two fur-trading companies, on whose supply lines he would be heavily dependent on his journey towards the unexplored area beyond Great Slave Lake. Those trading companies, however, had major difficulties of their own at the time of Franklin's expedition. Throughout almost the whole length of the route that Franklin chose to adopt, the two companies were locked in intense rivalry that was damaging the efficiency of both. As recently as 1815, the North West Company had abandoned all its posts in the Mackenzie River district, and the company only began fully to reoccupy the district between 1818 and 1820. At the same time, in 1818, the Hudson's Bay Company was launching the last and most successful of its major expeditions to establish itself in rivalry to the North West Company in the Athabasca and Mackenzie districts; in 1818-19, the HBC established rival posts on Lake Athabasca and at Fort Resolution on Great Slave Lake. Rivalry was so intense that each side abused the other and prisoners were taken at several posts. Franklin arrived in the midst of the dispute to find supply lines stretched and the trading posts undermanned and understocked, and he clearly needed to exercise great diplomacy to secure the maximum cooperation from both sides on his passage towards the North.

Returning now to London, we find that the origins and planning stages of the expedition themselves have some extraordinary elements. The first short note proposing such an expedition to the Admiralty and the Colonial Office was written by John Barrow, the Admiralty's second secretary, on February 22, 1819 — just three months before the expedition was expected to depart for Hudson Bay.[1] It appears that Franklin and his officers were appointed in late March and early April, and Franklin did not seriously begin to seek advice and information, and to requisition supplies, until the middle of April, little more than a month before he set off. Even today, with instant communications and a thorough knowledge of northern geography, that would be a very short time scale on which to plan such a venture. For Franklin, at least a year would have been needed even to communicate his intentions to the northern posts, let alone to prepare himself fully for his journey. (This was, indeed, one of the main lessons that Franklin was to learn from his first overland expedition; for his second, he began to prepare, and even to send out men and supplies, more than a year in advance.) When Franklin left London, he was, on the one hand, thoroughly ill-prepared for a journey of such magnitude, and on the other hand, he carried with him an ill-informed and over optimistic impression of the circumstances prevailing in the North at that time.

Two of his main sources of misinformation were, surprisingly, the London headquarters of the two trading companies. Possibly from anxiety to please the government, or perhaps from ignorance, neither seems to have given Franklin any warning of the difficulties and shortages in the North resulting from recent events. On the contrary, both sent out letters to their northern staff exhorting them to offer Franklin all the help he needed along his route, almost as if nothing were amiss. As examples, I extract two quotes from a letter from Simon McGillivray in London, which Franklin carried with him to each of the North West Company posts. First he writes:

> I have to inform you that upon an application from His Majesty's Government, I have on behalf of the North West Company promised that he and his party shall be well received by any of you, Gentlemen; whom he may meet or visit in his progress through the Interior of the Country; and also that you will afford him every facility and assistance in your power for the prosecution of the undertaking on which he is engaged.

Then later:

> I trust that you will afford Lieutenant Franklin every assistance and information in your power, and I trust that you can be at no loss to provide such conveyance and supplies as may be deemed the fittest for the purpose.[2]

Franklin must, from the outset, have derived much comfort and reassurance from those orders, and from similar orders sent out by the Hudson's Bay Company, for both exuded the same confidence that the companies' employees would have not only the will but also the means to convey the expedition comfortably along its route. Perhaps as a consequence, Franklin made few special arrangements in advance for the conveyance of his party through the inhabited region of the North, trusting to the two companies' resources to provide for him. Yet he was to find from the moment of his arrival at York Factory that whilst goodwill was plentiful enough, the means of assisting him were often almost entirely lacking.

A second source of misleading information was the preliminary advice that Franklin sought from northern travellers resident in London. Apart from acquiring a few books, such as Hearne's *Journey* of 1769-72, Franklin appears to have received firsthand advice from only two genuine northern travellers before he left: Sir Alexander Mackenzie and John Pritchard.[3] Pritchard had behind him the distinction of a 2000-mile winter journey from Moose and York factories to the Red River colony, but appears to have had little practical knowledge of northern travel in 1819. It was he, for example, who advocated bacon as the main item of provision, and on that advice Franklin set out with seven hundred weight of bacon, more than all other meats put together. Yet on leaving York Factory for the interior he had to abandon the whole consignment. "The bacon," he recorded, "was too bulky an item to be forwarded in any circumstances."[4] In fairness to Franklin's advisers, Mackenzie had some far more practical suggestions to offer; indeed, as events turned out, he outlined a plan of proceeding that Franklin followed almost to the letter, even to the extent that, on occasion, one wonders whether he was really exercising his own judgement, or was simply rereading Mackenzie's proposals. We shall return to Mackenzie later; the main point that emerges at this stage is that, however sound or unsound the advice, Franklin seems to have felt compelled to adopt it for want of any other guidance. We should also note, however, that innovation and personal initiative were never Franklin's outstanding talents as an arctic explorer; unswerving obedience to instructions and naive acceptance of the advice of his betters guided him from 1819 right through until 1847, when blind observance of instructions led a whole expedition into an impasse from which no one returned.

We have mentioned that Franklin's problems began as soon as he landed in North America, but in fact one problem arose even earlier than that. The expedition sailed on the Hudson's Bay Company's ship *Prince of Wales* on May 23, 1819. When only two days out from Gravesend, Franklin learned from experienced trading officers that he would not, as expected, find boatmen available for the expedition at York Factory; they would all be too busy. So he had to pen a hasty letter back to the Colonial Office requesting permission to recruit Orkneymen at Stromness.[5] Permission was granted, but in the Orkneys he found nearly all the experienced men engaged in the whale and herring fisheries. He managed to recruit only four men, which in the event turned out to be too few.

The party arrived at York Factory to be greeted most cordially by Governor William Williams of the Hudson's Bay Company and by two North West Company officers held under detention there, John George McTavish and Angus Shaw. Almost at once Franklin encountered the kind of problem that was to dog him over much of his route, for whilst the welcome was sincere enough and officers of both companies were all too willing to advise him on the details of his route, the predicted shortage of men to convey him along that route was all too apparent. Williams could offer only one steersman, who, with Franklin's two seamen and four Orkneymen, completed a crew for only one boat, whereas Franklin needed at least two boats. Williams provided his largest boat, which, though heavily laden, was inadequate to carry all Franklin's supplies, and he was obliged at this early stage to leave in store a total of thirty-five packages, including the bacon and much of his rum, tobacco, and ammunition. These three latter items, Williams assured him, could be forwarded the following year and were anyway plentiful enough in the interior. But Franklin was to find this assurance misleading to say the least; he was to find shortage of spirits, tobacco, and ammunition a problem throughout his journey.

Further problems awaited after he finally embarked on Hayes River on September 9. Hayes River had been for many years the Hudson's Bay Company's main line of communication into the western interior, but even this well-travelled highway offered the explorers a harsh initiation into the daily routine of travel in Rupert's Land, and it was in terms of hardship and danger above all else that the explorers began to record their first impressions of this new environment. George Back's journal presents a particularly vivid account of their hazardous, exhausting, and frustrating task in making progress up this shallow, swift-flowing stream; on September 13, for example, he describes a day's tracking, or hauling the boat upstream with tow lines:

> At 6 am the tents were struck and we resumed the tracking afresh, but with greater difficulty than ever from the steepness and excessive softness of the earth, the Men sinking deep each step, that it was hard work to get along without any other incumbrance — nor were the intermediate parts any relief, being a composition of sharp pointed stones which from the crew having their country shoes on (made of moose skin) cut their feet in all directions.... The current continued to grow more rapid, and with great labour we only got 13 miles.[6]

Two days later Franklin felt obliged to fire an irate letter back to Governor Williams complaining of the Hudson's Bay Company brigade's reluctance to stay back and help him through such difficult episodes — thus illustrating another problem that Franklin was to encounter more than once: that goodwill by the companies' senior officers was not necessarily matched by more junior servants, who tended to view the expedition more as an unnecessary encumbrance to their own progress.

On September 17 the expedition reached a staging post at the Rock Depot where more bad news awaited them, namely, that the river beyond that point would be quite unnavigable to a boat so heavily laden. Thus, unavoidably, they had to lighten their load by leaving behind a further sixteen packages, this time mainly of food. This was a disquieting state of affairs so early in the expedition, for they had now either abandoned or deposited for later shipment a total of fifty-one packages, or nearly two-thirds of their original supplies. This left the trading companies with the unwelcome burden of bringing on supplies in the following year and in the meantime left Franklin heavily dependent on the meagre resources of the inland posts. Both factors would later contribute to tension between the expedition and the traders.

Beyond the Rock Depot they made steadier progress with their lightened load, and after a total of forty-four days' tracking, portaging, and rowing, they reached Cumberland House on the Saskatchewan River, where they were to spend their first winter.

Both companies had a trading post at Cumberland House, and the explorers were hospitably received at each establishment. But once more Franklin found that goodwill was rather wanting in practical support. This time it was information he required most:

> My anxious enquiries were early directed to gain whatever information I could respecting the Countries North of the Athabasca from the Gentlemen whom I found here but to my regret I learnt that neither the person in charge of this or the NW Company's post...had ever been employed in that department and they therefore were unable to give me any.[7]

Being anxious to procure that information, and having now learned the necessity of forewarning the traders of the expedition's approach, Franklin therefore announced his intention to make a winter journey to Fort Chipewyan in the company of Back and Hepburn. It would be pleasant to record that, in announcing that bold move, Franklin was acting on his own initiative and beginning to show some independence from his fur-trade advisers. But it was not so: behind this decision, as with many other crucial decisions, was the guiding hand of Sir Alexander Mackenzie, whose letter of advice to Franklin prescribed just such a journey. Mackenzie had conjectured that the expedition would not get beyond Île-à-la-Crosse in the first season, and wrote: "In that event I would recommend that yourself and two or three of your party with proper Guides should proceed as soon as the ice would permit on foot to Athabasca to make your arrangements for the ensuing spring."[8] Although the plan was not as original as Franklin would have had us believe, it was, to give him his due, a much longer journey than Mackenzie had envisaged, and it proved as hard an initiation into overland travel as Hayes River had been into boat travel. They set out with carioles, sledges, dogs, and drivers on January 18, 1820, and Franklin neatly encapsulated the nature of their discomfort on the journey in a few lines of his report to the Colonial Office:

The mode of travelling in winter with Sledges and Dogs has been so often described, that I imagine any repetition would be useless: I will only therefore bear my testimony to the painful initiation into the daily practice of walking on Snow Shoes—a species of suffering and fatigue which greatly exercises the temper and patience of a Novice, and which practice alone will enable him to surmount. I wish to correct also a generally received opinion respecting the Place where the Parties sleep termed a Hut or Encampment. Its preparation simply consists in clearing the Snow away to the Ground, and placing a covering of Pine Branches, on which the Travellers spread their Blankets, Coats &c and sleep in warmth and tolerable comfort even in the coldest night, before a large Fire which is kept constantly burning at their Feet.[9]

After two weeks march up the Saskatchewan River, they welcomed the opportunity of a few days' rest at Carlton House, being considerably fatigued by the constant use of the snowshoe; but by February 16 at Green Lake they had "completely surmounted the pains which the walking in snow shoes has occasioned,"[10] and on their arrival at Île à-la-Crosse on February 23, George Back declared himself "in every manner more capable of undergoing fatigue than at the commencement."[11]

Thus, by patiently mastering this painful and alien mode of travel, the explorers finally reached Fort Chipewyan on March 26, after a journey of 790 miles, completed in sixty-nine days. They had covered a daily average of about sixteen miles, excluding rest days, which quite negates George Simpson's later disparaging—and much quoted—remark that Franklin "with the utmost exertion...cannot walk above Eight miles in one day."[12]

On his arrival at Lake Athabasca, Franklin was, of course, at the very heart of the prevailing bitter dispute between the two companies. This imposed on him a need to be even more tactful than previously in his dealings with them and to show no favour to either side. In this he was largely successful: he arranged a meeting-place on neutral ground and carefully made equal demands on both sides for opinions, provisions, and men. Opinions on his further progress were plentiful enough, but the much-needed provisions and men were almost impossible to obtain. The hostilities of the past year had left both trading posts severely short of supplies, and even the most careful diplomacy could not help him to acquire what the traders simply did not have. Here, more than ever before, the traders' attitude of sincere goodwill and evident desire to please was countered by a frank admission of inability to meet the expedition's considerable needs. The traders' dilemma is perhaps best portrayed in this passage of a letter from the North West Company partners at Fort Chipewyan:

> No endeavours will be wanting on our part to promote the object in view as far as the nature and severity of the circumstances under which we are at present placed will admit; and we are extremely sorry to find that the existing troubles in the country, and more particularly the recent extraordinary transactions taken place in this quarter, has already deprived us and may deprive us still more, of the means of contributing towards the successful issue of the expedition to the extent we most ardently desire.

And then there creeps into the letter the first hint, if not of resentment, then at least of irritation, at the expedition's demands. Referring to the boatmen required by Franklin, it continues:

> for whether the seizure of our people is by legal authority or not does not the less deprive us of their services, and those who are most useful to us would be of most service to you.[13]

Despite that reluctance, Franklin did eventually recruit enough boatmen to enable him to continue his journey, but he still remained desperately short of supplies. Among the worst shortages were those very items that had been left behind at York Factory on Governor Williams's assurance that they were plentiful in the interior: spirits, tobacco, and ammunition. But food supplies, too, were very short, and even the arrival of Richardson and Hood with their supplies and extra pemmican from Cumberland House brought little relief, for the pemmican turned out to be mouldy and uneatable. Thus, when they left Fort Chipewyan for the North on July 18, 1820, they had food remaining for only one day!

Not all their transactions at Lake Athabasca were ineffective, however. From there, Franklin had written to both companies' representatives on Great Slave Lake, Edward Smith and Robert McVicar, asking for assistance in procuring Indian guides and hunters. Smith, in turn, had forwarded his request to Ferdinand Wentzel at Fort Providence on the North Arm of the lake. In Wentzel, Franklin at last found a true asset—a veteran of the Athabasca and Mackenzie districts since 1806 who took real pride in his knowledge of the North and in his familiarity with the Indians. On May 22, 1820, Wentzel responded with "sincere pleasure" that he had recruited those essential guides and hunters, in the form of Akaitcho and his Copper Indian tribe. He went on to describe his plans for the expedition at considerable length and then concluded by hinting, with almost touching bashfulness, that perhaps he might be recruited as a sort of intermediary between the Indians and the expedition.[14] Franklin received that letter before leaving Fort Chipewyan, took the meaning of Wentzel's gentle hint, and responded with alacrity that "there appeared nothing else wanting to complete the happiness of our present prospect, than the assistance of an experienced Gentleman who is conversant with the Red Knife Tribe."[15] In other words, Wentzel could most certainly have the job he wanted, and Franklin recognized that he had at last found a truly knowledgeable ally in the North.

We can now move quickly over the next stage of the expedition, in the summer of 1820, when they continued by boat from Lake Athabasca to Fort Providence. Though short of provisions, they were greatly aided on their arrival at Moose Deer Island on Great Slave Lake — where both companies had trading posts — by the provision of 550 pounds of meat.

They joined Wentzel at Fort Providence about July 27 and with him, for the first time, embarked into unknown territory on the river to which Franklin gave the name of Yellowknife, after the tribe that lived there. Of that journey, Franklin records chiefly that it was "performed under the mortifying circumstances of being very short of Provision, and almost in want of the more encouraging stimulus to exertion with the Canadian Voyageur, Rum or other Spirits."[16] They arrived at the site the Indians had chosen for their wintering, which they named Winter Lake, on August 20, and immediately began preparations to build their house there, Fort Enterprise.

So far, then, so good. Franklin had successfully brought his expedition through the territory occupied by the fur traders and had handled his relations with them with diplomacy and discretion. He had found a secure base for his journey of exploration, had met a reliable group of Indians to hunt for him, and had recruited a worthy adviser in Ferdinand Wentzel. Were it not for the vexatious problem of the large quantity of essential supplies left behind at York Factory and the Rock Depot, he would have been able to look forward with unqualified optimism to the work that was to come, and there would have been no need to test the continuing goodwill of the fur traders. But ammunition for the hunters, tobacco for the voyageurs and the Indians, cloth, and ironworks were still in very short supply. For that reason, on October 18, Franklin asked George Back to return to Great Slave Lake to bring on the expedition's own supplies and to procure whatever he could from the trading posts.

It was at this stage that relations between the two trading companies and the expedition, hitherto amicable, took an unexpected turn for the worse. The reason for that change, though not fully made clear in the literature, can probably be ascribed to the impetuous character of the young George Back; to the stringent economies imposed by the Hudson's Bay Company's new governor in the North, George Simpson; and to the strange behaviour of a rather mysterious character, Wentzel's replacement at Fort Providence, one Mr. Weekes.

Certainly, Robert McVicar, the HBC representative on Great Slave Lake, was not to blame, for he gave George Back almost all the goods he had in his possession, an act of considerable generosity for which he was later to be soundly rebuked by George Simpson. But Back appears to have adopted a very much more aggressive approach towards the traders than Franklin had done, and there is evidence that his aggression was poorly received by most of them. Back himself wrote to Franklin from Great Slave Lake that "I have discovered...a great lukewarmness on the part of the NW Company absolutely amounting to a denial of further service to the Expedition. Be this as it may I shall soon have an opportunity of proving it, and be assured that nothing but a positive refusal communicated to me by letter will enforce me to return without some part of the requisite supplies."[17] Elsewhere in the same letter Back reported to Franklin in equally belligerent terms "the non arrival of our most important articles" owing apparently to a dispute between the two companies at Grand Rapid, and in another letter that has unfortunately not survived, he made accusations of uncooperativeness against both Weekes at Fort Providence and Edward Smith, the North West Company's partner on Great Slave Lake. These reports provoked the usually mild-tempered Franklin into firing off indignant letters to both Edward Smith and George Keith on Lake Athabasca in which he intemperately asserted that "a weight of odium will undoubtedly be attached by an indignant Country"[18] should the North West Company fail further to support the expedition. That letter in turn brought forth a deeply offended response from the partners of the North West Company at Fort Chipewyan, which reads in part:

> We leave you to imagine . . . Sir what was our astonishment on perusing an accusation against our associate Mr. Smith (who of all men living deserves it least) charging him with having forbid any supplies being furnished to the expedition. It appears further we regret to observe that you are strongly impressed with an Idea that it is the determination of the North-West Company "to limit their assistance within very narrow bounds." At the same time that we

should think some attention due to the information on which you ground the accusation against our Friend, we must be permitted to insist that it was incorrect, and that your decision on it betrays an unguarded precipitation and want of discernment little corresponding with your experience and high station and character in life. Your other charge so unjustly applied to the Members of the Concern is entirely groundless. In short Sir to enter into a refutation of these calumnies, must appear to every reflecting person concerned, a mere waste of time.

The letter continues:

We trust when it is considered that the Company had no anticipation whatever of being called upon by the Expedition for supplies of Goods, exclusive of other considerations of vital importance to the Concern, the proportion, promptly and cheerfully furnished on various occasions will ultimately elicit a correspondent estimation, or at all events shield the Members from the future Calumny or Abuse from the Officers of the Expedition.[19]

If a full apology from Franklin was expected, as it evidently was, it was not forthcoming. Franklin simply responded with further accusations against Weekes, though he did write a rather lame retraction to Edward Smith, and confessed privately in a letter to Back his regret at having written in such strong terms to the company's partners. If there is any point at which it might be said that relations between the expedition and the North West Company suffered enduring damage, then it occurred in that exchange of letters. In fairness to Franklin it might be said that his accusations against Weekes, if not those against Smith, were possibly justified. Franklin gathered evidence from more than one quarter that Weekes not only withdrew his cooperation from the expedition but also discouraged the Indians from cooperating. Indeed, right up until the moment of his departure from Rupert's Land at the end of the expedition in September 1822, Franklin was still writing indignantly to Simon McGillivray that Weekes had sought to undermine the success of the expedition. So it has to be said that, however justified the accusation against Weekes, the expedition and the North West Company parted under unhappy circumstances. George Back's journey south did scarcely more good for relations between the expedition and the Hudson's Bay Company. Because the supplies had not arrived, Back was forced to travel as far south as Fort Chipewyan, where he came face to face with the indomitable George Simpson.

Simpson had just arrived as the Hudson's Bay Company's new governor-in-chief in the North, and unfortunately for the expedition, he brought with him new demands for extreme economy and discipline. In one of his earliest letters to Robert McVicar, who had already been generous to the expedition, he wrote: "Economy must now be the order of the day, indeed our means are this season so limited, that we cannot follow up the extravagant system which has hitherto been adopted."[20] Thus, when Back tried the same bullying tactics with Simpson as he had already tried with others, he found himself facing a much harder man. Back's confrontation with Simpson is already well known thanks to the publication of this correspondence in the first volume of the Hudson's Bay Record Society. Perhaps just two extracts will give the flavour of it. Badgering Simpson for his supplies from the South, Back observed impertinently that "you have had several arrivals during my residence here and I imagine they were not all empty,"[21] to which Simpson replied sharply that "the arrivals you allude to have no connection with the goods expected from Isle à la Crosse and your conjecture that 'they were not empty' is perfectly just, but I presume you will give me leave to know the purposes for which they were intended."[22]

This and other exchanges prompted Franklin into a further injudicious and uncharacteristic correspondence in which at one point he remarked to Simpson: "I am not aware whence you could have drawn the conclusion...'that you have done more than was expected or required by Lieut. Franklin' because I left England under the impression that all our wants were to be supplied by the Hudson's Bay Company and have ever since remained in that opinion."[23] Such direct accusations, however, were of little avail, and Back was obliged to return to Fort Enterprise with only a small proportion of the expedition's supplies. We are not told what was in those supplies, but certainly they cannot have contained much ammunition or food. In his very last communication with the Colonial Office before his departure for his coastal exploration, Franklin wrote: "Though our stock of Ammunition is scanty, I trust with strict economy it will suffice to procure provision for the party until we shall arrive at some Establishment."[24]

Franklin was now, by his own admission, heavily dependent on establishing friendly relations with the Inuit along the coast, as he needed them to supply adequate provisions for his party of twenty men. In this, as is now well known, he was entirely unsuccessful. Though he encountered Inuit, they were frightened off before he could even begin to establish relations, and he had to struggle on with his own meagre supplies.

The rest is well-recorded history. He did explore a stretch of coast but at the cost of the lives of half his party.

This brings us to our conclusion. Was the effort worth the suffering and loss of life? Did Franklin make a major miscalculation in continuing his exploration with what he knew to be inadequate supplies and ammunition? The answer must be that in our eyes he was wrong to carry on; the fur trade support that had been promised had proved inadequate, and he could reasonably and honourably have retreated. It was the discipline of his naval training and perhaps the fear of defeat that drove him on.

It would be difficult to concur with Vilhjalmur Stefansson's well-known view that Franklin's failure was somehow the progenitor of a long line of British naval failures in polar exploration, reaching down even to Scott of the Antarctic. This expedition was unique in naval history and took place in circumstances that were never to be repeated. The expedition was invited and expected to rely on trading company support that proved to be wholly unreliable. Nor is it easy to agree with Stefansson's statement that Franklin failed to learn by his mistakes, or to learn from local or native experience. He did learn those very lessons, though the solutions he found were almost the very opposite of Stefansson's concept of living off the land. He learned for his second expedition not to trust anyone but tried and tested naval personnel, to plan more than a year in advance, and to make his own arrangements to ensure that his own supplies and his own boats arrived safely at his northern base. However, there is some truth in Stefansson's remark that Franklin's naval training had been "the sort of life that develops discipline and courage rather than initiative or self-reliance."[25] The events related in this paper seem to show that Franklin was quite lacking in personal initiative and was all too reliant on support expected but not forthcoming from the trading companies. But discipline and courage carried him onward into the unknown, when a more cautious man would almost certainly have turned back. For that we can hardly commend him, for he lost many men's lives, but we must at least admire his tenacity in overcoming many obstacles to carry out the instructions which he, as a naval officer, was bound by his own self-discipline to follow.

Notes

1. John Barrow to Lord Melville, 22 February 1819. Public Record Office (PRO), London, volume CO.6/15, pp. 113-14. (This volume contains all Colonial Office correspondence and minutes, including Franklin's incoming correspondence, for the expedition of 1819-22. Henceforward it will be referred to simply as PRO CO.6/15.)

2. Simon McGillivray to the North West Company's agents, 21 May 1819. PRO CO.6/15, pp. 99-101.

3. John Pritchard and Sir Alexander Mackenzie to John Franklin, 17 April and 21 May 1819. Scott Polar Research Institute (SPRI), Cambridge, Manuscript 248/276, pp. 29-33. (This manuscript is Franklin's personal letter-book of the expedition, containing copies of much of his own correspondence and incoming letters, victualling lists, etc. Henceforward it will be referred to as SPRI MS 248/276.)

4. John Franklin, *Narrative of a journey to the shores of the polar sea, in the years 1819, 20, 21 and 22* (London: John Murray, 1823), 27.

5. John Franklin to Henry Goulburn (Colonial Office), 25 May 1819. PRO CO.6/15, pp. 11-12.

6. George Back, journal, 1819-20; 13 September 1819. McCord Museum, McGill University, Montreal.

7. John Franklin to Henry Goulburn, 24 December 1819. PRO CO.6/15, pp. 28-31.

8. Sir Alexander Mackenzie to John Franklin, 21 May 1819. SPRI MS 248/276, pp. 29-31.

9. John Franklin to Henry Goulburn, 8 May 1820. PRO CO.6/15, pp. 34-38.

10. Franklin, *Narrative of a Journey*, 124.

11. George Back, journal, 1819-20; 26 February 1820. McCord Museum, McGill University, Montreal.

12. E.E. Rich, ed., *Journal of Occurrences in the Athabasca Department by George Simpson, 1820 and 1821, and Report* (London: Hudson's Bay Record Society, 1938) 1:261.

13. North West Company Partners at Fort Chipewyan to John Franklin, May 1820. SPRI MS 248/276, p. 146.

14. W.F. Wentzel to Edward Smith, 22 May 1820. PRO CO.6/15, pp. 39-40.

15. John Franklin to W.F. Wentzel, 20 June 1820. SPRI MS 248/276, pp. 149-51.

16. John Franklin to Henry Goulburn, 18 October 1820. PRO CO.6/15, pp. 52-55.

17. George Back to John Franklin, 8 November 1820. SPRI MS 248/276, pp. 198-99.

18. John Franklin to Edward Smith, 24 November 1820, SPRI MS 248/276, pp. 183-84.

19. Partners of the North West Company, Fort Chipewyan, to John Franklin, February 1821. SPRI MS 248/276, pp. 192-94.

20. Rich, ed., *Occurrences in the Athabasca Department*, 57.

21. Rich, ed., *Occurrences in the Athabasca Department*, 255.

22. Rich, ed., *Occurrences in the Athabasca Department*, 256.

23. John Franklin to George Simpson, 7 April 1821. SPRI MS 248/276, pp. 190-91.

24. John Franklin to Henry Goulburn, 16 April 1821. SPRI MS 248/276.

25. Vilhjalmur Stefansson, *Unsolved Mysteries of the Arctic* (New York: Macmillan, 1938), p. 104.

Chapter 5

"THIS RASCALLY & UNGRATEFUL COUNTRY": GEORGE NELSON'S RESPONSE TO RUPERT'S LAND

Sylvia Van Kirk

The papers of George Nelson, a rich collection of journals, letters, and reminiscences,[1] provide a fascinating opportunity to begin developing a framework for evaluating the nature and authenticity of the response of the officers of the North West Company to the western regions through which they travelled and to the native people with whom they interacted. Although most of Nelson's fur-trade career was spent as a Nor'Wester around Lake Winnipeg in the heart of Rupert's Land, he, in fact, served three companies. He first journeyed west in 1802 at the age of sixteen as a clerk with the XY Company, and he ultimately left the service of the Hudson's Bay Company in 1823, still at the rank of clerk. Unlike most of his contemporaries who have left well-known accounts of their experiences—men such as Alexander Henry the Younger and Daniel Harmon—Nelson did not progress through the ranks to become a wintering partner or commissioned officer; he thus offers the perspective of a man who was on the periphery of the fur-trade elite.

The first question to be addressed is "What was the nature of journal-keeping among the Nor'Westers?" In studying the journals of a Henry, a Harmon, or a Nelson, one is struck not only by the lavish attention to detail and the introspection (especially in Harmon's writing), but by the fact that the authors obviously considered these accounts their own private property. These do not seem to be official journals intended for the perusal of the agents in Montreal, as the journals of HBC men were meant for the edification of its London Committee. Instead, the writings of many of the Nor'Westers seem to fall very much within the genre of the travel-adventure narratives, so popular in late-eighteenth-century Europe. In writing his narrative, Nelson was influenced by Laurence Sterne's famous *Sentimental Journey*. Further, the title pages of the original editions of Alexander Henry the Elder's and Daniel Harmon's accounts are notably similar to the format used in Tobias Smollett's *Travels through France and Italy*, published in 1766. In the preface to *Travels and Adventures in the Indian Country*, the elder Henry sets out his purpose, which remarkably parallels Smollett's. First, he wants to give a factual account of his own personal experience in foreign climes (which in his case was particularly adventurous); second, he intends to record the geography and natural history of the country; and third, he wishes to present his views of the society and manners of the Indian people he encountered.[2] All Nor'Wester narratives are concerned with these three components, although they certainly vary in the degree to which the authors feel compelled to moralize on what they experience or witness.

It remains to ask why they write, considering the physical difficulties of doing so. In penning a long letter-journal to his parents in 1811 from Lake Winnipeg, Nelson apologizes for the deficiencies of his manuscript. Apart from the problem of keeping his pens sharpened, the environment was hardly ideal:

> I have wrote this in a small room of 12 or 13 foot square where we cook, eat, drink, & sleep altogether besides the trouble of indians & the noise of troublesome & unruly children.[3]

Undoubtedly, the Nor'Westers' highly personalized journals were written in part for their own amusement, perhaps to while away monotonous hours. Other motivations, however, were also at play. In the first place, they were often intended for the entertainment and edification of relatives and friends back home in the "civilized" world. In 1816, for example, Daniel Harmon sent home a copy of his journal of sixteen years, so that his family might know "how their long absent Relative has been employed both as to Body & Mind while in this Savage Country."[4] He was obviously not averse to having his comments read by others, and indeed this prospect may have shaped what he wrote. Certainly, it is evident that when George Nelson copied out his journals to send home to his parents in Sorel, Lower Canada, he added information and moral observations that would not have been part of his original record. Secondly, in a more metaphysical sense, as Professor Germaine Warkentin has observed, the narratives of many Nor'Westers serve not only as "a more general reading of nature and human experience" but as vehicles for expatiation on their authors' own lives.[5] Certainly Nelson's later narrative can be interpreted in this light — as a tale of his own wanderings and testing in the wilderness, thanking God for his ultimate preservation, and lamenting his own sins and weakness.[6]

The Nor'Westers were not divorced from more worldly considerations, however. Although it seems to be almost a convention among them to modestly eschew any interest in publication for a wider audience and to lament their deficiencies in terms of literary style, they were aware of a lucrative European and eastern American market for accounts of the wilds of the interior.[7] Alexander Mackenzie's journals of exploration, published in 1801, were an instant success, and Alexander Henry the Elder followed suit by transforming his journals into an exciting narrative. Even before Henry's narrative was published in 1809, his adventures had brought him public notice both in Montreal and fashionable circles in Europe. The prospect that their own writings might generate similar interest and, hopefully, financial reward may have been an added impetus to the literary labours of Nelson and his contemporaries. Possibly, Nelson was personally inspired by Mackenzie, for he had the privilege of being taken into "the Great Man's" light canoe in 1802 when he first travelled with the XY brigade to Grand Portage; the young man's initial efforts at journal-keeping apparently met with Mackenzie's approbation the next summer at the rendezvous.[8]

While this complex of purposes helped to shape the Nor'Westers' responses to Rupert's Land, so too did their individual backgrounds and education. In Nelson's case, although he was only sixteen when he first ventured into the Indian Country, his upbringing set the stage for his expectations and his response. Nelson's parents, William and Jane, were Loyalists who settled in Sorel, where his father, the schoolmaster for the British garrison, was given land. Thus young George received the rudiments of a classical education, but what gripped his imagination most were the tales of adventure he had read, such as the story of Telemachus and Daniel Defoe's *Robinson Crusoe*. Of his introduction to Telemachus, he recalled.

> I well remember when, between the age of 12 & 13 I was engaged in translating Telemachus, how my young mind would rise & my little heart would swell at the beautiful recital of the adventures of that fictitious hero. I knew it was a work of the *mind*: but the incidents are so graphically told, with so much poetry, yet so very natural that *we* often wished we had been of the party.[9]

Nelson's enthusiasm for seeking his fortune in the fur trade was fired not only by this kind of fiction, but by the real-life tales of adventure told by the voyageurs returning to Sorel. He later wrote:

> The example was infectious, the Stories thrilling, and I was in that period of life remarkable for thoughtlessness & anxious to be engaged in busy life. I was seized with the delirium.[10]

This spirit of adventure definitely pervades Nelson's writings, but he also carried more weighty cultural baggage with him. Even adventure tales such as *Robinson Crusoe* contained their moral precepts: the wanderings of the hero were meant to test and temper his courage and virtue, to bring him to a better understanding of God's grace and the human condition. Nelson found the example of Robinson Crusoe fortifying, recording that "more than once, when real difficulties overtook me, did I recall Robinson, & found the benefit of his advice & example."[11] Raised an Anglican, Nelson also set off into the wilderness armed with his Bible and prayer book. When seeking solace after an initial frightening encounter with a band of Saulteaux, he found consolation in his prayer book, which propitiously fell open at Psalm 120: "Woe is me, indeed! that I am constrained to dwell with Mesheck & have my habitation among the tents of Kedar!"[12] He took this as a sign that he was not altogether "cast off," and throughout his career, his Christian beliefs increasingly shaped his outlook.

Nelson's literary education, like that of many other Nor'Westers, continued informally during his sojourn in Rupert's Land. His family sent him volumes from home for his instruction and amusement. Among them were the popular French adventure-cum-morality tale *Gil Blas de Santillane* and a seventeenth-century treatise *The Whole Duty of Man according to the Law of Nature*, written specifically "that the Minds, of Youth especially, should be early embu'd with *Moral Learning*."[13] Nelson was always grateful to other Nor'Westers, especially Charles Oakes Ermatinger with whom he summered in 1806, for lending him books and encouraging him to more serious study. Various references from his Lake Winnipeg days suggest that he was particularly enthralled with borrowed volumes of Hume and Smollett's *History of England*.[14] Thus by the time he came to write his reminiscences, Nelson was quite well versed in contemporary literature, history, and philosophy. What he read influenced both his style and moral outlook, creating an intellectual framework of considerable importance in shaping his response to Rupert's Land.

As will be demonstrated, Nelson's view of Rupert's Land was not static, however. There are some important differences between his original journals and the more considered reflections contained in both his reminiscences and the fragments of his narrative which have survived. Nelson began penning his reminiscences in the fall of 1836 after a chance encounter with Dominique Ducharme, an old comrade from his Lake Winnipeg days, brought back a flood of memories. By the early 1850s when he set about to write a more formal narrative of his life and adventures in the Indian Country, it is apparent that the lapse of time and the disappointments of his troubled subsequent life back in Quebec had coloured his view of those long-lost days.[15]

*   *   *

The title of this paper underscores Nelson's characterization of Rupert's Land as "this rascally & ungrateful Country." Such a reaction was very much on his mind by 1811-12 after he had spent nearly a decade in the Lake Winnipeg area.[16] His response was prompted not only by the physical environment and the often cruel hardships it imposed, but by what Nelson considered the destructive elements of the fur trade itself: the deceitful and unchristian way in which the competition turned man against his fellow man. It was particularly unfortunate, he felt, that in Rupert's Land, "where every step was beset with difficulties, themselves sufficient to exert every faculty & try the nerve," that "even here, the Demon of Ambition followed us, blinded our better judgement & sharpened our wits only to oppose, annoy & injure each other."[17]

In his response to the landscape, Nelson, like other Nor'Westers, was often awed by the varied and magnificent scenery he encountered. He recalled that even when a raw youth, "thoughtless and indifferent" to many things, he was not immune to "the numerous beauties of nature" he encountered in his travels.[18] It was in 1804 that Nelson first travelled the route from Grand Portage to Lake Winnipeg. This landscape combined, he wrote,

> every idea of beautiful, & grand, wild & romantic – some spots as it were, by the beautiful stillness & charming appearance of every thing around, *inviting* one to repose in enjoyment or contemplation. Others again, by the wild & frightful appearance of [their] mighty rocks, barren & parched with the heat of the Sun & fire of former years, leaving nothing but a few clusters of scattered heaps of dry & rotting trees – Seem to say "this is the land of evil spirits & demons – fly ye weake & helpless mortals nor presume to intrude on our domains"....What would not Milton, Fenelon or Chateaubriand have given to have had a view of such places at the time of their writing: these men had to *coin* objects to form their ideas – but here they are ready, in all the extravagance of fancy, requiring no aid or fiction.[19]

Nelson's post that year was at the mouth of the Red River. In the fall, he and John Sayer paddled up the Red to the Assiniboine for a hunting trip to the plains. The first sight of the open prairie made a lasting impression on Nelson:

> My eyes were not big enough...all my faculties as it were, were arrested - I was lost in amazement and admiration!...I stood rivited to my place & could [only] exclaim O beautiful, beautiful! what art can ever come up to nature? My companion laughed at my *foolishness*.[20]

Nelson claimed that the sight produced a strange, melancholy feeling that at one time this land, like the plains of Asia, must have thronged with people but that their civilizations had been obliterated by some disaster. Coming as he did from an agrarian society, Nelson was certainly impressed with the agricultural potential of the plains, which he maintained was vastly superior to that of Lower Canada. On a return trip in 1812, he found himself "almost agoing to grow envious of the *future inhabitants* of this place,"[21] but, like a good Nor'Wester, he was not favourably inclined toward the projected Selkirk colony. He knew the arrival of settlers was imminent, but did not expect the project to succeed because of its isolation, the difficulties of shipping goods and livestock via the Bay, and the hostility of the Sioux. Interestingly, Nelson recommended that if the English were so keen on planting colonies they should consider the Columbia region. He had been told by the recently-returned David Thompson that there was "a country & climate...not inferior to many of the Spanish provinces in America" where colonists could be assured of success and "of reaping much more benefit that they will ever be able in my humble opinion to do in Red River."[22]

For most of his own sojourn on Lake Winnipeg, however, Nelson wintered up the west side of the lake at the entrance of River Dauphine and at Tète au Brochet. The scenes here he found "picturesque," but the spot that really stuck in his mind was Pointe aux Lièvres, where the combination of the lake, smooth red granite, trees, and grass had been engineered so perfectly as to render it "little short of the enchanted residence of Calypso."[23] In his actual journals, Nelson was not given to rhapsodizing about the scenery, but this he later claims was not because he was unaffected but because he lacked the literary ability to do it justice. As he later reminisced:

> O! how often...have I selected a shady place & spreading my cloak or blanket on the Sward feasting my eyes & ears with this most splendid scenery, regretting I had none of my brothers, my Sisters,

> my father & mother to partake of this enjoyment with me; or that I was not blessed with a poetic vein, or sufficient literary abilities to note down these beauties & the delightful, tho' somewhat melancholy impression they left on my soul. In calm & Serene evenings, on the eve of a storm, the gulls & other water fowls would hover over & around us & the fish leaping in every direction on the placid bosom of the lake & a variety of birds flitting, warbling & chirping all around.[24]

Although Nelson enthusiastically responded to elements of both the picturesque and the sublime that he found in Rupert's Land, he certainly felt that much of the more northerly reaches of Lake Winnipeg had nothing to recommend them. The country approaching Grand Rapids on the west he described as exhibiting

> a picture vastly more dismal than the far famed Siberia. Rock after rock with a swamp intervening, & but here & there a few Small Shrubs or Stunted Spruce barely rearing their handsome green heads above the Snow....Yet, every object conveyed the idea of barrenness, solitude & wretchedness.[25]

He obviously felt that this land was not fit for human habitation and wrote that "it required all the energy, Spirit & ambition of youth to seclude ourselves for so many months in such regions."[26] The harsh landscape was rendered even more threatening in winter, when the lack of firewood and boughs for their night camps made them even more vulnerable to the freezing cold. Nelson frequently refers to the weather as "rascally"—emphasizing its unpredictability and severity.[27] He recorded in exasperation in early October 1810: "Cold & raw, & snow & rain, & hail & fair weather, all at once & each in their turns such is to-days weather."[28] But in spite of the perils of frostbite and violent summer storms, Nelson acknowledged that the bracing climate was basically healthy and one of their lesser worries.[29]

The spectre that most haunted the traders, and the native people as well, was starvation, one of the chief reasons Nelson chastized the country as "ungrateful." The traders were primarily dependent upon the food resources of Rupert's Land itself, but nature could be fickle and parsimonious in yielding up her bounty. Interestingly, time seemed to dull Nelson's remembrance of the ever-present cycle of "feast or famine." While his reminiscences contain references to the River Dauphine being the "land of milk and honey" because of the richness of the fishery,[30] his actual journals reveal the fluctuation in the availability of fish and other food resources and the constant preoccupation with getting enough to eat. Nelson's 1808 journal contains typical entries on the vagaries of fishing with nets and with spears by torchlight. In mid-October, Nelson records gloomily: "Our Nets are hardly able to maintain [us] in living, much less to put up a winter's stock."[31] Spear fishing at the rapids promised to be more productive but was hardly pleasant sport. After one outing Nelson and two of his men did spear almost five hundred fish, in spite of having "but few torches, a high wind, cold weather, a leaky Canoe & waiding up to our middle in water & ice and our hands so benumbed by the ice continually coming on our spear handles as hardly to be able to hold them." Shortly after this, the quantity of fish at the rapids fell off sharply, causing Nelson to lament that "if some extraordinary fishing from under the ice does not relieve us I am much afraid we shall starve." In fact, the fishery recovered to give the men a good winter supply, which was augmented by moose meat traded from the Indians.

River Dauphine was indeed a more bountiful post than some of the others on the lake, and there are frequent references to the men taking trains of fish and pounded meat to other posts. Nelson particularly pitied his colleagues who had to winter at Pigeon River up the east side of the lake. At that post, observed Nelson, "the greatest exertions, perserverance, prudence & economy were required [merely] to avoid starvation," and he relates the grim tale of how Angus Bethune and his people came near to perishing there in 1803-1804.[32] Nelson also observed firsthand the shocking state to which people living on "this miserable Lake"[33] could be reduced. In the winter of 1809, he was part of a mission to rescue Alexander Campbell and his people at Grand Rapids. Words hardly sufficed, declared Nelson, to convey the horrifying sight of the starving *engagé* Beaudry, whom they encountered first:

> He was warmly clad, but so filthy it was almost impossible to be more so. His beard of a reddish hue & nearly the length of his whiskers was full of the leaves of balsam (Sappin), fish Scales, ashes, the spittle of his tobacco frozen in icicles in several places: his head had not been combed perhaps since New Years day, also full of spruce & balsam leaves, fish scales and ashes; his eyes emitted a deadly glare and scarcely moving; emitting a most offensive odeur of *sour* smoke & fish—so strong that we had to keep several feet from him. The tout en Semble, his stare, voice, motions, language &c. &c. displayed a picture of idiocy & wretchedness indescribable.[34]

Although in this instance the suffering was partially occasioned by Campbell's drunken mismanagement, one gets the sense that Nelson blamed the country itself for reducing men to demented, shaggy beasts. As he said of another individual: "To look at this man [from] behind he had the appearance of a man but to look at him in the face all was lost."[35]

Apart from the dangers of starvation, Nelson was also mindful of "the peril" from the lakes and rivers over which they travelled. He pitied the hard lot of the voyageurs, numbers of whom perished in the dangerous rapids, and would have seconded Daniel Harmon's melancholy reflection on "the obstinancy & folly of man in persisting to follow a road which has led so many of his fellow creatures to sustain [so] unfortunate and premature an end!"[36] The parts of Rupert's Land that Nelson knew were really no place for a civilized man to pursue his livelihood; the country itself was "rascally and ungrateful," imposing numerous hardships and sometimes death.

The excesses of Rupert's Land might deprive a man of his civilized material state, but perhaps what concerned Nelson even more was that the fur-trade experience resulted in his moral degradation. Young men, Nelson lamented, were duped into entering the fur trade, thinking they would make their fortunes with no restraints on their liberty. In this he believed they were deluded; most, like himself, would never gain even a modest competence, and he was highly critical of the way in which the North West Company contrived to keep its *engagés* in perpetual debt.[37] In a ringing condemnation written to his parents in 1811, Nelson declared that even those who made money in "this brute Country" lost a great deal in terms of other riches such as "virtue, morality & the blessings of God"; there were few who did not deserve God's curses, having sunk into villainous and licentious behaviour of almost every description.[38] This is a particularly black sketch, and it may have been heightened by the fact that it is part of a series of letters that Nelson wrote to his parents. He emphasized that he would like to return to Lower Canada could he be assisted to purchase a farm—honest agrarian Christian toil being much preferable to the ill-gotten gains of the fur trade.

However, Nelson was especially ill-suited to the survival-of-the-fittest mentality that characterized the highly competitive period he experienced. He recalled quaking with fear when he learned that he was to be posted to the NORTH (his name for Lake Winnipeg) because he had heard many tales of how XY people had been abused by the dastardly Nor'Westers.[39] Owing to the union of these two rivals in 1804, Nelson was spared the full force of competition in his early Lake

Winnipeg years, but he was well aware of the growing threat of the Hudson's Bay Company. The destructive and demeaning nature of the competition he experienced, especially during his posting north of Lake Superior from 1813 to 1816, remained impressed upon his memory:

> In that country, & in those times, where the law of the Strongest i.e. violence always ruled, it became a *principle* who should *exert* himself the *best* [was] he who bro't in the "best returns" & most coerced his opponents. The ends, if Successful, always justified the means whereby they were obtained. On these, as on many other occasions the morality of course was never thought of....With *very* few exceptions, all, according to their respective temperaments "followed in the wake."[40]

Nelson's writings provide a valuable catalogue of the diverse tricks and violent deeds each side perpetrated against the other, and Nelson, especially in later life, obviously felt guilty that he had allowed himself to have been drawn in and corrupted, to have strayed so far from his Christian duty. He chides himself over his first evil deed of stealing some provisions: it was his "first act of baseness. But unfortunately not the *last*!!!"[41] Nelson's disgust over the depths to which he and other traders could sink was most evident during the three years he spent in opposition to the Hudson's Bay Company at Manitonamingan Lake, north of Lake Superior. "Deep villiany is not the least essential part of a trader's attributes here," he lamented.[42] In fact, Nelson appears to have quit the trade in 1816, taking his native family back to Sorel. But financial difficulties probably forced his return two years later, and he spent the dying years of the competition in the Cumberland House district. Nelson derived little satisfaction from the coalition of 1821, however, for he now found himself virtually redundant. In a fascinating coded journal, he gives vent to this sense of betrayal and despair—nothing to show for so many years service in "such a trade" and "such a country!"[43]

The extent to which Nelson thought life in Rupert's Land could make one forget one's Christian, civilized duty and regress to a barbaric state coloured his views of the *engagés* and especially the French-Canadian freemen, who adopted the life-style of the Indians after the expiry of their contracts. He considered that their much-vaunted desire for "freedom" was simply laziness, despising their primitive and often penurious existence with their large native families. Declared Nelson, the French-Canadian freemen "give me such a pitiful & contemptible *notion* of mankind in General that I would sometimes wish myself almost as distant as I am near them."[44] What perplexed Nelson, however, was that in spite of their wretchedness, most of the freemen seemed quite happy with their lot. Obviously Nelson's perceptions in such matters, like those of other Nor'Wester were commentators, structured by his personal religious, class, and ethnic concerns, which gave him little sympathy with the *engagés'* own response to Rupert's Land (a fruitful subject for investigation in itself).

Although Nelson was highly critical of white men who had fallen to the primitive level of the Indians, it is significant that he does not judge native people by the same criteria. As the work of Professors Jennifer Brown and Robert Brightman is beginning to show, the writings of George Nelson are a remarkably rich ethnographic source.[45] His journals give a highly personalized view of the Saulteaux and Swampy Cree bands that traded in the Lake Winnipeg area, providing new insights into the interconnectedness of the trader/ Indian worlds. In retrospect, Nelson appears to have possessed an unusual sense of cultural relativity, but this perspective developed over the years as he became more familiar with native languages and customs, as he matured, and as he reflected on Rupert's Land after experiencing life in the so-called civilized world.

In his journals, Nelson's reaction to the Indians was often conditioned by immediate commercial considerations. Some of the terms he uses in reference to his native visitors are hardly complimentary, such as "cursed wretches," "half-starved Devils," and "pulsillanimous band of rascally Vagabonds."[46] Certainly, several features of Indian behaviour horrified him. Their drinking bouts, he declared, "reminded me of Pandemonium, where all the wild passions man is susceptible to, succeed each other in the most wild & extravagant degrees."[47] Drunkenness often gave rise to hideous acts of violence, during which the women seem to have been particularly abused. Like other Nor'Westers, Nelson felt that Indian women had a particularly hard lot to bear: "the drudgery, trouble & misery some of them undergo is really astonishing," he lamented.[48]

Unlike his contemporaries, however, Nelson was also bitterly censorious of the traders' treatment of Indian women. He charged that the traders callously exploited native women for base purposes, and that the men's licentious behaviour led some Indians eventually to despise them.[49] While Nelson's is an overly negative assessment (for numerous lasting and devoted relationships between native women and Nor'Westers, both officers and *engagés*, can be cited),[50] his remarks do point to the social tragedy that could result. Again his comments may have been written partly to assuage a guilty conscience. During the course of his fur-trade career, Nelson had two Indian wives, his treatment of whom he later acknowledged was hardly commendable. Ironically, his Saulteaux wife Mary-Anne may have found life especially difficult after he took her to settle in Lower Canada, where she died in 1831. "I sincerely trust the Almighty has received & comforted her lacerated spirit," he grieved in his reminiscences.[51]

Although always fascinated with Indian tales and legends, Nelson, as an educated Christian, was quick to point out to his parents that such stories were riddled with superstition and foolishness. Yet when a legend about the reason for human mortality reminded him of the Greek myth of Oriander, he felt moved to observe: "Why not draw as good a moral from this Indian story as that of Oriander? Would it be because the one is savage & the other half civilized?"[52] An increased sympathy and tolerance for Indian customs and rituals becomes particularly noticeable following Nelson's return to Lake Winnipeg in 1818. On one occasion, honoured to be invited to a Midewiwin ceremony, he confessed that he could not help but admire their dances & speeches, "having now a far better idea of their *Theology*."[53] The use of the word *Theology* is significant, for it means that Nelson appreciated that the Indians were, indeed, a deeply spiritual people with their own system of religion. So interested had Nelson become in Indian religious beliefs and practices that, in 1823, he penned a remarkable record of his observations on this subject. He was motivated, he said, because although several accounts about the Indians had been published, he knew of none that gave sufficiently detailed insight into their "private life" and "ideas" to enable a reader to form a proper estimate of man in "his *natural* state."[54] He intended to send the manuscript to his father for safekeeping, hoping some day to write his own book on the Indians.

Nelson was apparently trying to achieve this objective in his later writings, as one of his chief concerns in his narrative was "to preserve a few traits of Indian character that deserve a more conspicuous place."[55] Although he claimed his purpose was simply to "*relate*" accurately, not to "*endorse*," he does not maintain this neutrality, for he feels compelled to decry the way in which those considering themselves Christian and civilized ridiculed the Indians for being superstitious barbarians. In spite of their ignorance of Christianity, the Indians, Nelson emphasized, were no strangers to virtue and fundamental human decency. This made him feel that, as Saint Paul said, "the knowledge of the Lord is in our hearts."[56] He found the Indians' attachment to their children especially praiseworthy:

The exhortations to their children...were truly edifying,...full of strong argument, beautiful comparisons & allegories....I have been astonished many a time by their shrewd remarks, the justice & correctness of their notions ....But [he says] I must not offend the pride of our educated folks here. Their dignity would be shocked by the comparison, tho' in substance they are far behind these Children of the Forest.[57]

White society should think twice about denouncing the Indians as savage, for with all its knowledge and advantages, the civilized world was guilty of "a catalogue of crimes never Surpassed & seldom equalled by those we so complacently call Barbarians."[58] By this time, Nelson, recoiling from the meanness and deceit he had experienced upon his return to Lower Canada and no doubt influenced by his reading of Rousseau, had begun to consider that civilization was "mere Polished barbarism" when compared with the "beautiful simplicity & truth of nature."[59] He found it significant that Indian society knew none of the invidious distinctions of class, which he considered a particularly corrupt and unchristian aspect of civilized life. The natives, he enthused, "consider every man equal, since every many comes into, & goes out of, the world in the same way. There is no precedency known but such as are acquired by the practice of the virtues."[60] Interestingly, Nelson wrote this in 1836 when Lower Canada was in great political turmoil; indeed, his own younger brothers Wolfred and Robert would go on to become the Anglophone leaders of the Rebellion of 1837.

Understandably, Nelson came to believe that the fur trade had sadly corrupted and exploited the Indians. While it can be argued that he had a romanticized view of the Indian past, he emphasized that the Indians themselves had often told him how much they regretted the coming of the traders. The animal resources that had once provided them with food and raiment were now rapidly diminishing, the Indians having been seduced by European technology and trinkets and fatally poisoned by that demon, rum.[61] Nelson gives tantalizing glimpses of Indian patterns of resistance — from an abortive plan on the part of the natives to drive the "pedlars" out of Rupert's Land in 1780 to the attempts of individual Indian leaders to chastise the Nor'Westers for their falseness and extortion. Of an Indian, "La Bezette," who often complained of the traders' exploitation, Nelson sardonically observed: "A Spirit of this Sort did not very well suit our ideas of Subordination — we therefore called him a bad fellow & a Scoundrel."[62]

This statement underscores how far Nelson had come in his appreciation of the Indian point of view.

In conclusion, even this preliminary analysis of the papers of one Nor'Wester poses some intriguing questions as to how we judge the authenticity of the fur traders' response to Rupert's Land. It has often been claimed that the fur traders were among the most accurate of European commentators because they lived and worked for extended periods in the Indian Country, living off the land as they found it in mutual interdependence with the native people, whose life-style they had no vested interest in trying to change. Like other Nor'Westers, Nelson is eager to emphasize the truthfulness of what he relates, as unbelievable as some of it may seem.[63]

Yet the truth is obviously filtered through the mind of the observer. The commercial purpose for which the traders came to Rupert's Land, the considerable cultural baggage they brought with them, even the literary conventions of their times — all shape the nature of the testimony those observers have left for future generations. Significantly, too, their response to Rupert's Land could also change with time. In the case of George Nelson, his opinion of Rupert's Land as being "a rascally & ungrateful Country" was considerably moderated. These terms do not appear in his later writings; instead, Rupert's Land has become the site of some of the best and most interesting days of his life, and its people the symbol of unspoiled living and human decency.

Notes

1. With one exception, the papers of George Nelson are to be found in the Manuscript Collection of the Metro Toronto Reference Library (Baldwin Room). The diary of September 1818-April 1819, however, is located at the Archives of Ontario, MU842. All references are to the original manuscripts, using Nelson's own pagination, wherever possible.

2. Alexander Henry, *Travels and Adventures in Canada and the Indian Territories between the Years 1760 and 1776*, ed. James Bain (1901; reprint, Edmonton: Hurtig, 1969), xiv-xlvi.

3. George Nelson Papers (GNP), Journal of 1803-04, transcribed in 1811: 42.

4. W. Kaye Lamb, ed., *Sixteen Years in the Indian Country: The Journal of Daniel Williams Harmon* (Toronto: Macmillan, 1957), xxiii.

5. Germaine Warkentin, "Exploration Literature in English" in William Toye, ed., *The Oxford Companion to Canadian Literature* (Toronto: Oxford University Press, 1983), 245.

6. GNP, Narrative, Pt. 1: 6.

7. Warkentin, "Exploration Literature in English," 243.

8. GNP, Narrative, Pt. 1: 14; Sorel Journal 1825-36 (contains reminiscences), 35.

9. GNP, Narrative, Pt. 1: 4.

10. Ibid., 5.

11. Ibid.

12. Ibid., 22.

13. Samuel Puffendorf, *The Whole Duty of Man according to the Law of Nature* (1673), preface.

14. GNP, Sorel Journal, p. 83; Narrative, Pt. 5: 198.

15. An interesting parallel might be drawn here with the well-known Nor'Wester David Thompson, whose impressive narrative was first published by the Champlain Society in 1916, edited by J.B. Tyrrell. Nelson and Thompson were, in fact, writing their narratives at approximately the same time; they were both in old age and would die within a few years of each other in the late 1850s. Since retirement, both had seen considerable tragedy befall the native families that they had brought to settle in eastern Canada, and both had failed in various business ventures that had left them in financial ruin. Thompson's original journals are extant, but a systematic comparison between them and the narrative has not been undertaken.

16. GNP, Nelson to his sister Rebecca, 4 June 1811: 4; Transcribed Journal 1803-04: 2.

17. GNP, Narrative, Pt. 1: 16.

18. GNP, Sorel Journal: 62.

19. Ibid., 56.

20. Ibid., 62.

21. GNP, Nelson to his parents, 9 February 1812: 13.

22. Ibid., 16.

23. GNP, Narrative, Pt. 5: 187.

24. Ibid., 187-88.

25. Ibid., 212.

26. Ibid.

27. GNP, Journal 1 September 1808-31 March 1810, 7 August 1809: 32; Journal 1 April 1810-1 May 1811, 5 October 1810, n.p.

28. GNP, Journal 1810-1811, 11 October 1810, n.p.

29. GNP, Nelson to his parents, 3 November 1811: 3.

30. GNP, Sorel Journal: 82.

31. GNP, Journal 1808-1810, 15 October 1808: 7 and following quotations 17-18 October and 20 October, 1808: 8.

32. GNP, Narrative, Pt. 5: 209-10.

33. GNP, Journal 1810-1811, 15 October 1810, n.p.

34. GNP, Narrative, Pt. 5: 213.

35. GNP, Journal 29 August 1805-8 March 1806, 24 January 1806, n.p.

36. Harmon, *Sixteen Years*, 15.

37. GNP, Nelson to his parents, 8 December 1811: 8.

38. Ibid., 7.

39. GNP, Narrative, Pt. 1: 29.

40. Ibid., Part 7: 279-80.

41. Ibid., Pt. 1: 39.

42. GNP, Journal 30 November 1815-13 January 1816, 31 December 1815: 93.

43. GNP, Journal 15 April-30 October 1821, 19 August 1821: 34 (decoded).

44. GNP, Nelson to his parents, 29 May 1812: 19; see also Nelson to his parents, 8 December 1811: 9-12.

45. See Jennifer Brown and Robert Brightman, eds., *The Orders of the Dreamed: George Nelson on Cree and Northern Ojibwa Religion and Myth* (Winnipeg, University of Manitoba Press, 1987).

46. GNP, Journal 1810-11, 8 July 1810, n.p.; Journal 1808-10, 14 November 1809 n.p.; Journal 1810-11, 14 October 1810. n.p.

47. GNP, Sorel Journal: 25.

48. GNP, Transcribed Journal 1803-04: 42.

49. GNP, Narrative, Pt. 5: 225.

50.   For a detailed examination of the marital relationships between Nor'Westers and native women, see Sylvia Van Kirk *"Many Tender Ties:" Women in Fur Trade Society in Western Canada, 1670-1870* (Winnipeg: Watson & Dwyer, 1980).

51.   GNP, Narrative, Pt. 1: 10.

52.   GNP, Transcribed Journal 1803-04: 43.

53.   GNP, Journal 1 May-8 June 1819, 7 June 1819: 12.

54.   GNP, Journal 1823, 16 April 1823: 62. (See Brown and Brightman volume cited above).

55.   GNP, Narrative, Pt. 1: 10.

56.   Ibid., Pt. 5: 223.

57.   GNP, Sorel Journal: 50.

58.   GNP, Narrative, Pt. 7: 288.

59.   GNP, Sorel Journal: 33.

60.   Ibid., 44.

61.   GNP, Narrative, Pt. 5: 201.

62.   Ibid., Pt. 5: 224.

63.   GNP, Sorel Journal: 22; Narrative, Pt. 1: 10-11.

Chapter 6

CHIPEWYAN AND FUR TRADER VIEWS OF RUPERT'S LAND

James G.E. Smith

The Caribou Eater Chipewyan were the original inhabitants of the taiga-tundra ecotone west of Hudson Bay, occupying a huge arc extending from the Seal River northwest to approximately the mouth of the Coppermine River. They were the first of the Northern Athapaskans to be encountered in their own lands by Europeans, and thus have the longest documented history, however fragmentary it may be. The initial contacts were made by Hudson's Bay Company men, followed much later by government explorers, missionaries, and scientists.

The term Chipewyan is derived from the Cree, meaning "pointed tails." According to Chipewyan legend, the Cree told the English at York Fort that they were less than human and had pointed tails, hence the name. To themselves they are *dènè*, people, as are other Athapaskan-speaking nations. To their Athapaskan neighbours they were *etθen-eldili-dènè*, the caribou-eater people. The English generally referred to them as the "Northern Indians," in contrast to the Cree, who were "Southern Indians." In some of the early literature they were termed "dog-ribbed Indians," derived from a widespread myth among Northeastern Athapaskans that they were descended from a woman and a miraculous dog who transformed himself into a handsome man at night.

I propose here to discuss Rupert's Land as seen by the Chipewyan, or rather, as an anthropologist interprets that point of view. This inevitably leads to a discussion of man's relationship to nature, and especially to the all-important caribou, the source of almost all food and raw material until recently. The moral significance of the caribou is symbolized in the legendary qualities of the arctic wolf, and the identity of wolf and man. The anomalous nature of man's relationship to woman also requires comment, and the metaphor of woman and dog is perhaps as significant as that of man and wolf. The fur traders' views of Rupert's Land lend another thread to the tapestry, essentially an inversion of the Chipewyan view.

The earliest published reference to the Chipewyan is in N. Jérémie's account of his twenty years at Fort Bourbon,[1] the French alternative to York Fort, from 1694 to 1714. His record indicates only that the "Dog-ribbed" Indians lived north of the Seal River. A few more of Jérémie's comments were recorded by Captain James Knight in the York Fort post journal for 1714, deriding Knight's plans to establish peace in the entire western hinterland of Hudson Bay.[2] During the winter of 1715-16 Captain Knight sent William Stewart,[3] guided by the remarkable Thanadelther of Chipewyan legend, known as the Slave Woman in the HBC records,[4] and accompanied by 150 Cree, to find the Northern Indians in their own territory, to make peace between the Chipewyan and the Cree, and to bring the Chipewyan to trade at the new Fort Churchill that was established for this purpose in 1717. Although Stewart kept no journal of their successful trip, both he and Thanadelther were frequently interrogated by Knight, and their responses recorded in the daily post journal of York.[5]

The route taken by Stewart, Thanadelther, and the Cree was along the edge of the forest, and generally marked by the seasonal absence of the barren-ground caribou (*Rangifer tarandus groenlandicus* L.) that typically spend the winter in the northern transitional zone of the boreal forest and the summer on the tundra. The scarcity of game caused Stewart's party to break into smaller groups, some of which subsequently returned to York in despair of ever accomplishing their mission. Stewart and Thanadelther, however, continued with some Cree and, after great hardship, encountered a major gathering of Chipewyan, probably somewhere near the east arm of Great Slave Lake. According to Thanadelther, she had found more than a hundred tents of her countrymen, indicating a population of eight hundred to one thousand, calculated at eight to ten persons per lodge. She returned to Stewart's camp with 400 of these, of whom 160 were men. The disproportionate number of men was created by many having remained back, fearing treachery on the part of the Cree and the unknown white man. The total number of almost one thousand individuals is huge by boreal forest standards, but the figure is explained by the occasional characteristic of several of the great herds of caribou to aggregate,[6] and several regional bands of Chipewyan to aggregate with them.[7]

The importance of the migratory and nomadic barren-ground caribou was made known to me at an early stage of my field research. One elder asserted that "in the old days [before 1958] we lived like the caribou," while another said it another way: "In the old days we lived like wolves." Both statements had great validity, I was to learn, but the latter was to introduce me to important truths about the moral commitment of the Caribou Eater People to the herds and about the mythology and the rich, natural imagery of the People.

Briefly stated, as the great herds congregated prior to the migrations from the barren lands to the forest in the early winter (November-December), and from the forest to the tundra at the end of winter (April-May), so did the regional bands of Caribou Eaters congregate along the anticipated migratory routes. Once in the winter foraging zone of the boreal forest or the summer foraging and calving grounds of the tundra, the great herds dispersed into smaller herds and then into bands of one or two dozen animals. So too with the People: The regional bands which made great kills at the time of the migrations dispersed into local bands that were then predatory upon smaller herds, and then into still smaller hunting groups, generally each made up of an extended family, that harvested the smallest caribou bands at the time of maximum dispersal.

I was told repeatedly that in those golden days before 1958 enough caribou could be killed or were killed in early winter to provide the basic subsistence to last through the winter, and enough were taken during the late winter migration to last through the summer. Hunting on the tundra in August and September was necessary to obtain the hides when at their best for making clothing, lodge coverings, *babiche* (dried rawhide thongs), and the multitude of uses to which the caribou were put. At this time the caribou congregated near the treeline, and their skins were not yet affected by the infestation of warble fly larvae. Unfortunately most of the caribou flesh was wasted, for the People had no technique of preserving meat at this time or place. During much of the winter and summer, hunting was done for the fresh meat and the delicacies – the tongue, brain, eyeballs, and head. For the caribou had the same overwhelming importance to the Caribou Eater People as the bison had to the hunters of the Great Plains. Clark Wissler pointed this out in a brilliant but virtually unknown essay,[8] probably based solely upon Samuel Hearne's narrative of his journey from Churchill overland to the Arctic Ocean. This narrative was so perceptive and full of insight that it remains a standard ethnological source for all anthropologists concerned with the North.

In general, the Chipewyan lived the life of an "original affluent society,"[9] one with simple needs, simply but adequately satisfied. If the migratory patterns or the foraging zones were sometimes erratic and unpredictable, Chipewyan society had a reasonable explanation and had devised a workable strategy. The seasonally dispersed local bands and hunting groups were so distributed as to monitor the gathering caribou bands and herds as they prepared for the migrations and began their movements, and to communicate this information to neighbouring local bands and hunting groups. Chipewyan social structure can be viewed as an efficient communications system, evolved over a long time to monitor caribou movements and to prepare the People for the major kills of the migrations. Should the caribou move in unusual directions, this information was quickly transmitted through the widely dispersed and anticipating hunting groups. It is no accident that the Cree *wihtiko* or the Ojibwa *windigo* or Cannibal Giant myths are missing from Chipewyan mythology, for true starvation, resulting in death, is rare in the historical legends.[10]

The adaptation of Chipewyan society and culture to the caribou developed over a long period. Archaeological excavations and surveys demonstrate that this basic adaptation to the caribou had occurred about 700 B.C.[11] By historical times the commitment had taken on a moral character that pervaded life. It included the excitement that built up when the migration of the caribou was anticipated, a growing distaste for fish, and in very recent years, for food purchased from the HBC. The thought of real meat, *tɵen,* not store bought exotic meat (*ber*) or fish, was tantalizing.

There was no recognition among these subarctic hunters that there might be oscillation or periodic variation in the total number of caribou. Scarcity of caribou in any region was attributed to maltreatment of the animals by humans, information about which was transmitted by the Spirit of the Caribou, who informed all the individual caribou, which therefore remained away from the area of human mistreatment.

In Chipewyan belief, caribou never die, but they may stay away. Caribou—and some other animals—may be "killed" properly and legitimately, to provide food and raw materials to the People, but only if they choose to be "killed." By remaining away, any species indicates its displeasure at being mistreated. When the Canadian Wildlife Service in the mid-1960s began their great study of caribou population decline, the People believed that the flagging, tagging, and attaching of radio transmitters to the caribou were types of humiliation and maltreatment that caused the herds to remain far away in the Keewatin District. The blame for game shortages was thus placed upon the well-meaning but perplexed biologists who were repeatedly berated by the band chief and council. If animals are to cooperate with humans, they must be treated with respect.

Caribou never die in the sense that the animal that gives its body for food, clothing, and other good things for the People does not give its spirit or soul. The spirit is immediately reborn or reincarnated as a new-born calf. Other animals, too, can be reincarnated. The wolf, an important example, may be reincarnated either as a human or as a wolf.

There are numerous variations on the theme of reincarnation. True People, meaning Chipewyan, may be reincarnated immediately among band members, as can be seen in physical or behavioural similarities of a new-born infant to a recently deceased older person. It is, of course, possible for the Chipewyan to be reborn into another band. More importantly, the Chipewyan may be reborn as a wolf, subsequently as a human, and then again as a wolf. Such humans were believed to have enormous supernatural powers. I should observe that among the western bands of Caribou Eaters only men may go through the wolf transformation, but among the eastern bands from Lake Wollaston to Churchill, women too may be reincarnated as wolves. Samuel Hearne noted that both wolf and wolverine were more than ordinary animals, but did not specify in what ways they surpassed the ordinary.[12] While the wolf remained important in Chipewyan imagery in the 1960s and 1970s, the supernatural status of the wolverine has apparently disappeared or at least grown obscure.

The archives of the Hudson's Bay Company show again and again the commitment and the priority given to the caribou. If caribou were scarce, the Chipewyan went to where they could be found, and trapping and fur returns declined. If caribou were abundant, trapping results returned to normal, although "normal" reflected the limited number of trade goods the Chipewyan considered necessary. Higher prices for fur or the abundance of fur bearers made little difference to the Chipewyan, who trapped only enough to satisfy their limited needs. There was no regard for economists' notions of maximizing income or profits, or of elastic or inelastic demand, or of a nebulous standard of living as evidenced in a consumer-oriented society.

H.S. Sharp has stressed the significance of the moral commitment of the Caribou Eaters to the caribou.[13] Caribou were not only the principal source of food and raw materials without which the Chipewyan could not survive, but the pursuit of the animal, the treatment of the living or the dead animal, was a moral imperative. The distinction between the hunting by men and the processing by women was fundamental to their conceptualization of the sexes; it underlay their entire social structure.[14]

In some sense the subjective relationship of the Chipewyan to the caribou is reflected in the frustrated comment of Father Joseph Egenolf, O.M.I., to P.G. Downes on the teaching of the catechism to Chipewyan children: "There is one long passage which asks, 'What is the most beautiful thing our Lord has created?' The automatic answer according to the Catechism is 'angels and man.' Time and again when he went through this formula, all the children could mumble it correctly—all but one little girl, who insisted on replying each time, 'Idthen'—the caribou."[15]

With the advent of sedentary life in 1967-68, it is impossible to describe adequately the excitement with which the migration of the caribou was anticipated. Hunters first returned with no reports of caribou traces, but as the days followed, the return of every hunter was anxiously awaited. The first report that caribou tracks had been seen, even of one animal, was a signal that a herd must be on the move, that soon real meat (*tθen*) would again be available. While most other foods were not scorned, caribou was the supreme food. If eating caribou was a supreme pleasure, quartering, distribution, preparation, and eating was the expression of the most basic values of a hunting society.

The values embodied in the social use of the caribou can only be hinted at in these pages. To be a good hunter was assurance that the hunter possessed "good luck" or *i^{n}ko^{n}ze^n*, the supernatural power that comes through dreams.[16] To quarter the carcass with minimal loss and with respect for the bones and offal was an expression of proper respect between man and caribou. The distribution of meat to less fortunate hunters and their families, to widows and orphans and others, embodied the greatest virtue, generosity, for it was only through sharing that the well being of a hunting society could be maintained. As the hunter gave his meat and hides into the possession of his wife, he expressed acknowledgement of the division of labour and of woman's part in society. Perhaps in the eating of caribou, with the males served first, there was an expression of social priorities, but perhaps in the act there was also a sense of primitive communion.

Caribou was the only big game animal upon which the Chipewyan depended, other animals contributing minor quantities to the food supply. Bears were numerically not a major part of the diet, although their fat was valuable in a diet that was largely deficient in fats. But as it did throughout the northern circumpolar zones, the bear served a greater ritual than dietary function. Muskoxen were once plentiful on the tundra and the edge of the forest, but were not considered proper food.[17] Moose were rare, found principally in the very southern margin of Chipewyan occupancy of the forest and considered a poor alternative to caribou. Beaver were of some importance for their fatty tails, but became much more important with the advent of the fur trade. Fish were caught in gill nets made from *babiche* or by angling, primarily during the spawning seasons during the autumn or spring. The most important species were whitefish, lake trout, northern pike, and pickerel.

Subarctic winters are among the most severe in the world, yet elderly Chipewyan men did not stress the severity or discomfort until recent decades. Then they became familiar with the housing of the modern *banlai* (buttons, as non-Indians are known), with good insulation, central heating, and other conveniences. The Elders point out the great advantages of several layers of caribou-skin clothing, with the hollow, insulating hair in, noting that even in the most severe winter weather they were never cold. And it is true that the traditional caribou clothing of the original peoples of the circumpolar regions created almost tropical, mobile microenvironments that made a mockery of most winter weather.

The advent of the fur trade made small fur-bearing animals – such as marten (Canadian sable), mink, ermine, arctic fox, squirrel, and muskrat – of great economic value. Formerly, they were of no importance, as they were too small to be useful and as they involved too much work for their negligible food value. In contrast to the migratory and nomadic caribou, the fur bearers were essentially sedentary. Moreover, the fur bearers became more scarce in the northern transitional zone of the forest and on the tundra itself. To the fur trader the solution was obvious: the Chipewyan should move into the full boreal forest, where fur bearers were more abundant.

The Chipewyan had another solution. They became middlemen in the fur trade, exchanging English trade goods from Bayside to the Copper Indians (or Yellowknives) and the Dogribs for furs in the distant hinterland of Hudson Bay. During this period, trading bands developed and became a prominent feature of life. The trading Indians were headed by leaders whom the English recognized as chiefs. They were given titles such as captain and lieutenant, and gifts and gun salutes at the forts were bestowed upon them according to their rank, which was in turn based on the size of their trading bands. Samuel Hearne described the limits of the trading chiefs' authority beyond the coastal forts (*Journey*, 186-87). He expressed his appreciation of the trading band chief Matonabbee (*Journey*, 222-28), who, after guiding Hearne overland to the Arctic Ocean, was recognized by the HBC as head chief of the Northern Indian nation – but was he acknowledged such by the Northern Indians?

The trading band became a feature of Indian life in Rupert's Land during most of the eighteenth century. But the lucrative middleman position was soon eliminated as the North West Company and the HBC established forts in the interior and thus were able to deal directly with the once-distant bands. This coincided in part with the great smallpox epidemic of 1781, introduced by the Cree, who had received this devastating disease from the Ojibwa and Sioux.[18] The death toll, however exaggerated in fur traders' accounts, made possible the expansion of some Chipewyan into the full boreal forest, lands that had previously been exploited by the Cree.

Who these Chipewyan were who relocated will always remain a mystery, but the ever-reliable Hearne provides some clues. He wrote that while almost all Chipewyan men had been to Churchill at least once in their lives, most preferred not to take the long and arduous trek across the Barren Lands to Churchill. They preferred the more leisurely life amidst the plenty provided by the caribou, but there were those who chose the life of trading Indians, repeatedly making the trip to Bayside to enjoy the prestige accorded them by the English and by their relatives and friends in the interior to whom they distributed trade goods. These hardy and adventurous souls must have provided the backbone of those who colonized the boreal forest, became moose hunters, and developed a riverine adjustment similar to that of the Western Woods Cree.

But let us return to the fur-bearing animals and the change in man-animal relationships. In the days before the Chipewyan became Christians, men and animals could talk together. This occurred principally in dreams and visions in which animals transferred important "supernatural" powers to humans, the transference and power of which were known as i^n ko^n ze^n. (I place "supernatural" within quotation marks, for it was quite natural to elderly Chipewyan. The notion that animals do not have souls is limited to some religions.) The concept of guardian spirits was, of course, common to most of the original peoples of the Americas, and involved the cooperation of humans with animate nature, and including as animate many types of phenomena that are strange to Euroamericans. Perhaps the spirits of the small animals were offended as the tradition of ignoring them was suddenly replaced by brutal overkill. One is tempted by the empirically unacceptable historical hypotheses of Calvin Martin on the breaking of the "covenant" between man and animals,[19] but I refrain from pursuing this line of thought for fear of becoming as anthropomorphic as a Disney film.

The status of women among the Chipewyan also warrants discussion. The picture of the Chipewyan woman in the literature presents the appearance that she occupied the lowest status of any known society. This interpretation stems from inferences drawn from Hearne's discussions of the importance of women's work, interpreted by many as sheer drudgery. There are, however, hints that the status may be interpreted differently. What the situation was prior to the development of the trading band of Hearne's time we shall never know, but during the period when the Chipewyan were middlemen in the trade, more information is available. Women were needed to carry the loads of fur pelts, equipment, and supplies to the environs of Fort Churchill and to carry the loads of trade goods on the return trip. The fur trade undoubtedly placed a premium on women as necessary beasts of burden. It also probably led to an increase in the rate of polygyny for successful trading chiefs, and to the development or intensification of the habit of wrestling contests in which young women, unburdened by children, were the prizes.

The first and only Chipewyan woman to enter history was Thanadelther, who is known as the Slave Woman in the HBC archives. She stands in stark contrast to the portrait of women as drudges. She was captured and enslaved by the Cree as a girl, but she escaped to the English at York Fort. She became Captain Knight's instrument in his plans for the development of Rupert's Land. In 1715-16 she successfully led William Stewart and the Cree to find the Chipewyan, to make peace between Cree and Chipewyan, and to bring the Chipewyan to trade at Fort Churchill. The fort was built for that purpose in 1717. Knight recognized her enormous contribution to the Company and praised her as a brave guide, leader, ambassador, and rhetorician. Her abilities, indeed, would have made her an outstanding person in any society.

Until the use of dogs became common in the twentieth century, the woman's role as the one who hauled the toboggan was not merely menial, it was important and necessary. She contributed little to the food supply except seasonal berries or small game snared near the camp. But if she was unimportant in this respect, the Chipewyan had evolved a system of complementarity in which men hunted and women processed the food. Once the caribou flesh and hides were delivered to the woman in the tent or lodge, they were hers, and she alone had the right to dispose of them. All the tools essential to the processing of food, clothing, lodge coverings, bedding, etc., were hers, while spears, knives, muskets or rifles, traps and deadfalls, toboggans, dogs, and other things used in the hunt were the property of the man.

As I witnessed the demise of the traditional hunting and trapping culture during the late 1960s, and the emergence of the "microurban" village of the Canadian welfare state,[20] I saw many hints that the place of women was perhaps more significant or could be so interpreted. This case was ably stated by Sharp,[21] and it can be inferred from Irimoto's study of Chipewyan sociospatial concepts.[22]

I had always been told that important decision making was solely the right of the man, as in the betrothal of a daughter to a young man selected as a son-in-law. I found, in fact, that a wife's opinion or judgement was taken seriously, although not publicly acknowledged. In fact, over a period of years the wife became an important companion and confidant, although the husband remained the *de jure* head of the family. When polygamy was in flower, the bestowal of a second daughter on a hunter was a signal of high approval by the wife's father (and mother), and possibly by both daughters.

I must not turn from this brief discussion of the complementary nature of men's and women's worlds without pointing to the traditional past and the untraditional future. In the past, women's complementary role was expressed in the disposition of the caribou supply as it came into the lodge, the woman's realm. Sharp found special interest in "the structuring of the division of labour upon systematic symbolic oppositions between male and female [acted] in such a manner as to keep the social system in a balance between conflicting forces, and hence in a better position to respond to changes in the physical and social environment."[23]

It would be an error to understate the hardships falling to women. Among the Chipewyan, female infanticide was practised until the early nineteenth century,[24] and women consoled themselves in the belief that infant death saved the babies from the hard life that would otherwise befall them. As late as the 1970s, women complained of the hard life, much alleviated as it was. Men, too, complained of the hard life, but perhaps this was partly the result of increasing awareness of the relatively easy life and the comfortable quarters of the Whites. They did not, however, think of hunting as a heavy burden!

Since World War II the Canadian welfare state developed, and its impact on the small and isolated societies of the Canadian colonial empire has accelerated. Hunting as a way of life appears to be doomed, and trapping is becoming marginal. Distances are often too great and costs too high to make commercial fishing a feasible alternative where good lakes are to be found. Increasingly, the cash economy has eroded the emphasis upon generosity and sharing. The introduction of Family Allowances payable to the mother and of Old Age Pensions payable to the individual, the conceptualization of family responsibilities and authority along a model of Eurocanadian society, the impact of political notions based upon British Parliamentary democracy and majority rule (rather than the development of a consensus), the immersion in a technological and industrial world beyond the comprehension of hunters emerging from an almost Upper Palaeolithic pattern—all these forces have produced enormous structural changes that I cannot dwell upon here. And if Christianity did not effectively eliminate the Chipewyan belief system and the impressive oral literature, they are being obliterated by the school system and will probably not long out last the introduction of television.

Let me turn to a brief discussion of Rupert's Land as seen by a few fur traders of more than common knowledge and insight. Captain James Knight was an old man when appointed governor-in-chief in the Bay in 1714, but he was an old man with the vision and ambition of the young when he assumed command at York.[25] He believed that the lands to the North and West would be of great profit to the Company and, perhaps, would be the basis for his reputation in the following centuries. He was confident that this northwestern hinterland inhabited by the Northern Indians would be the source of fur, and he was determined to make peace throughout the region and to develop a great fur trade. As well, he believed in the existence of a Northwest Passage, in the search for which he soon lost his life. And he was excited by the possibility that not only copper was to be found in the far Northwest, but perhaps other more precious yellow metal, for which he was eager to sponsor exploration. To Captain Knight, Rupert's Land was a land of opportunity, but to William Stewart, his emissary to the Chipewyan, it was a land of incredible hardship.

In the years 1769-72, Samuel Hearne made his remarkable journey overland from Prince of Wales Fort (Churchill) to the mouth of the Coppermine River. He was led by Matonabbee, whose many wives made the trip logistically possible. He determined, finally, that no easy Northwest Passage lay this way, that the amount of copper at its source was very limited, and that fur production in the domain of the Northern Indians was restricted. But above all, he was perceptive of the people and of their relationship to the caribou, pointing out how simple were their needs, how few furs were needed to procure necessary trade goods, and what relative ease their lives held without much reliance on European technology. What he perceived in Rupert's Land was a relationship between man and nature, rather than a simple image of the land itself.

Early in the nineteenth century, the HBC began requiring districts to submit annual reports to London that contained information on the Indians and the advantages and disadvantages of the districts. We repeatedly find the remark from the districts in or near Chipewyan territory that the proximity to the caribou country is the major disadvantage. The Chipewyan who hunted furs in the full boreal forest at the behest of the traders almost regularly returned to the caribou country for the hunting, companionship, and what they considered a normal life. Even those who supposedly left the taiga-tundra ecotone permanently in the late eighteenth century were periodically returning to their own lands. The commitment to the caribou was recognized, but the moral commitment was unrecognized. The traders' attention was principally oriented to overcoming this commitment.

Hugh Leslie, writing in his District Report for 1819-20 on Reindeer Lake, noted that the Chipewyan lived to the north, in the edge of the forest and on the tundra.[26] They lived a nomadic life, which elicited Leslie's complaint: "The Northern Indians being such a wandering set [trading] never takes place at any one place above a year or two at the utmost." In his District Report for 1820-21, he wrote they intended to visit "their country," and few furs were to be expected.[27]

Sir George Simpson noted in 1821-22 noted that the Chipewyan were strangers in the lands south of Lake Athabasca, and their own lands were far to the north. He was the first to use, in print, the term "carribeau eaters."[28]

In his Great Slave Lake District Report for 1825-26, Chief Factor Robert McIvor wrote under the heading of disadvantages: "The most serious and lasting obstacle to the profitable employment of the resources of this district is the vicinity of the Rein Deer/or Chipewyan Lands." He observed that these lands lacked the fur-bearing animals, and that the native people resisted efforts to "resort to the beaver country and encounter the additional labour, hardships and privations they so often experience in the pursuit of furs."[29] The tension between hunting and trapping is a theme that recurs frequently in the archives. That hunting won the contest so often was the traders' lament, and in the region of the Caribou Eaters, the caribou continued to win until the very collapse of the traditional subsistence economy.

To the Caribou Eater Chipewyan, the chief and most beneficial characteristic of Rupert's Land was the presence of the migratory and nomadic barren-ground caribou, on which they depended for food and essential raw materials. The relationship of Chipewyan and caribou was an ancient one, with a well-developed hunting strategy and a moral dimension. The division of labour and the most important social structural features were related to the caribou and their pursuit.

The fur traders' view of Rupert's Land was an inversion of the Chipewyan's view: the hunting of the migratory and nomadic caribou so necessary for the Chipewyan interfered with the intensive hunting or trapping of the sedentary fur-bearing animals. If caribou were lacking in the fur areas, the Chipewyan would follow the distribution of the herds, and fur returns would suffer. Moreover, the plenty supplied by the caribou limited the dependence of the hunters on the goods that could be provided by the traders.

To the cultural ecologist, the relationship of humans to animals and the changing relationship of the native peoples to the European newcomers are of paramount importance.

Notes

1. Nicolas Jérémie, *Twenty Years of York Factory, 1694-1714* (Ottawa: Thorburn and Abbott, 1926).

2. York Fort Post Journal, 1714-1717, B.239/a/1, HBC Archives.

3. K.G. Davies, ed., *Letters from Hudson Bay, 1703-1740* (London: Hudson's Bay Record Society, 1965), 413-17.

4. Alice Johnson, "Ambassadress of Peace" *The Beaver* 283 (December 1952): 42-45; Davies, 410-13; Sylvia Van Kirk, "Thanadelthur" *The Beaver* 304 (Spring 1974): 40-45; James G.E. Smith, "Thanadelther" *Arctic* 37 (1984), 296-97.

5. York Fort Post Journal, 1714-1717, B.239/a/2-3, HBC Archives.

6. G.R. Parker, "Total Numbers, Mortality, Recruitment, and Seasonal Distribution." Part One of *Biology of the Kaminuriak Population of Barren Ground Caribou* (Ottawa: Canadian Wildlife Service Report Series 20, 1972); Frazier Symington, *Tuktu: The Caribou of the Northern Mainland* (Ottawa: Canadian Wildlife Service, 1965).

7. James G.E. Smith, "Economic Uncertainty in an 'Original Affluent Society': Caribou and Caribou Eater Adaptive Strategies," *Arctic Anthropology* 15 (1978), 68-88.

8. Clark Wissler, "Culture of the North American Indians Occupying the Caribou Area and Its Relationship to the Other Types of Culture." Proceedings, National Academy of Sciences I:51-54.

9. Marshall Sahlins, "Notes on the Original Affluent Society," in Richard E. Lee and Irven DeVore, eds., *Man, the Hunter* (Chicago: Aldine, 1968), 85-89.

10. Smith, "Economic Uncertainty," 68-88.

11. William C. Noble, "The Taltheilei Shale Tradition," in J.W. Helmer, S. Van Dyke, and F.J. Kenze (eds.), *Problems in the Prehistory of the North American Subarctic: The Athapaskan Question* (Calgary: University of Calgary Archaeological Association, 1977), 65-71.

12.   Samuel Hearne, *A Journey from Prince of Wales's Fort in Hudson's Bay to the Northern Ocean 1769, 1770, 1771, 1772*, ed. Richard Glover (Toronto: Macmillan Company of Canada, 1958), 135-36.

13.   Henry S. Sharp, "The Caribou Eater Chipewyan: Bilaterality, Strategies of Caribou Hunting, and the Fur Trade," *Arctic Anthropology*, 14 (1977): 35-40.

14.   Henry S. Sharp, "The Null Case: The Chipewyan," in F. Dahlberg (ed.), *Woman, the Gatherer* (New Haven: Yale University Press, 1981), 221-44.

15.   See R.H. Cockburn, "After-Images of Rupert's Land" in this volume, page 283.

16.   See David M. Smith, "$I^n ko^n ze^n$: Magico-religious Beliefs of Contract-Traditional Chipewyan Trading at Fort Resolution, NWT, Canada." Ethnology Service Paper No. 6 (Ottawa: National Museum of Man, 1973).

17.   Hearne, *Journey*; Ernest S. Burch, Jr., "Muskox and Man in the Central Canadian Subarctic, 1689-1974," *Arctic* 30 (1977), 135-154.

18.   J.B. Tyrrell, ed., *David Thompson's Narrative of His Explorations in Western America, 1784-1812.* (Toronto: Champlain Society, 1916), 321-25.

19.   Calvin Martin, *Keepers of the Game: Indian-Animal Relations and the Fur Trade* (Berkeley: University of California Press, 1978). See also Shepard Krech III, *Indians, Animals, and the Fur Trade: A Critique of Keepers of the Game* (Athens: University of Georgia Press, 1981); James G.E. Smith, Review of Calvin Martin's *Keepers of the Game*, *American Ethnologist* 7 (1980), 810-12.

20.   James G.E. Smith, "The Emergence of the Micro-Urban Village among the Caribou Eater Chipewyan," *Human Organization* 37 (1978), 38-49.

21.   Sharp, "The Null Case," 221-44.

22.   Takashi Irimoto, *Chipewyan Ecology: Group Structure and Caribou Hunting System.* Senri Ethnological Studies 8. Osaka: National Museum of Ethnology.

23. Sharp, "The Null Case," 241.

24. June Helm, "Female Infanticide, European Diseases, and Population Levels among the Mackenzie Dènè," *American Ethnologist* 7 (1981), 259-85.

25. York Fort Post Journal, 1714-1717, B.239/a/1, HBC Archives; Davies, ed., *Letters*, 394-410.

26. Reindeer Lake District Report, 1819-20, B.179/e/1, HBC Archives.

27. Reindeer Lake District Report, 1819-20, B.179/e/2, HBC Archives.

28. George Simpson.

29. Great Slave Lake District Report, 1826, B.181/e/1, HBC Archives.

Chapter 7

FROM "ICY PICTURE" TO "EXTENSIVE PROSPECT:" THE PANORAMA OF RUPERT'S LAND AND THE FAR NORTH IN THE ARTIST'S EYE, 1770-1870

Robert Stacey

The perception of landscapes as *landscapes* — that is, as pictorial constructs rendered according both to the laws of perspective and topographical draughtsmanship and in response to the impulses of the imagination — is a recent development in the history of human consciousness. By chance, this perceptual revolution came into its own at the same time that commercial interests charted and colonized the upper half of the Northern Hemisphere, interests whose combined financial, national, and explorational zeal was crystallized in the Royal Charter granted by Charles II to Prince Rupert in 1670.

The creation of the Hudson's Bay Company occurred on the eve of the aesthetic phase we know as the Picturesque Movement. Although the Picturesque phase proper extends from 1730 to 1830, its origins can be traced to the closing years of the seventeenth century, while its lingering influence is evident in the writing and picture-making of tourists and explorers well into the Victorian period.

The Picturesque manner has been defined simply as a "habit of viewing and criticizing nature as if it were an infinite series of more or less well composed subjects for painting."[1] Implicit in this practice is the position of the viewer on a moderate rise looking out over a foreground, a middle ground, and a background, to each of which, according to the theory devised by the Rev. William Gilpin, were consigned suitable natural and man-made objects. In a Picturesque composition these divisions were harmonized by the modulating effects of light and shade and united by the presence of a single vanishing-point on the horizon to which the viewer's gaze was drawn, not directly but along a meandering "line of beauty" that could take the form of a road or pathway, or the gentle folds of a river valley leading to distant, unprecipitous hills.

Although the mode's most prolific flowering took place in the mid-eighteenth century, it was an inevitable consequence of cultural and economic phenomena of the era immediately preceding: culturally, the fashionable passion for travel and, economically, the defeat of Napoleon. The travel passion made familiar the digressive routes of the Grand Tour and, later, of the English Lake District, and it reflected the recently acquired taste for the landscape paintings of Claude Lorraine, Salvator Rosa, Jacob Ruysdael, Aelbert Cuyp and Meindert Hobbema, and their British followers. Scenery—particularly untamed scenery—that had previously been regarded with dread or boredom had now become the object of pleasure and curiosity.

Economically, the final victory over the French in 1815 freed Britain to channel its aggressive energy into expeditionary assaults on natural and geographical forces. All such endeavours since the inception of graphically recorded history have attracted their pictorial annalists. Yet the number of painted or indeed written masterpieces inspired by the entire adventure that was Rupert's Land and the charting of the arctic regions is disproportionately small. Few such momentous events in the course of human endeavour have been so mundane and narrow-focused in the imaginative response their unfolding has evoked. Perhaps only historical illustrators of the latter third of Victoria's reign were drawn to the story of the HBC because of the mercantile nature of the enterprise, but surely no more romantic subject could be proposed than those misguided and tragic crusades in pursuit of that boreal chimera, the Northwest Passage.

The reasons for this are numerous and complex, although perhaps not surprising. The small volume of genuine art that did manage to survive the unfriendly conditions of its specific production and reception is the more to be cherished—both for its rarity and for the odds against its very coming into being.[2]

Rupert's Land and its arctic extensions failed to capture the fancy of Europe's cultural arbiters because its explorers failed to do justice to the reality that lay before them. The image they created of the land and its inhabitants did not convey the potency and potential of the New World; instead, it could be said that nothing has changed in the essential mind-set since Voltaire's notorious dismissal of Canada of 1759 as *"quelques arpents de neige"* and the observation by R.B. Cunninghame Graham of 1898 that "Canada is said to have got its name from the two Spanish words 'Aca' and 'Nada' as signifying 'there is nothing here'," except that the acreage of ice and snow—of palpable nothingness—has expanded exponentially.

Besides northern Canada's inhospitality and lack of conformation to aesthetic rules, three major forces stood in the way of its appreciation: the British Admiralty, the Royal Geographical Society, and the Hudson's Bay Company. The former two bodies took little cognizance of the great land-mass immediately to the south, which they looked upon merely as a source of provisions and manpower for their various programmes of discovery, conquest, and exploitation amid the floating alps of ice. For the overland explorers, Rupert's Land constituted a hindrance to be overcome, an irritation of thousands of miles of bush and rock, muskeg and moose pasture, sea-sized expanses of lake, and ladders of rapids to be negotiated before the true objective hoved into sight—the Pacific or Arctic coastline.

The HBC's policy of building posts on Hudson and James bays and letting the Indians come to them with their furs is emblematic of the limits of vision that circumscribed the colonizing and exploratorial enterprises themselves. Though these two latter projects may have had differing (George Simpson would have said incompatible) aims, their ends were alike determined by their beginnings, which lay more in material and military agendas than in the heroic designs of the Enlightenment. Blinkered thinking led, inevitably, to blinkered seeing. What was to become the Dominion of Canada remained largely invisible except to the odd sojourner who chose to stop and look, at least for the duration of an on-site sketch of a waterfall or a floe.

The following piece of paradoxical hyperbole is quoted in *S.W. Silver & Co.'s Handbook to Canada*, published in 1881: "'Distance!' said a Yankee trader, when appealed to on the probable width of the seemingly limitless expanse of prairie which everywhere confronted him; 'distance! I should think so—distance till you can't see!'" An endemic inability to see the forest for the trees is supplanted, in wide landscapes deemed wastelands by those who have yet to figure out how to covert them to gardens, by an induced blindness to what is there through too much concentration on what is not.

The aesthetic concept of the Sublime—rather than the Picturesque—is the characteristic of Romanticism that dominated the literary, theatrical, musical, and visual arts between 1817 and 1854. In the fall of 1817, whaler and scientist William Scoresby wrote his famous letter to the Royal Geographical Society, stating his opinion that "between 74°N and 80°N the Greenland Sea is now unexpectedly free of ice." Within three weeks of the receipt of this missive, the prime minister authorized the expeditions of Buchan and Parry. The era thus inaugurated came to an abrupt close in September of 1854, when Robert McClure laid claim to the £10,000 Admiralty prize for the discovery of the Northwest Passage. This is not to say that the aesthetic ethos of Romanticism failed to survive this devastating epochal moment; but its imported perpetuation depended, after Canada's Confederation in 1867, on a nascent sense of national identity on the part of new-world immigrants and natives rather than on the imperial longings and old-world nostalgia of the mother countries, which had more or less given up on their wayward children.

William Wordsworth, among others, connected the northerly regions with the Sublime. His definition of "Sublimity," in his *Guide Through the District of the Lakes in the North of England* (first published in 1810), as "the result of Nature's first great dealings with the superficies of the earth," suggests why the connection should have appealed to his age. His qualifying clause — "but the general tendency of her subsequent operations is towards the production of beauty, by a multiplicity of symmetrical parts, uniting in a consistent whole" — offers a reason why the High Arctic of the British navigators and the lakes, forests, and tundras of the fur traders and overland explorers did not fulfil the requirements of Picturesque taste in landscapes. A helpful differentiation of Sublime and Picturesque is offered by S.T. Coleridge:

> When the parts by their harmony produce an effect of a whole, but there is no seen form of a whole producing or explaining the parts, i.e. when the parts only are seen and distinguished, but the whole is felt — the picturesque. When neither whole nor parts, but unity, as boundless or endless *allness* — the Sublime.[3]

The "endless *allness*" of the elemental landscapes of Rupert's Land and points north spelt interminable, uninhabitable monotony to its wayfaring European observers, an infinity of parts that never amounted to a coherent, geographically comprehensive totality.

This is not to suggest that individual expressions of awe, wonder, and admiration for the Sublime latitudes were entirely lacking, even at the apogee of Picturesque reconnaissance. One of the first nineteenth-century accounts of Arctic travel, published in 1817, describes a stormy summer's night in Hudson Bay:

> August 6th. — In the middle of the night, the prospect from the ship was one of the most awful and sublime that I ever remember having witnessed, during a life spent entirely upon the ocean: and I regret that no language of mine can give an adequate idea of the grandeur of the scene. As far as the eye could reach, a vast alabaster pavement overspread the surface of the sea, whose dark blue waters could only be seen at intervals, where parts of the pavement appeared to have been convulsively torn up, and heaped upon each other in ruined fragments. The snow-white surface of this immense plain formed a most striking contrast to the deep black clouds of a stormy night; through which,

uninterrupted flashes of forky lightning succeeded each other in great rapidity, as if intending, by their fiery glare, to shew us the horrors of our situation, and then to magnify them by leaving us in utter darkness. Add to this, the reiterated peals of thunder that burst forth, in a thousand roaring echoes, over the surrounding ice; also the heavy plashing of the rain; the distant growling of affrighted bears, the screams of sea-birds, and the loud whistling of the wind; — the whole forming a midnight prospect which I would have gone any distance to see; but having once beheld, never wish to witness again.[4]

It is impossible, reading this, not to call to mind the painter John Martin (1789-1854), who in 1812 exhibited at the Royal Academy, London, the first of his sixteen "sublime" canvases, depicting "immeasureable spaces, innumerable multitudes, and gorgeous prodigies of architecture and landscape."

Though most direct apprehension of the Sublime takes place in nature, under trying, sometimes life-threatening circumstances, Sublimity can be contemplated and savoured only in reflective repose. When harsh reality impinges, displacing the necessary aesthetic distance between observer and observed, the terror lurking at the heart of the observer comes to the fore, and the *frisson* experienced at the threshold of very existence itself is no longer associated with pleasing anticipation.

The motif of travel is integral to the notion of the Picturesque, and this, too, had its effect on visual representations of Rupert's Land and the Arctic archipelago. From the days of Isham and Hearne, to those of Rindisbacher and Kane, the principle modes of transportation changed but marginally: when in the civilized world, the view was framed by the carriage window; when in the wilds, the surrounding scene was admitted from above and on all sides. For the ship-borne artists — almost all of whom were officers — the "floating-hotel" school of polar exploration had its equivalent in a floating-hotel school of art. Officer status, however, afforded those rare moments of repose that are essential for the contemplative observation out of which comes art. The access of emotion in the face of both the grandeur and the terribleness of icy seas under the midnight sun, which found expression in the American Sublime of Frederick Edwin Church, James Hamilton, and William Bradford, was the prerogative of only a minute sampling of the thousands who saw the aurora borealis and the paraselenae but were not moved by the phenomena to declamation or delineation, having either no opportunity or no desire to give utterance.

I

My title suggests a movement from a frozen landscape to a still point, toward which the observer advances or from which he stands back in order to take in the whole picture. Movement, however, is not just lateral but longitudinal or circumferal when the delineator elects to ape the cycloramist by dividing the 360° horizontal sweep visible from the height of land or from the crow's nest and rendering it in connected sections. Or the artist might anticipate the cinematographer in "panning" along a horizon or shoreline and breaking it down into a continuous, linear sequence of discrete images according to the dimensions of the bound sketchpad or watercolour-block. If, since 1885, the word "panorama" applies (in the *Shorter OED*'s phrasing) to "a place which affords an open view; a look-out," a much earlier definition is more contextually pertinent. In 1538, the concept meant "an extensive sight or view; the view of the landscape from any position;" in 1633, "the visible landscape;" and in 1771, "a picture, a sketch of a scene or the like." It was in search of "pleasing prospects" that the first Picturesque travellers set forth.

As I hope to reveal, "panoramic thinking" in the depiction of such landscapes as concern us evolved, if not naturally, then as a popular reaction to the artists who paused long enough in their headlong traverses westward and northward to record the scenery — such of it, that is, as they were capable of seeing. There was, to begin with, a venerable precedent in the couching of long views in theatrical or amphitheatrical terms, giving the horizontal sweep the illusion of depth through the interposition of rocks, trees, and shrubberies so rendered as to resemble the *coulisses* or flies and sliding screens of the proscenium-arched stage. This combination of the retreating horizon and the flattened foreground is an observable characteristic of North American topography and atmospherics. Whether by instinct or by inclination, painters of the Canadian prairies and boreal forest have resorted *en masse* since the 1820s and '30s to a compositional format that could be described as a panoramic prospect. Staggered by a vastness of space dwarfing the observing consciousness, and in vain search of the beguiling variety of shape and surface called for by the doctrinarians of the Picturesque, again and again they sought out valleys, ranges of hills, and promontory-hemmed shorelines whose contours literally made the picture.

Since certain land-routes and sea-lanes tended to be pursued as more efficient and reliable than others, the same prospects were noted and commented on in journal after journal, sketchbook after sketchbook, over a period encompassing the lifespans and professional careers of Samuel Hearne and George Simpson. It is not that there was, or is, a paucity of scenes as worthy of celebration as the familiar touchstones—the Thunder Capes, the Kakabeka Falls, the Qu'Appelle Valleys, the Vales of the Clearwater River, the Cape Yorks, and the Bylot Islands. From the scarcity of representations of these alternative magnets, we must therefore assume that the compulsion of the beaten track considerably affected individuality of creative expression.

The advent of the locomotive and the paddle-wheeler occurred at the height of the popularity of an entertainment device that in itself foreshadowed the motion picture even as it harked back to the hieroglyphic frieze: the moving panorama. The panorama did as much as paintings, prints, or published explorers' journals to convey an image of Rupert's Land and the Far North—an image that, however inaccurate, continues to enjoy the status of a universally accredited truth which no amount of contrary evidence can displace or disprove. The viewer of a moving panorama stood stationary before a slow revelation of geography, hidden but audible machinery turning the endless shroud on which was painted, more crudely than was admissible in salon or academy, the length and breadth of the Mississippi, the St. Lawrence, the Hudson, or the Rhine.

Among the letters of John Franklin to his sister is one dated April 12, 1819 in which he reports that

> the Panorama opens for public exhibition this day.... I have not seen it, for some weeks when about half finished. I do not expect to see it again, since my likeness is said to be strong. I shall not venture to approach very near Leicester Square for the passers-by should say there goes the fellow in the Panorama! I have just learnt Sir Joseph Banks has seen it and approves of it highly.[5]

The year before, Capt. (later Sir John) Ross was the first to enter the renewed Northwest Passage stakes, sailing home not with the much-coveted trophy but with the rediscovery of Baffin Bay—a triumph angrily deprecated by the Admiralty's Sir John Barrow, who had hoped for a confirmation of his *idée fixe* about an open polar sea. Despite the mockery Ross had to endure from his rivals on account of his having mistaken a refractory mirage for the phantom Croker Mountains erroneously supposed by him to block Lancaster Sound—the true entrance to the Passage—his expedition was a popular success, confirmed by the appearance of his *Voyage of Discovery* in 1819.

The artists on board the *Isabella* and the *Alexander* had been, besides Ross himself, a representative of that race whose graphic and sculptural art today best captures the spirit of the Arctic: John Saccheuse or Sackhouse, a mixed-blood Greenland Inuk and former stowaway who accompanied the expedition as an interpreter, at the wage of three pounds per week. Both Ross and Saccheuse are credited as the authors of sketches from which Messrs Marshall's *Grand Peristrephic* — i.e., revolving — *Panorama of the Polar Regions* was painted. Lieut. Frederick W. Beechey, who had served as draughtsman on the *Trent*, commanded by John Franklin, on the abortive North Pole expedition sent out by the Admiralty to coincide with Ross's Northwest Passage attempt, is cited as the originator of the views of Spitzbergen.

The first of Messrs Marshall's two Baffin Bay panoramas, based on a folding plate in Ross's *A Voyage of Discovery* (1819) (Fig. 1), or else on Saccheuse's original drawing for it, represents Ross's *Isabella*, and the *Alexander*, captained by his second-in-command, Lieut. W.E. Parry, "at the new discovered land in Baffin's Bay, named by Captain Ross the Arctic Highlands. Captain Ross, Lieutenant Parry, Saccheuse the Esquimaux, and some of the crew, in conference with the natives, &c." The published description further explains that Capt. Ross and Lieut. Parry (depicted wearing their cocked hats, dress uniforms, swords, and white gloves; the artist portrays himself in the background in a beaver hat) are presenting the never-before-encountered Regent's Bay Inuit "with looking-glasses, knives &c; their astonishment is extreme, at beholding their faces in the mirrors; others of the natives are flogging their dogs to preserve order."[6]

The letterpress goes on to relate how Saccheuse, having bravely volunteered to act as an emissary between his adoptive party and the Arctic Highlanders, was so impressed by the ludicrousness of the natives' fascination with the proffered looking-glasses that

> some time after he made a drawing of it, being the first specimen we had of his talents for historical composition. His practice in the art of design, which he had cultivated, in addition to all the other branches of knowledge engrafted on his Esquimaux education, having hitherto limited to copying such prints of single figures or ships, as he could procure, as he never received any hint or assistance in this performance.[7]

The spiky blue-grey mountain backdrop of the published aquatint (and presumably of the panoramic blow-up) after Ross's original watercolour evoke the Bylot and Baffin island peaks painted by Lawren Harris in pursuit of the Theosophists' Ultima Thule in 1930.

Ross's contribution to the panorama, *Crimson Cliffs — Captain Ross, Lieutenant Parry, Saccheuse, and part of the crews, playing at football with the natives*, must have been sensational, if it bore any resemblance to its hand-coloured source plate in his *Voyage of Discovery* — arguably the first example of painting that combines prophesies of both the Fauvist and Surrealist movements to have been inspired by a Canadian landscape (Fig. 2). The claret-hued cliffs, which in Ross's words "presented an appearance both novel and interesting," of the newly named Sir Byam Martin range, sighted on August 17 at lat. 75° 54' N., long. 67° 15' W., mundanely turn out to have been discoloured by *Protococcus nivalis*, a unicellular plant also common to the Rockies.[8] Oblivious of the spectacle looming garishly above them, whites and natives in the panorama's foreground were intent on "kicking at each other an inflated seal skin bag, behind which are more natives taking care of the sledges." As for the middle distance, Ross (or his presumed ghostwriter) could anthropomorphically commend it as representing "the most magnificent chain of mountains, which I had ever beheld.... In one place,...two rocks, resembling human figures of a gigantic size, were seen in a sitting posture on the very highest peak; and, as it was considerably above the clouds, their appearance was both extraordinary and interesting."[9]

Subjected to special questioning by sceptics was the aquatint by R. Havell and Son, *Passage through the Ice* (Fig. 3), based on another Ross watercolour, which graces his 1819 narrative, and his other illustrations of "remarkable icebergs." The tilting, jagged, ship-dwarfing floes were criticized as gross exaggerations, but more reliable witnesses than Ross were to bring home tales and images of bergs no less improbable in size and shape: consider, for instance, George Back's *Boats in a Swell amongst Ice*, engraved by Edward Finden for John Franklin's Narrative of a *Second Expedition to the Shores of the Polar Sea* (1828).

Messrs Marshall were not the only panoramists to latch onto the 1818-19 expeditions. Perhaps the most singular and at the same time most archetypal image of shipwreck is suspected of owing at least a minor debt to Antonio Secchetti's hemicycloramic painting *North Pole Expedition* and to Johann Carl Enslen's panorama *Winter Sojourn of the North Pole Expedition*, which were exhibited respectively in Prague in 1821 and Dresden in 1822. This is Kaspar David Friedrich's *The Sea of Ice (The Failed North Pole Expedition)*, formerly confused with a lost painting known as *The Wreck of the "Hope,"* which Alexandra

Feodorovna (later empress of Russia) ordered from the German Romantic artist in 1821.[10] Painted in 1822-23, this symbol-charged canvas, which features so many of what were to become the constants of the more mundane and documentary renderings of Arctic seagoing disaster, from the stratified slabs of dirty ice to the battered ship, seems to have been based on an historical incident. Though the floes in the right foreground have their source in sketches made during the winter of 1820-21 when the Elbe froze over, Friedrich might possibly have received his primary inspiration for this work from newspaper reports or from the published account of Parry's 1819-19 expedition with Ross to Baffin's Bay, his journal recounting which also appeared in 1821. The wrecked vessel is thus thought to be the *Griper*, which participated in a second polar thrust in 1824. And may not word of this same expedition, and of the concurrent assault on the Pole led by David Buchan and his second-in-command, the young John Franklin, have reached the ears or eyes of Mary Shelley as she penned her *Frankenstein* in Italy? How Shelley could have continued, in the face of contradictive testimony, to allow the dying count to rave on about the pole being not "the seat of frost and desolation" but rather—at least in his fevered imagination—"the region of beauty and delight" remains problematical.[11] Remember, though, that Frankenstein's poleward-sledging creature managed to wreak his revenge on his crazed maker within the intervening "'land of mist and snow'" where the Modern Prometheus's Faustian designs were at last exposed as folly.

From what sources did Mary Shelley derive her alternatively benign and malign notions of the realm to which, long before Milton mapped the geography of Hell, the demons and fallen angels of the world were consigned?[12] Her narrator confides to his sister that his polar expedition from Archangel had been a favourite dream of his early years: "I have read with ardour the accounts of the various voyages which have been made in the prospect of arriving at the North Pacific Ocean through the seas which surround the Pole. You may remember that a history of all the voyages made for purposes of discovery composed the whole of our good Uncle Thomas' library.... These volumes were my study day and night."[13]

Walton's "history" would likely have been Hakluyt's and Purchas's *Principal Navigations, Voyages, Traffiques and Discoveries of the English Nations*, which records the exploits of the early Arctic probers, among them Luke Foxe, William Barents, Frederick Martens, John Harris, and Thomas James. It was from such authorities that Coleridge derived the imagery contained in his button-holing mariner's advisory:

Listen, Stranger! Mist and snow,
And it grew wond'rous cauld:
And Ice mast-high came floating by
As green as Emerauld

—lines that have been identified as a pastiche of Marten, Harris, and James.[14]

In outlining his mission, Robert Walton also cites *The Rime of the Ancient Mariner* as a cautionary tale for explorers. The poem was first published in 1798—the same year, coincidentally, that Kaspar David Friedrich (if indeed it was he) painted his allegorical *Wreck in the Polar Sea*, in the Kunsthalle, Hamburg. Such rhapsodies as Frankenstein's hymn to the sunny polar paradise as "a land surpassing in wonders and in beauty every region hitherto discovered on the habitable globe" would not return to the literature of boreal description until the arrival on the scene of such early twentieth-century champions of pan-arcticism as Vilhjalmur Stefansson, Robert Flaherty, Peter Freuchen, Edmund Carpenter, and Barry Lopez.

Successor to Messrs Marshall's above-described 1819 panorama was one advertised by Robert Burford as the *View of the Continent of Boothia, Discovered by Captain Ross, In his late Expedition to the Polar Regions*. Exhibited at Leicester Square in 1834, the panorama was painted by Burford from drawings by John Ross made for his *Narrative of a Second Voyage in Search of a North-West Passage, and of a Residence in the Arctic Regions during the years 1829, 1830, 1831, 1832, 1833*. Those given the vapours by the spectacle could turn their attention to Exhibit No. II, a panorama, appropriately enough, of Niagara Falls. We may presume that Burford chose to inflate on canvas one or more of Ross's naive but haunting watercolour records of the purpureal polar sky contrasted by the creamy white of floes and igloos, which Day and Son lithographically rendered for his *Narrative*, published in 1835. Novel though such images may have been to the readers of his account and its spinoffs, Ross's sympathetic portraits of Inuit men and women hark back to the first depictions of these aborigines, credited to the father of the Arctic documentary tradition, John White, who may have accompanied Frobisher to South Baffin Island in 1577.

The failure of Sir George Back's 1836-37 Northwest Passage cruise, financed by the Royal Geographical Society as an attempt to complete the charting of the coastline between Prince Regent Inlet and Point Turnagain, put an effective end to nearly three decades of intensive if frustrated Arctic probes. Significantly, perhaps, Back—whose artistic exploits during the Arctic overland expeditions of 1819-22 and 1825-27 will be discussed later—himself produced only a handful of watercolours during this terrible voyage, but instead relied on the sketches of his able first lieutenant, William Smyth, for the plates reproduced in his narrative. This account, tellingly, is that of a defeated, disappointed man for whom both art and science had foundered in the grip of an immoveable natural Will. The lesson of the *Terror*'s unsuitability for further arctic service was lost on Franklin, of course, with results that possess, in retrospect, a Sophoclean tragic inevitability.

One unexpected outcome of the response to Franklin's disappearance was a revival of artistic interest in the farthest North. This fascination would burn over the course of a decade before turning into abhorrence and bitter disillusionment on confirmation of the pessimists' worst fears. So long as the lucrative Admiralty reward for settling once and for all the fate of Franklin and his crew remained unclaimed, the idea—if not the reality—of the region containing Franklin's elusive goal retained its allure.

The mid-century year marked a kind of watershed in the history of far-northern and arctic exploration. The first of some forty missions in search of the vanished *Terror* and *Erebus* had been dispatched three years earlier. Eighteen-fifty alone saw some fifteen search expeditions, including a private venture in the yacht *Felix* led by that seventy-year-old veteran of the second great wave of arctic travel and exploration, Sir John Ross. The Victorian Penelope was not amused to be informed by this tactless seadog of the rumour that her wandering Ulysses and his men had been devoured by cannibal aborigines on the northwest coast of Greenland. Convinced that Sir John had obeyed his orders and concentrated his efforts on Lancaster Sound and Prince Regent Inlet, she sent forth the *Prince Albert* under the command of a latter-day Telemachus in the person of her adoptive son, the French naval lieutenant, Joseph René Bellot, a gifted amateur artist whose death by drowning in 1853 during a second mission further exacerbated the national fit of fear and trembling.

The media circus revolving round these nautical events had from the outset been whipped into a frenzy of morbid speculation and patriotic zeal by two phenomena of the age: the steam-driven printing press and the invention of efficient and economical modes of engraving and lithography that allowed for the mass-proliferation of cheap images expressive of national hopes, resolves, nightmares, and delusions. This iconographic industry in turn was fed by a pictorial tradition traceable to a custom established by the second wave's heroes, Constantine Phipps and James Cook. Both seamen, in their respective North Pole and Northwest Passage pushes of 1773 and 1776-80, had included topographically trained artists in their companies: John Clevely II and John Webber. A disproportionate number of participants in the Franklin search who recorded their experiences in published narratives illustrated them, in demonstration of the graphic skills in which they had been drilled at military school or on shipboard by senior officers adept in the observational practices of ordnance surveying, chartmaking, and sketching in line and wash.

Nor were the impresarios and hacks who gained from Arctic Fever content simply to profit from print, book, periodical, and theatrical forms. Medium fed medium, on a perhaps declining scale of quality of reproduction. An instance of such cannibalism is a sequence of hand-coloured lantern-slides, in the possession of Montreal's Notman Photographic Archives, which were based on published arctic images: in the example reproduced in Figure 4, the sources of the vignette was the tint-stone lithograph after Walter William May's watercolour *H.M.S. Assistance and Pioneer in Winter Quarters. Returning Daylight* (Fig. 5), published in 1855.

It was in reaction to the electrifying *Arctic Regions* panorama painted by Robert Burford and exhibited at his premises in Leicester Square, London, in the benchmark year of 1850, that William Makepeace Thackeray, writing as "Goliah Muff," voiced his tongue-in-cheek minority view of the pictorial wares so exposed for public titillation:

> Ah, Sir, of what clay are mortals supposed to be made, that they can visit that exhibition? Dreams I have had in my life, but as that view of the Arctic Regions nothing so terrible. My blood freezes as I think of that frightful *summer* even — but what to say of the winter? By heavens, Sir! I could not face the sight — the icy picture of eternal snow — the livid northern lights, the killing glitter of the stars; the wretched mariners groping about in the snow round the ship; they caused me such a shudder of surprise and fright, that I don't blush to own I popped down the curtain after one single peep, and would not allow my children to witness it.[15]

"Panorama" and "panic," the resident sceptic of *Punch* seems to be reminding us, have the same Greek root. Some idea of what had elicited this horrified exclamation is provided by an engraving bearing the caption: "Burford's Panorama of the Polar Regions — the 'Investigator' Snow-walled in for the Winter," which appeared in the February 23,

1850, issue of the *Illustrated London News* (Fig. 6). Accompanying the exhibition was a descriptive pamphlet entitled *Panorama Royal, Leicester Square. Now Exhibiting Sublime Views of the Arctic Regions, as seen During Summer and Winter*. The featured topic was the expedition of Captains James C. Ross, of the *Enterprise*, and E.J. Bird, of the *Investigator*, in 1848. As Richard Altick, in his *The Shows of London*, informs us,

> in the three years beginning late in 1849, the already protracted search for Sir John Franklin—it would go on for another twenty years—was the subject of several panoramas. The quest was one in which the nation had a deep emotional involvement: not only was British prestige at stake, but the shock of Franklin's total disappearance, after the confidence that had surrounded the departure of his elaborately equipped expedition, was an upsetting national experience. At Leicester Square, Burford provided a pictorial supplement to the growing literature on Arctic exploration which the Franklin drama had evoked by producing a show composed of two "hemiramas," as the diarist Crabb Robinson called them, one portraying Ross, a would-be rescuer, on the coast of Greenland in July, the other showing his ships, the *Enterprise* and the *Investigator*, iced in during the winter at Port Leopold. The existence of a rival panorama led Lieutenant Browne, an officer of the *Enterprise*, to notify the press (doubtless prompted by Burford) that he alone had many any sketches during the late expedition, and that it was these sketches the Admiralty had given Burford exclusive permission to use. Later (1852) Vauxhall Gardens erected an enormous outdoor "diorama" of Arctic scenery.[16]

The Browne alluded to by Altick was the Dublin-born Lieut. William H. J. Browne, who executed the backdrop for Burford's huddling figures on the basis of an on-site sketch. Browne, who had served as second lieutenant to James C. Ross on H.M.S. *Enterprise* in 1848-49 and returned the following year with Capt. Austin on H.M.S. *Resolute*, had acted as a scene-painter for the Royal Arctic Theatre on board that vessel. Probably in May or June, 1849, he had led a daring sledge-trek from Port Leopold to the coast of Prince William Island, crossing Prince Regent Inlet and returning to the ships after an absence of eight days. He depicted this journey in a series of watercolours—including the panorama's source image of the iced-in ship (Fig. 7)—which Charles Haghe lithographed for publication by Ackermann and Co. in 1850 under the title *Ten Coloured Views taken during the Arctic Expedition of Her Majesty's Ships "Enterprise" and "Investigator."*

Renderings of "scenery" and scene-painting seemed to have gone hand-in-hand in the Arctic of that theatrical, not to say melodramatic, era. Browne suggests this symbiotic relationship even in the course of assuring his readers in his folio's introduction of the faithfulness of these "delineations of the most interesting scenery in the Arctic regions." His claims to accuracy were backed up, however, by at least one colleague who had witnessed not only the giant enlargements of these images, but the actual places depicted. Capt. W. Parker Snow, before setting forth in command of Lady Franklin's *Prince Albert*, took in the show at Leicester Square and testified to its effectiveness, declaring that he had seen the spot near Leopold Island illustrated by Browne and that he recognized every detail:

> As we neared the shore, the whole features of the place came fresh upon me, so truthful is the representation given of them by Lieut. Browne in Burford's Panorama. I could not mistake, and, I almost fancied that I was again in London, viewing the artistic sketch, but for certain undeniable facts in the temperature and aspect of the ice which banished such an idea.[17]

Snow, who went on to illustrate his own expeditionary narrative,was not alone in responding creatively to Browne's example: the leading American entrant in the Franklin stakes, Dr. Elisha Kent Kane, examined the folio of *Ten Coloured Views* before departing with the first U.S. Grinnell Expedition in 1850. Observing an already venerable tradition, he returned with his own thick sketchbooks, which were used by the professional landscape painter James Hamilton, a disciple of J.M.W. Turner and Clarkson Stanfield, to prepare atmospheric watercolours for translation into engravings for Kane's *The U.S. Grinnell Expedition in Search of Sir John Franklin, 1850-51* and its even more lavish follow-up, *Arctic Explorations: The Second Grinnell Expedition in Search of Sir John Franklin.* Hamilton did not himself voyage northward, except spiritually; his visionary landscapes and seascapes, however, anticipate those of his compatriots William Bradford (1823-1892) and F.E. Church (1826-1900), who would paint the polar regions not as topographical or editorial illustrators but as exponents of the luministic, transcendental Sublime; his undated *Berg off Cape Melville* (Glenbow Museum, Calgary) is a direct lineal ancestor of Lawren Harris's 1930 canvas *Icebergs, Davis Strait.*

This susceptibility to Arctic sublimity may have been unavailable to contemporary British artists for emotional and patriotic reasons, as much as it was alien to them because of perceptual biases against visionary light that had been fostered in military landscape instruction. The imaginative blockage that was to plunge the Canadian Far North into a permanent polar night, so far as European sensibilities were concerned, is summed up in the following obituary to an imperial quest that had outlived Franklin's mysterious disappearance but that could not survive the cold fact of his proven defeat:

> No; there are no more sunny continents—no more islands of the blest—hidden under the far horizons, tempting the dreamer over the undiscovered sea; nothing but those weird and tragic shores, those cliffs of everlasting ice and mainlands of frozen snow, which have never produced anything to us but a late and sad discovery of the depths of human heroism, patience, and bravery, such as imagination could scarely dream of.

Thus lamented *Blackwood's Edinburgh Magazine* in November 1855. Doubtless this blanket dismissal of the colossal spoil of empire stemmed from the news that the hotly contested Admiralty prize had been won the previous year by an illustrious fellow countryman and Edinburgh University graduate, Dr. John Rae, a HBC surgeon based at Moose Factory.

Franklin's failure and death, within sight of his reward, vindicated the nay-sayers, especially those who considered whoring after strange latitudes to be a manifestation of hubris, if not of dementia. At the same time that it created a new cause for national mourning and posthumous hero-worship, it put paid to any hopes for the hyperborean realm ever again fully engaging the British imagination. The poetry and drama inspired by the catastrophe invariably emphasized the sacrificial aspect of the pursuit of knowledge into *meta incognita* that too often proved fatal to its seekers, more than it stressed the possible outcome or instigating rationale of that inquiry.

In a sense, the oblivion found by Franklin came to stand for the clime in which he met his nemesis. The uncertainty of the exact nature of his fate or his final resting-place led his poet-laureate cousin, Lord Tennyson, epitaphically to consign his bones to "the white North," and at the same time to project his "Heroic sailor-soul" toward "no earthly pole." Charles Dickens, in his prologue to the dramatization of Wilkie Collins's *The Frozen Deep*, reduced the entire theatre of arctic action to "One savage footprint on the lonely shore/ Where one man listen'd to the surge's roar." Having been invited to "Pause on the footprints of heroic men,/ Making a garden of the desert wide/ Where Parry conquer'd death and Franklin died," the reader is asked to accompany the players

> To that white region where the Lost lie low,
> Wrapt in their mantles of eternal snow, —
> Unvisited by change, nothing to mock
> Statues sculptured in the icy rock.[18]

The play's intention, we are told, is not to dwell on such macabre images and grisly episodes for their own sakes, but rather

> ...that the secrets of the vast Profound
> Within us, an exploring hand may sound,
> Testing the region of the ice-bound soul,
> Seeking the passage at its northern pole,
> Softening the horrors of its wintry sleep,
> Melting the surface of that "Frozen Deep."[19]

The inward journey into the metaphysicality symbolized by Thackeray's and Dickens's "eternal snow" could take the painter along with him only if he were prepared (like Lawren Harris and the colour-field abstractionists of the prairies in the following century) to sail the uncharted waters of non-representation. In its appeal to sensation and reverie, the panoramic Sublime seems in its own way to be pointed in that directionless direction. But along the way there are scattered landmarks — cairns and shrines raised, as it were, to an absconded or indifferent *genius loci* — that merit our breaking our journey and emulating the Picturesque topographers by mounting the summit to survey the prospect spreading extensively before us.

II

Despite what I have presented as the obstacles that prevented major European painters from seeing the far-northern regions of Canada with their own eyes, a canvassing of contemporary illustrated sources, and of the archives and marine museums where most of this little-appreciated material is housed, reveals that there were at least as many pictorial approaches to Rupert's Land and the Arctic Archipelago as there were, in Stefansson's notorious analysis, phases of arctic exploration and corresponding emotional reactions to the frozen zone. These reactions range, as we have seen, from dread to friendly accommodation, and encompass fear and the grudging respect that came with technical sophistication.

The stylistic method imparted to the artillery and engineering trainees at Woolwich, which boasted a fairly extensive art course, and to the more haphazardly instructed students at Sandwich and the Royal Naval College, Portsmouth, tended to produce painstaking copyists after nature—as nature was supposed to appear, that is, if not through the naked eye then through the composition-framing lens of the *camera lucida* or the Claude glass. At the same time, the aesthetic laws of the previous century, as laid down by Edmund Burke, Uvedale Price, Richard Payne Knight, and Gilpin, prevailed over the freer instincts of the officer-artists who literally drew on their experiences in the field or on the high seas. Artist after artist sought to adapt the irregular features of the Canadian wilds according to the ordering and organizing tenets to which they subscribed. Trouble ensued when essential elements for any one of these modes of representation, such as the "high colouring" prescribed by Gilpin, or the *parerga*—that is, adjuncts or additional graces, such as watermills, farm-houses, woods, flocks of sheep, herd of cattle, pilgrims, ruins of temples, castles, and monuments—appropriate to a proper Claudian "landskip," were found to be lacking in the actual far-flown prospect. The absence of these features did not prevent the attempted superimposition of substitutes on the uncooperative wilderness, though such transplantings were less efforts to make northern North America conform to European standards and presumptions than they were unconscious habits of vision.

Thus it is that, well into the Victorian era, interpreters of the Canadian Northlands were drawing and painting as if Paul Sandby, R.A., chief drawing-master at Woolwich Military School from 1768 to 1799, were peering over their shoulders, even as back at home the likes of Richard Wilson, James Ward, Thomas Girton, Francis Danby, Philip James de Loutherbourg, John Martin, J.M.W. Turner, Clarkson Stanfield, John Constable, David Cox, John Crome, John Sell Cotman, Samuel Palmer, and, latterly, the Pre-Raphaelites were revolutionizing landscape painting by imbuing it with an unprecedented scope for expressiveness and implied meaning. With Sandby, wrote Christopher Hussey, "'all the world's a stage,' and its scenery—scenery. An appreciation of Dutch painting is equally evident in his gnarled trees and crumbling edifices... Between them the brothers [Paul and Thomas Sandby] represent consistently and over a long period the type of the picturesque artist."[20]

The inappropriatness of the Sandby-Gilpinian schema to these latitudes is demonstrated in a sardonic aside issuing from the pen of a seasoned explorer and outdoorsman adept at living off the land as well as rendering it, both verbally and visually. "Dear Back," wrote Dr. John Richardson on June 9, 1821, while on a supply trip to the Coppermine River,

> Gilpin himself, that celebrated picturesque hunter, would have made a fruitless journey had he come with us. We followed the lakes & low ground, which...were so deeply covered with snow, that it was impossible to distinguish lake from moor— Frequently, when I was congratulating myself on crossing a wide lake I discovered my mistake by sinking to the middle through the snow and sticking amongst the large stones which cover the bottoms of the vallies— I have said this much that you may judge if the sameness of the views that occurred in our journey—[the sentence is incomplete]— The only variety that we had was in crossing two extensive ridges of sand, which occur at the distance of 7 or 8 miles from each other & nearly half way to the river— I should suppose them to form the height of land between [illegible] & Coppermine Rivers, as all the heights of land that I have seen in this country consist of sand— Amongst these hills you may observe some curious basons, but nowhere did I discover anything worthy of your pencil—
>
> So much for the country— It is a barren subject and deserves to be thus briefly dismissed— Not so, the motley group of which we were composed— it afforded ample scope for the most able pencil or pen....[21]

such as the recipient of this missive, George Back, undoubtedly possessed.

The unPicturesque and yet unSublime barrenlands scene here described, however, answers in certain details to one drawn by Samuel Hearne in 1771, during his traverse to the Coppermine River and the Arctic Ocean: *A Winter View in the Athapuscow Lake* (Fig. 8). This impression of what is now known as Great Bear Lake was engraved by J. Saunders from Hearne's sketch for his posthumously published *A Journey from Prince of Wales's Fort in Hudson's Bay to the Northern Ocean* (1795). The neat, precise, symmetrical, almost parklike appearance of the snowcovered lake and its poplar-, birch-, and pine-clad islands may owe as much to the HBC employee's lack of artistic sophistication as to any cognizance on Hearne's part of the Picturesque formulae observed by his near namesake, Thomas Hearne, a Payne Knightian topographer who abhorred Turner's painting as entirely lacking in "sentiment."

Sentiment and imagination both, of course, were adjudged inappropriate to the recording of explorational expeditions and their findings. Enjoined to fidelity to appearances and minute attention to detail by their superiors in the Admiralty and by the directives of the Royal Geographical Society, the officer-artists stuck, by and large, to objective renderings of topography, however much they may have been tempted in the direction of decorativeness, fantasy, or romantic feeling by the extraordinary sights that met their gaze. After all, the official occasion for drawings and watercolours "taken" during the course of journeys was strategic and scientific, and the majority of the draughtsmen who kept private journals and sketchbooks did not choose to let themselves go in these more intimate formats. Often where stylistic individuality and intensified dramatic effect are introduced into a scene, it is at the hands of the unsung engravers and lithographers responsible for translating field-sketches into prints and plates for books and periodicals.[22]

The transformational process whereby a rough field-sketch was first worked up by the original artist, then further manipulated by the publisher's agent for the purposes for mechanical reproduction, is nicely illustrated in a sequence of images generated by George Back on Franklin's second land expedition to the shores of the Arctic Ocean in 1825-27. The subject was an exception to the rule about the inherently unaesthetic quality of northern Canadian topography— one that exerted a strong appeal on the successive legions of fur brigaders and explorers who witnessed the scene in their transits north and south across the height of land: the dramatic Vale of the Clearwater River, in what is now northern Saskatchewan.

A "most extensive, romantic, and ravishing prospect:" the very epithets applied to this celebrated panoramic vista by Sir Alexander Mackenzie (or by the suspected ghostwriter of his *Voyages*, William Combe), in recollection of his viewing it in 1789, show the picturesque sensibility at work in retrospect on a view that on contemplation from a distance, at least, could be allowed to possess the fundamental properties of a true landscape.

The taste that induced Mackenzie or his abettor to describe the "meandering" Clearwater, as seen from the north side of the 1,500-foot-high precipice at the termination of the Portage La Loche (also known as the Methye Portage), as "displaying a most delightful intermixture of wood and lawn, and stretching on till the blue mist obscures the prospect,"[23] still prevailed three decades later when Lieut. Robert Hood, a topographer who accompanied Franklin under Admiralty instructions on his first expedition to the Arctic Ocean in 1819-22, recorded in his journal:

> We were prepared to expect an extensive prospect, but the magnificant scene before us was so superior to what the nature of the country had promised, that it banished even our sense of suffering from the mosquitos which hovered in clouds about our heads. Two parallel chains of hills extended towards the setting sun, their various projecting outlines exhibiting the several gradations of distance, and the opposite closing on the horizon. On the nearest eminence, the objects were clearly defined by their dark shadows, the yellow rays blending their softening hues with brilliant green on the next, and beyond it, all distinction melted into grey and purple. In the long valley between, the smooth and colourless Clearwater River wound its spiral course, broken and scattered by encroaching woods. An exuberance of rich herbage covered the soil, and lofty trees climbed the precipice at our feet, hiding its brink with their summits. Impatient as we were, and blinded with pain, we paid tribute of admiration which this beautiful landscape is capable of exciting, unaided by the borrowed charms of a calm atmosphere glowing with the vivid tints of evening.[24]

Hood was at least the equal of George Back both as a prose stylist and as a painter of watercolours, which in their refined yet muscular treatment of northern lakes and rapids herald the direction Canada's national landscape movement would take in the first two decades of the next century (Fig. 9). The more is it to be regretted that Hood seems not to have been able or inclined to set down this scene in line and colours. His description, though, accords in virtually every detail with Back's treatment, five years later, of the same entrancing subject, seen by him and his leader now for the third time.

Franklin, more circumspect in his appreciations than were his younger official draughtsmen, simply noted in his *Narrative of a Second Expedition to the Shores of the Polar Sea* that "the annexed accurate drawing, taken by Lieutenant Back, from the highest part of this Portage, gives a beautiful delineation of one of the most picturesque scenes in the northern parts of America."[25] Back's entry for July 16-19 in his unpublished 1825 journal is also somewhat restrained in its lyricism — perhaps because it was written with the prospect of the thirty-six-mile portage ahead, and with the memory still fresh of the torment administered two nights previous by "those unceasing labourers after Blood, the Mosquitos". He simply reports that "The view here...was beheld with fresh Pleasure, and during the three days the Men were occupied in transporting the Canoes &c across, we [i.e., Back and the expedition's other artist, Edward Kendall] took a patient and we think an accurate sketch of it."[26]

The Finden engraving reproduced in Franklin's *Narrative of a Second Expedition* was not in fact taken directly from Back's on-site watercolour sketch, dated July 16, 1825, but from a larger and more finished "replica" completed on his return to England, presumably on the request of Franklin or his publisher, John Murray. As a comparison of the two watercolours (Figs. 10, 11) reveals, Back was at pains to tidy up the unkempt appearance of the valley in the image painted for replication. The colours are brighter, the forms clearer, the foreground trees more definitely shaped, so that their appearance is now almost Italianate. Both the breadth and the declivity of the valley have been increased, to convey a sense of endlessly retreating and yet expanding space. In deepening the foreground shadows and augmenting the radiance of the background as it recedes to the vanishing-point, Finden has converted what began as a roughfield-note into an epiphany in stipple and hatchwork that is worthy of the engravers employed by Turner for his *Liber Studiorum* (Fig. 12).[27]

Capt. Back returned to the scene in the summer of 1833, toward the beginning of his journey to the Great Fish River and Coronation Gulf in search of the missing Sir John Ross. The July 21 entry in his *Narrative of the Arctic Land Expedition* pays obligatory homage to "a spectacle so novel and magnificant," but there is a new note in his tone: that of a veteran of hard slogging for whom novelty and magnificence in themselves, devoid of the civilizing influences of history and the comforts of human companionship, are no longer enough. "My own sensations," he confesses,

> had not the keenness of those of a stranger to the sight; and it was not without a sort of melancholy, such as results from satiety, that I contrasted my present feelings with the rapture which I had formerly experienced. It was, to me, Portage la Loche, and nothing more, — the same beautiful and romantic solitude through which I had passed and repassed on two former expeditions.... I looked upon it as I should look upon an exquisite but familiar picture — with pleasure, but without emotion.

Then he continues, as if awakened to the insight that *his* own *loneliness* is what haunts the vista with the ghost of Absence, and shadows it with the prospect of his own mortality: "There is something appalling in the vastness of a solitude like this."[28] Yet he does recognize the presence of "the genius of the place," which he is reluctant to disturb. His own men, labouring along the portage with their burdens, were screened from his sight, but the sound of their tread comforted him — as did the "moving scenery of human occupation" which for Mackenzie completed the picture of "this wonderful display of uncultivated nature."[29]

From our remote perspective, it is just such written and painted responses as Hood's and Back's, amounting to a conjoint anthology and gallery of witnessings over time, that invests such wilderness landscapes with the richer dimensionality of those parts of the earth that have been seen and felt, described and invoked by successive generations of beholders. Out of such raw materials, as out of the wilderness itself, we forge a mythology, carve a culture.

In keeping with the titular theme, my final cluster of images is by choice a kind of outdoor-sketcher's makeshift panorama *in potentia*, but a very different one in content and feeling from the melodramatic spectacles of Leicester Square. In March 1821 George Back climbed a lightly treed hill eight miles from Fort Franklin, overlooking Great Bear Lake,[30] where with pencil and watercolours no doubt mixed with melted snow he executed a four-part, four-directional "Panoramic View" (Figs. 13-16).

What is so remarkable — and prophetic — about this technically modest investigation of place is its unaffected straight-forwardness, its lack of any kind of narrational pretext or emotive subtext. It is a statement in pure vision, as uncompromising in its directness as it is naked of mannerism. Diminuitive in actual size, the connected sketches are as vast in scope as the vista depicted. Dr. J. Russell Harper states that "Sir George Back was the most important Arctic topographer from the Canadian viewpoint."[31] Back was more than that; he is a true if still unacknowledged forerunner of an indigenous Canadian art.

Though they themselves were trammelled by stylistic biases no less artificial than those of the Picturesque, the home-bred painters who, led by A.Y. Jackson, Lawren Harris, and F.H. Varley, would claim these remote latitudes for their own a hundred years hence, understood that Eldorado lay all around them, in the very trees, snow, lakes, cliffs and clouds that composed the scene. It was to be found, in other words, not at the end of the portage or the mouth of the river, on the other side of the mountains or past the open polar sea, but here and now, in that most extensive of prospects, the artist's all-encompassing imagination.

Notes

1. Christopher Hussey, *The Picturesque: Studies in a Point of View* (1927; reprint, London: Frank Cass, 1967), 1.

2. Two pioneering studies of the high Arctic as seen through artists' eyes are Chauncey C. Loomis's "The Arctic Sublime," in *Nature and the Victorian Imagination*, ed. U.C. Knoepflmacher and G.B. Tennyson (Berkeley: University of California Press, 1977), 95-112, and Constance Martin's unpublished University of Calgary MA thesis, "Perceptions of Arctic Landscapes in the Art of the British Explorers, 1818-1859" (1981). The subject was introduced to Canadian readers by the late Dr. J. Russell Harper, who in 1967 delivered a lecture at the National Gallery of Canada entitled "Arctic Ice: A Romantic Theme," which in turn was an amplification of "The Last Frozen Barrier," a chapter in his *Painting in Canada: A History* (Toronto: University of Toronto Press, 1966), 163-68. Recent years have seen the publication of several essays by I.S. MacLaren, University of Alberta, Edmonton, notably his "'...where nothing moves and nothing changes': the second Arctic expedition of John Ross (1829-1833)," *Dalhousie Review* 62 (1982), 485-94; "Retaining captaincy of the soul: responses to nature in the first Franklin expedition," *Essays in Canadian Writing* 28 (1984), 57-92; "The Grandest Tour: The Aesthetics of Landscape in Sir George Back's Explorations of the Eastern Arctic 1833-1837," *English Studies in Canada* 10 (1984), 436-455; "The Limits of the Picturesque in British North America," *Journal of Garden History* 5 (1985), 97-111; "The Aesthetic Mapping of Nature in the Second Franklin Expedition," *Journal of Canadian Studies 20 (1985), 39-57; and* "The Aesthetic Map of the North, 1845-1859," *Arctic 38 (1985), 89-103.* MacLaren concentrates, however, more on the verbal than on the visual interpretation of the Arctic by expeditionary witnesses.

3. S.T. Coleridge, *The Table Talk and Omniana of Samuel Taylor Coleridge* (Oxford: Oxford University Press, 1917), 443.

4. Lieutenant Edward Chappell, R.N., *Narrative of a Voyage to Hudson's Bay in His Majesty's Ship Rosamond...* (London, 1817; reprint, Toronto: Coles Publishing, 1970), 123-25.

5. John Franklin to Mrs. Cracroft, 12 April 1819. Scott Polar Research Institute, MS 248/298/9.

6.   *Description of Messrs Marshall's Peristrephic Panorama of the Polar Regions....* (Leith, Scotland: Printed by William Heriot, 1821), 12-13.

7.   *Description*, 18-19.

8.   This natural anomaly was no doubt responsible for the similarly outlandish shading of James Hamilton's c. 1853 watercolour *Crimson Cliffs of Beverly*, reproduced in colour in Constance Martin's 1983 Glenbow Museum Exhibition catalogue, *James Hamilton: Arctic Watercolours*, as plate 16.

        Hamilton's *Refraction*, a watercolour of c. 1852 in the Glenbow Museum (Martin, pl. 11), depicts the same effect that so misled Ross, who added an appendix on the subject to his *Narrative of a Second Voyage* (1835). Thus is encapsulated the distinction between the priorities of the documentary artist and those the self-expressive landscape painter whose objective is the production of art, not information: an optical effect that Ross cited as an impediment to the making of accurate sketches would be celebrated by Hamilton, not twenty years later, as being eminently paintable.

9.   John Ross, *A Voyage of Discovery made under the Orders of the Admiralty in His Majesty's Ships Isabella and Alexander of the Purpose of exploring Baffin's Bay and enquiring into the Probability of a North-West Passage....* (London: John Murray, 1819), 170.

10. See *German Masters of the Nineteenth Century: Paintings and Drawings from the Federal Republic of Germany* (New York: The Metropolitan Museum of Art, 1981), 112.

11. Mary Shelley, *Frankenstein* (London: 1819; reprint, New York: Bantam, 1965), 15-16.

12. See I.S. MacLaren, "Arctic Exploration and Milton's 'Frozen Continent,'" *Notes and Queries*, new series, 31 (1984), 325-26.

13. Shelley, *Frankenstein*, 16.

14. See John Livingston Lowes, *The Road to Xanadu: A Study in the Ways of the Imagination* (New York: Vintage Books, 1959), 130.

15.   W.M. Thackeray, "The Sights of London," *Punch* (April 1850). Reprinted in *The Works of William Makepeace Thackeray. Volume 24: Contributions to "Punch"* (London: Smith, Elder, 1886), 245.

16.   Richard Altick, *The Shows of London* (Cambridge, Mass.: The Belknap Press of Harvard University Press, 1978), 177.

     The Crabb Robinson reference is to his *The London Theatre*, 1811-1866, ed. Eluned Brown (London, 1966), 191, while Browne's claim to primogeniture is found in the *Athenaeum*, 12 January 1850, 52.

     I.S. MacLaren, in his above-cited "The Aesthetic Map of the North" (see endnote 2), observes of Charles Haghe's tint-stone lithograph after Browne's sketch *Noon in Mid-Winter at Point Leopold*, which served as the basis for the second of Burford's two Leicester Square "hemiramas," that "Darkness at noon provides him with the opportunity of exhibiting perhaps nature's own most sublime example of chiaroscuro — the balance of light and shadow in a picture....[T]he scene's moonlight and the slightest hint of sun on the horizon combine to provide a most uncommon array of lighting over a windswept, desolate scene" (p. 92).

17.   W. Parker Snow, *Voyage of the Prince Albert in Search of Sir John Franklin* (London: 1851), 249.

18.   Charles Dickens, "Prologue to Wilkie Collins's Play 'The Frozen Deep'" [1856], *Complete Plays and Selected Poems of Charles Dickens* (London: Vision Press, 1970), 243.

     Almost as if in illustration of these prophetic lines is an anonymous watercolour in the Royal Ontario Museum's Canadiana Collection, entitled *The Fate of Sir John Franklin's Land Expedition*, which owes its details to Sir Francis McClintock's report, in his *The Voyage of the 'Fox' in Arctic Seas, a Narrative of the Discovery of the Fate of Sir John Franklin and his Companions* (London, 1860), of the finding of the skeletons of two men, two guns, a rowboat and some small articles at Point Victory, King William's Island, in 1859; it is possible that the painter of the picture, and of the two related works in the same collection, was one of the artists who accompanied McClintock on this last official Franklin search mission.

     As for Dickens' sources: by his own confession he was a "diligent and enthusiastic reader of the narratives of Polar Voyages," and an admirer of George Back's in particular, as he remarked in a July 1857 letter to Back (Royal Geographical Society, London) in which he invited him to attend a private performance of *The Frozen Deep*, to be played before the Queen. This invitation was extended at the request of Clarkson Stanfield, the marine painter, who had executed the act-drop and scenery for the London and Manchester productions of the melodrama, and whom Back had met and travelled with in Germany during his continental tour of 1830-31. "I fear," wrote Stanfield to Back on 5 July 1857, "what you saw last night gave a sorry notion of the sublime realities of those terrific scenes which <u>you</u> have so well and sympathetically described" (RGS).

19.   Dickens, "Prologue," 243.

20.   Hussey, *The Picturesque*, 255.

21.   Dr. John Richardson to George Back, 9 June 1821, quoted in J. McIlwraith, *Life of Sir John Richardson...* (London: Longmans, Green, 1868), 82-83.

       On the other hand, Richardson was enough taken with the picturesque but impractical hilltop situation of Fort Enterprise to write to his mother (McIlwraith, p. 63), "We could not have selected a more convenient or beautiful spot. The surrounding country is finely varied by hill and dale and interspersed with numerous lakes connected by small streams."

22.   One random though typical example of this transformation occurs between the original drawing for Walter William May's *Division of Sledges, Passing Lady Franklin's* — a product of the last naval armada in search of Franklin, that of 1852-54, in the incompetent command of Sir Edward Belcher — and the lithographic version published in 1855 by Day and Son, London. Not only has the lithographer heightened and sharpened the "Extraordinary Masses of Ice Pressed Against the North Shore of Bathurst Land" that were observed by May in the course of the 1853 sledge party from the *Resolute* to rescue the stranded crew of Robert McClure's *Investigator*, but the sky has acquired a foreboding storm-cloudiness not present in May's white-heightened drawing (which may itself have been from memory).

23.   Sir Alexander Mackenzie, *Voyages from Montreal on the River St. Lawrence through the Continent of North America to the Frozen and Pacific Oceans In the Years 1789 and 1793...* (1801; reprinted, Edmonton: M.G. Hurtig and Rutland, Vt.: Charles E. Tuttle, 1971), lxxxvi.

24. Robert Hood, *To the Arctic by Canoe, 1819-1821: The Journal and Paintings of Robert Hood, Midshipman with Franklin*, ed. C. Stuart Houston (Montreal and London: McGill-Queen's University Press/The Arctic Institute of North America, 1974), 115-16.

25. John Franklin, *Narrative of a Second Expedition to the Shores of the Polar Sea in the Years 1825, 1826, and 1827* (London: John Murray, 1828; reprinted, Edmonton: M.G. Hurtig, 1971), 4.

26. George Back, "A Journal of the proceedings of the Land Arctic Expedition under the command of John Franklin Esquire Captain R.M., F.R.S. &c. &c." Unpublished holograph manuscript on deposit at Scott Polar Research Institute, Cambridge, MS 395/6.

27. Edward Finden (1792-1857) was to have direct professional involvement with the greatest British painter, collaborating with his older brother, William, on a number of publications featuring engravings after pictures by Turner.

28. George Back, *Narrative of the Arctic Land Expedition to the Mouth of the Great Fish River, and Along the Shores of the Arctic Ocean in the Years 1833, 1834, and 1835* (London: John Murray, 1836; reprinted, Edmonton: M.G. Hurtig, 1970), 71-72.

29. For a more detailed register of aesthetic encounters with the Vale, see W.O. Kupsch, "A Valley View in Verdant Prose: The Clearwater Valley from Portage La Loche," *Musk-Ox* 20 (1977), 28-49.

30. The four views can probably be connected with a passage in Franklin's *Narrative of a Second Expedition* (pp. 73-74), covering the period 11-21 March 1826: "The description he [Dr. Richardson] gave of a view from an eminence nine miles behind the fort, induced Lieutenant Back and me to visit the spot, and we were amply repaid for the walk. The view embraced the mountains on the borders of the Mackenzie to the west, a considerable portion of Great Bear River, and the mountains near its rapids, Clark's Hill to the south, and the range of elevated land stretching to the east till they were lost in the distance. To the N.E. there appeared several small lakes, and the view was terminated by a portion of Bear Lake."

31. J.R. Harper, *Painting in Canada: A History* (Toronto: University of Toronto Press, 1977), 131.

TEXTUAL FIGURES

Figure 1
John Sackheouse [i.e., Sackhouse or Saccheuse] (after)
First Communication with the Natives of Prince Regents Bay...Augt 10. 1818
Aquatint and outline etching, printed in colours
Published by John Murray, London, 1819
Photo: Metropolitan Toronto Library, Canadian History Department
Note: the Metropolitan Toronto Library's copy of Ross's *Voyage of Discovery* belonged to Sir John Barrow

Figure 2
Sir John Ross (after)
Crimson Cliffs — Captain Ross, Lieutenant Parry, Saccheuse, and part of the crews, playing at foot-ball with the natives
Aquatint and outline etching, printed in colours, with watercolour, Engraved by D. Havell
Published by John Murray, London, 1819
Photo: Metropolitan Toronto Library, Canadian History Department

Figure 3
Sir John Ross
Passage through the Ice
Aquatint by R. Havell and Son, London
Printed by John Murray, London, 1819
Photo: Metropolitan Toronto Library, Canadian History Department

Figure 4
Anonymous
Winter Quarters (after W.W. May)
Hand-painted glass lantern slide
Manufactured by Smith and Back, c. 1855
Notman Photographic Archives, McCord Museum, McGill University, Montreal
Note: Of the Notman Photographic Archives' set of 112 Smith and Beck lantern slides, twelve are of the search for Franklin.

Figure 5
Walter William May (after)
H.M.S. Assistance and Pioneer in Winter Quarters. Returning Daylight
Tint-stone lithograph
Published by Day and Son, London, 1855
Note: May wrote in the letterpress for his *A Series of Fourteen Sketches...*, "This plate is intended to represent a curious effect of the power of the moonlight before the return of sun...on a clear day in the end of January."

Figure 6
Burford's Panorama of the Polar Regions — the "Investigator" Snow-walled in for the Winter
Wood-engraving
Published in *Illustrated London News*, 23 February 1850

Figure 7
W.H. Browne (after)
Noon in Mid-Winter at Point Leopold
Tint-stone lithograph by Charles Haghe
Published by Ackermann and Co., London, 1850
Photo: Metropolitan Toronto Library, Canadian History Department

Figure 8
Samuel Hearne (after)
A Winter View in the Athapuscow Lake
Engraving by J. Saunders
Published by Cadell and Davies, London, 1795
Photo: Royal Ontario Museum, Canadiana Department, Toronto.

Figure 9
Robert Hood
Trout Fall and Portage on the Trout River, Northwest Territories
1819
Watercolour on paper (25.4 x 38.6 cm)
Public Archives of Canada, Ottawa (C-15257)

Figure 10
George Back
The View from Portage la Loche... 16 July 1825
Watercolour on paper (13 x 21 cm)
Photo: Public Archives of Canada, Ottawa (C-2477)
Note: in Back's "Sketch Book - Views from Upper Canada along the
        McKenzies [sic] River to Great Bear Lake, 1825-1826"

Figure 11
George Back
*View from the Ridge of Portage la Loche, including the Clearwater River,
and the Valley...* (c. 1825-26)
Watercolour on paper (dimensions unknown)
Private Collection, England

Figure 12
George Back (after)
Vale of the Clearwater River from the Methye Portage...
Engraved by Edward Finden
Published by John Murray, London, 1828
Photo: Public Archives of Canada, Ottawa (C-94110)

Figures 13-16
George Back
Panoramic View 8 Miles from Fort Franklin 11-12 March 1826
Watercolour on paper over graphite (each: 13 x 21 cm)
Photos: Public Archives of Canada, Ottawa (C-93035 to C-93038)
Note: in Back's "Sketch Book - Views from Upper Canada along the
        McKenzies River to Great Bear Lake, 1825-1826"

FIGURE 1

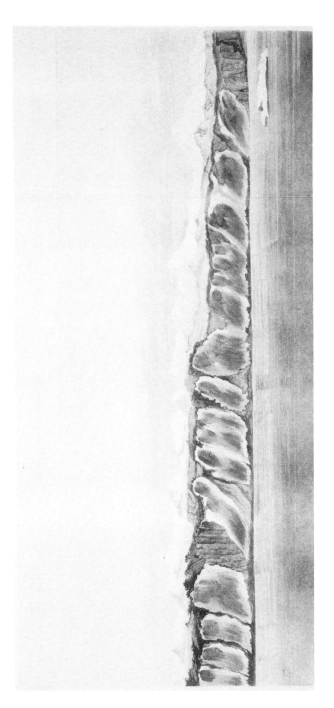

Figure 2

FIGURE 3

FIGURE 4

FIGURE 5

FIGURE 6

FIGURE 7

FIGURE 8

FIGURE 9

FIGURE 10

FIGURE 11

FIGURE 12

FIGURE 13

FIGURE 15

FIGURE 14

FIGURE 16

Chapter 8

THE PALLISER EXPEDITION

Irene M. Spry

John Palliser was the son and heir of a great Irish landowner. The family had originated in Yorkshire. The founder of the Irish branch into which the explorer was born had come to the country in 1660. He studied at Trinity College, Dublin, and became the Most Reverend Archbishop of Cashel. His descendants were among the social élite of the Protestant Ascendancy, with estates in County Tipperary, County Longford, County Waterford, and elsewhere. The explorer's grandfather, another John Palliser, was the guardian of an heiress, Anne Gledstanes, whose property, Annesgift, adjoined the Pallisers' Derryluskan estate. She married the senior John Palliser's heir, Wray Palliser. With their large family they lived, not only on their Irish estates, but in Dublin, London, and Rome.[1]

In the family tradition, young John attended Trinity College, Dublin, though only intermittently. He does not appear to have been an enthusiastic student, but he probably acquired the rudiments of a scientific education before dropping out without taking his degree. He discharged the family and social obligations proper to his class, becoming a captain in the Waterford Artillery Militia, of which regiment his father was colonel and in which he saw only a few scattered months of service (Spry, ed., *Palliser Papers*, xvi-xvii, cxxv, cxxxiii). He may have worked with the Ordinance Survey when it mapped County Waterford.[2] His dominating interests, as with most of his brothers, friends, and relatives, were travel and sport, especially big game hunting. He was also a gifted musician. The whole family travelled widely in Europe. Brothers, brothers-in-law, and close friends ventured to Australia, the China Seas (where Wray Palliser, Jr., rescued a French lady from pirates), Ceylon (now Sri Lanka), Central Africa, and the Arctic, where a brother-in-law was lost with Franklin.

Besides his exploration in what is now western Canada, John Palliser himself made extensive journeys in the United States, crossed the Panama Isthmus, voyaged among the Caribbean Islands, hunted in Spitzbergen and the Kara Sea in the Eastern Arctic, and apparently in emulation of a Scottish friend, William Fairholme, who was to marry his older sister, Grace, spent eleven months (from September 1847 to July 1848) hunting buffalo and grizzly bear in the Missouri country.[3]

This adventure fired him with a resolve to explore the prairies of British North America – and to do some more buffalo hunting, which he considered "a noble sport." The Palliser brothers had grown up in the comfortable assurance of family wealth. By mid-century, however, the family fortune was being depleted as a result of the desperate situation created by the Irish potato famine and Colonel Wray Palliser's attempts to help his tenants,[4] as well as by Frederick Palliser's unlucky coffee planting project in Ceylon,[5] which cost Col. Wray some thousands of pounds, to say nothing of the expense of John's American adventures and of other brothers' activities. Evidently the family's private fortune could not stand the strain of another North American expedition for the heir.

John Palliser secured election as a Fellow of the Royal Geographical Society (RGS) in London. To this august body he submitted a plan to explore the country along the as yet unsurveyed and unmarked international boundary between Red River (south of modern Winnipeg) to the Rocky Mountains and possible passes through the southern Rockies in British territory. He intended to get hold of a couple of half-breed guides, with whom he had travelled on the prairies of the Missouri, and to cross the plains directly from east to west, as near to the 49th parallel as possible.

There was good reason to think that a survey of this little-known border country should be undertaken. Even the Hudson's Bay Company had given up any attempt to maintain trading posts on the South Saskatchewan River after the Bow River expedition of 1822-23 and the lack of success of Peigan Post (Old Bow Fort) in the 1840s. The Americans had, in the early 1850s, mounted a series of explorations to find possible routes for transcontinental railroads, and the Russians had been exploring Siberia, but the British knew almost nothing about the country they claimed south of the North Saskatchewan, between Red River and the Rockies, and through and beyond the Rockies to the Pacific Coast along the American boundary.

The RGS was much interested in Palliser's plan but decided that a solitary journey across the plains was too limited a venture. What was needed was a scientific expedition manned by a team of experts and equipped with up-to-date instruments. The Society, therefore, enlarged the scheme and laid it before the Colonial Office with a request for £5,000 to fund it (xxi-xxiii). The under-secretary of state for the colonies was an Irish friend of Palliser's, John Ball. He managed to extract the required sum from a reluctant British Treasury, but added a further responsibility to what the expedition was instructed to do: This was to examine the old North West Company canoe route from the Head of

Lake Superior to Red River Colony, to find out whether there was any possibility that it might be developed as a means of communication between the little Colony of the United Canadas and the British prairies. Palliser knew nothing about canoeing and did not want to undertake this extra assignment, but the Colonial Office insisted that it should be carried out.[6]

The help of Sir George Simpson, North American governor of the HBC, was enlisted to give advice and to provide canoes with their crews, as well as to recruit men, carts, and horses for the expedition's overland journey west of Red River. Leading scientists were consulted about what the expedition should try to find out and about possible personnel. Sir Roderick Murchison, president of the RGS and an eminent geologist, recruited Dr. James Hector, a recent medical graduate of the University of Edinburgh, to act as geologist, naturalist, and physician to the expedition. Major-General (later Sir Edward) Sabine of the Royal Society recommended Lieutenant (later Captain) Thomas W. Blakiston, R.A., as a magnetical observer. Sir William Hooker, of the Royal Botanical Gardens at Kew, found a charming, industrious, and experienced little Frenchman, Eugéne Bourgeau, to be the botanical collector. Dr. Edward Purcell of the Royal Naval College at Greenwich nominated John W. Sullivan to be astronomical observer and secretary for the expedition.[7]

Blakiston was to bring the delicate magnetical instruments to the prairies by Hudson Bay and the "inland navigation" from York Factory to Carlton House on the North Saskatchewan, where he was to meet the other members of the expedition. They crossed the Atlantic to New York, travelling on via Niagara Falls and Detroit to a rendezvous at Sault Ste Marie with the canoes and their crews that were to take them to Red River.[8]

At Red River Settlement the party sought information and advice from old timers, such as C.F. Edward Harriott, and made preparations for their overland exploration. With the help of Chief Factor Swanston, they hired voyageurs, horses, and carts, though with considerable difficulty, as the twice-yearly buffalo hunt had already left, taking with it most able-bodied men, good horses, and carts.[9]

While the carts carrying the expedition's main supplies set off by the Carlton Trail to Fort Ellice, Palliser, with Hector, Bourgeau, and Sullivan, went south up Red River to the American boundary at Pembina. There they found an American surveyor working for a land company. With him they made observations to discover the exact position of the boundary line on the 49th parallel. They decided that earlier surveys had not been perfectly accurate and left a new marker.

Then they travelled westward along the border, with a digression to St. Joe's (now Walhalla, N. Dakota), to Turtle Mountain, noting swarms of grasshoppers and a lack of wood and water when they had ascended "Pembina Mountain," the escarpment that took them up to the Second Prairie Level or "Steppe," in Hector's alternative term. At the west end of Turtle Mountain they turned northwest to Fort Ellice on Beaver Creek near the junction of the Qu'Appelle River with the Assiniboine. Again, Palliser and Hector, guided by the famous plainsman, James McKay[10] (then in the service of the HBC), made a "branch expedition" to the southwest via Moose Mountain to La Roche Perée on the Souris River. There Hector had a geological field day, examining the coal beds and the strange rock formations.

From Fort Ellice, again with McKay as counsellor and guide, they made their way west to the South Branch of the Saskatchewan via Pile of Bones Creek, near modern Regina. They studied the connection of the headwater valley of the Qu'Appelle with the Elbow of the South Saskatchewan, now drowned in Diefenbaker Lake. Having reached the foot of the Missouri Coteau, some sixteen miles upriver from the Elbow, they were now at the eastern limit of the Third Prairie Level. From the Elbow they went northeast to Fort Carlton, where the main party was to winter, while Palliser went back to Montreal and New York in the hope of getting permission from the British Colonial Office to spend more time and more money on what was by then clearly an enormous task.

Blakiston—after a week's magnetical observing at York Factory and the difficult upriver journey—soon arrived at Carlton. He set everyone to work on his meticulous, hourly magnetical observations, but he found time to pursue notable ornithological studies as well as to do some hunting.[11]

Hector was busy with preparations for the coming season of further exploration and with geological investigations. He went to Fort Pitt and Fort Edmonton to recruit men and horses for the projected journey in 1858 through Blackfoot country and across mountain passes. He travelled on to Rocky Mountain House, where he made friends with the Blackfoot, and afterwards to the south of Edmonton, over the Beaver Hills, to find the Lac Ste Anne buffalo hunters, freemen, of whom he engaged twelve, including Gabriel Dumont, senior, uncle of Louis Riel's commander. Hector returned to Carlton by the North Saskatchewan, mapping the whole river from Rocky Mountain House to Carlton. As he travelled, he made geological, meteorological, and geographical observations.

Meanwhile Palliser had made the journey via St. Paul to Montreal and New York, returning by St. Paul and Red River in the spring to meet the rest of the expedition. He had arranged for men and horses for the 1858 season to go from Red River up to Carlton and had dealt with problems of supplies for the expedition and its accounts with Simpson at Lachine, as well as sending off another letter to the Colonial Office. His journey back down Red River to the Settlement was by canoe. He walked most of the way from Red River Settlement to Carlton, 550 miles or so, hunting as he went to help feed his men.

The united party set out again as soon as there was enough new grass for their horses. The explorers worked their way westward, via the Eagle Hills and Battle River, to the neighbourhood of modern Irricana, Alberta. There, after a splendid buffalo hunt, the party split up. Palliser and Sullivan made a quick dash to the boundary at Chief Mountain and then crossed the Rockies by the North Kananaskis Pass,[12] returning to the prairies by the North Kootenay Pass and then going northward to Edmonton. Blakiston skirted the Rockies to the entrance to the Crow's Nest Pass, which he noted but passed by, as the Indians reported it was a very bad road. He crossed the mountains by the North Kootenay Pass and came back by a route that took him into American territory to reach the South Kootenay (Boundary) Pass, by which he returned to the plains.[13] Hector and Bourgeau probed up the Bow Valley. Bourgeau stayed in the mountains to botanize, delighted to be back in alpine country, like his own Haute Savoie, after what to him were wearisome plains. Hector crossed the Rockies by the Vermilion Pass and returned by the Kicking Horse Pass, from which he found his way to Edmonton by the Bow Pass, the Mistaya Valley, and the North Saskatchewan.

At Edmonton, Blakiston left the expedition in a huff.[14] Hector made further geological and mapping explorations, first to the east and northeast of Edmonton and then along the edge of the Rockies north of the Bow Valley. After that he travelled north to the Athabasca River and the entrance to the traditional fur-trade route over the mountains, the so-called "Athabasca Portage" from the headwaters of the Athabasca to the Boat Encampment at the apex of the Big Bend of the Columbia River.

Meanwhile Palliser had been joined by two sporting friends. The three of them spent the winter hunting, examining the country around Edmonton, and making friends with the Blackfoot Indians at Rocky Mountain House.[15] One of the chiefs, Old Swan, named Palliser his grandson (409). With Mrs. Christie, the explorers gave a magnificent

Christmas ball at Edmonton House, for which Bourgeau made a splendid lustre and other decorations.[16]

When spring came, Bourgeau (to his colleagues' great regret) had to leave the expedition to keep an earlier engagement in the Caucasus. The party, already reinforced by Palliser's friends, was further strengthened by some American miners who had been delayed by the onset of winter in their journey to the gold diggings on the Fraser River. Hector and Peter Erasmus waited at Edmonton for the expedition's servant, James Beads, who had made a trip to Red River during the winter because his brother had been killed by the Sioux, and who was to bring despatches Palliser was expecting from the Colonial Office. Palliser and the rest of the party travelled southeast by Buffalo Lake to the Hand Hills. There Hector joined them to geologize on the Red Deer River. Sadly, he failed to find any dinosaur remains. The party crossed the Sand Hills, south of the Red Deer, to Bow River. Palliser made a side trip to the junction of the Red Deer with the South Saskatchewan (Bow River) at modern Empress on the Alberta-Saskatchewan border. There, he was satisfied that they were not far from the westernmost point they had reached in their first season and was confident they had achieved a fair idea of the whole spread of prairie country along the South Saskatchewan River.

Now they turned south to the Cypress Hills which they found to be a delightful oasis in the middle of the dry plains, with wood, water, and good pasture. There, they replenished their stocks of food, and their horses ate well. Sullivan made a branch trip to the boundary south of the hills. There, too, Palliser's friends left them to travel home by way of the Missouri. Hector struck off to the northwest, crossing the mountains by Howse Pass to the Columbia Valley. He could not find any practicable way from that valley across the mountains to the west of it and turned up the Columbia to rejoin Palliser.

Palliser and Sullivan had meanwhile travelled westward to the Rockies, which they crossed once more by the North Kootenay Pass to the Tobacco Plains in the Kootenay Valley, a continuation of the Columbia Valley. They struggled with the problem of finding a feasible route to the Pacific Coast from that valley. Like Hector, they were out of food. They went south through American territory, Sullivan taking the men and horses on to Fort Colville, while Palliser traversed Kootenay Lake (in British territory) by canoe to Fort Shepherd. There, he made astronomical observations to establish whether the fort was in British territory. He reported that a circle of Scotchmen, Americans, and Indians, surrounded me, anxiously awaiting my decision as to whether the diggings were in the American territory or not; strange to say the Americans were quite as much pleased at my pronouncing in favour of Her Majesty, as the Scotchmen; and the Indians began cheering for King George (478-79).

From Fort Shepherd, Sullivan made a difficult journey through British territory eastward, almost to the Tobacco Plains, while Palliser forced his way westward to Lake Osoyoos. There he met an American party of the Boundary Commission of 1857-60. He had learned from HBC officers and Lieutenant Palmer, R.E., that an all-British trail led from that point to the Pacific.

In their three seasons of work, the explorers had examined the canoe route to Red River Settlement and the route through Minnesota, as well as the river route connecting York Factory and Carlton House. They had zigzagged across the plains from Red River to the mountains, and from the American border to Athabasca River. They had traversed six passes through the southern Rockies. What kind of a report did they bring back to the Imperial Government?

The immensity of the country astonished the explorers, whose members took astronomical observations whenever possible, thereby producing the materials for the great map of 1865, which was published in the fourth of the Blue Books containing their reports. There were errors and gaps in this map, but it was a great improvement on earlier maps, and it served newcomers, such as the NWMP, until new and more accurate maps could be made, based on detailed surveys by the Geological Survey of Canada, the Dominion Land Surveyors, and the Mounties' own observations. The expedition plotted the location of such important geographical features as the North and South branches of the Saskatchewan River, Turtle Mountain, and the Cypress Hills, the latter having been earlier confused with the Porcupine Hills of modern Alberta. They had mapped the basic geographical structure of the vast stretch of country that they traversed.[17]

Besides mapping the country, the expedition described its salient features. Hector noted that there were three Prairie Levels: one at the altitude of Red River and Lake Winnipeg, one stretching from the top of Pembina Mountain to the Missouri Coteau, and one from the summit of the Coteau to the Foothills of the Rockies. The central plains thus rose in a series of three "Steppes" to the foot of the mountains (cvii-cviii, 8, 20, 104-5, 108). The expedition also described the main river systems and appraised the "capability" for agriculture and settlement of the country through which they flow.[18]

Hector described its essential geological structure. As well, he identified useful mineral resources, notably coal deposits, such as those on the Souris River and on the Red Deer and North Saskatchewan, and oil, which he called "black unctuous mud," that oozed from a round hole so deep that no one had ever found its bottom (199). This was in the Vermilion River area, to the south of the Cold Lake region of modern Alberta. He also identified clay, suitable for making bricks and pottery; rock, useful for building; salt springs; and rock salt. He was, however, unduly optimistic about rich deposits of iron ore.[19]

The explorers kept records of temperature and precipitation (and persuaded local residents to keep additional meteorological records). These records shed new light on the vexed question of whether Rupert's Land was a frozen wilderness, fit for nothing but the fur trade, or a potential Garden of Eden, only awaiting the hands of industrious husbandmen to produce a wealth of agricultural produce.

The expedition made exhaustive lists and collected specimens of the rocks, fossils, fauna and flora, and products of the country. Bourgeau alone collected ten thousand botanical specimens (ciii). Some of these may still be seen in the Royal Botanical Gardens at Kew and elsewhere. Some new species were discovered that now bear the names of Bourgeau and Blakiston. The party noted a rich variety of game, fur-bearing animals, fish, and wildfowl. The explorers saw immense herds of buffalo, but also recorded that the Indians were beginning "to apprehend scarcity of buffalo" (137).

The party met and got to know the peoples of the country. They met Governor Sir George Simpson and other HBC officers and missionaries of the Catholic, Anglican, and Methodist persuasions. They established a friendship with the redoubtable mixed-blood guide, James McKay. Earlier, on the Missouri in 1848, Palliser had met the equally redoubtable and "very intelligent half breed," James Sinclair (260). As well, they got to know the Red River voyageurs and the buffalo hunters from Lac Ste. Anne. They met a great many Indians, including the Assiniboine encountered in the Souris Valley; many Cree; Blackfoot, Blood, Peigan, and Sarcee; Mountain Stoneys; Kootenay; and Shuswap.

Besides instructing the explorers to keep detailed factual records, the Imperial Government had asked them to give their opinions on a number of contentious issues:

(1)   Whether it would be possible to establish an all-British communication between the Canadas and the prairies and between the prairies and the Pacific Coast?
They concluded that

> the unfortunate choice of an astronomical boundary line has completely isolated the Central American possessions of Great Britain from Canada in the east, and also almost debarred them from any eligible access from the Pacific coast on the west. (30)

The canoe route would

> be always too arduous and expensive a route of transport for emigrants, and never could be used for the introduction of stock, both from the broken nature of the country passed through, and also from the very small extent of available pasture. (7)

Palliser felt he could not advise any such heavy expenditure of capital as would be required to force an all-British thoroughfare through the country either by land or water. Only the discovery of mineral wealth would be likely to make this region attractive to settlers. Access through the United States was much cheaper and more convenient than a British route could be (7, 524). The ill-fated Dawson Route later fully confirmed this judgement. Even the CPR had great difficulty in pushing its line through this broken country.

Palliser thought that Canada must give up any idea of annexing Rupert's Land. It was too far away, and the obstacles to communication were too great for the little colony on the St. Lawrence to try to govern that remote and immense territory. The Imperial Government should take responsibility for it as a crown colony.[20]

Similarly, though it would be possible to build a wagon road or even a railway from the prairies to the Pacific Coast in British territory, such a project would be extremely costly. The expedition had discovered feasible passes through the Rockies to the valley of the Columbia and Kootenay rivers, but the mountains beyond—the Selkirk and Purcell ranges—presented enormous difficulties. There were easier and cheaper routes through American territory (30).

(2)   On the other hand, it would be easy to provide a means of transportation across the plains. Palliser wrote that, apart from a few creeks, "you might drive a coach and four from Fort Ellice to the Elbow" [of the South Saskatchewan].[21]

(3)   What were the capabilities of the country for agriculture and for settlement?

The expedition reported that the Great American Desert extended only a little way into British territory in a semi-arid area reaching from a base on the United States boundary some three hundred miles northward in what is now known as "Palliser's Triangle"[22] — or, if you are a botanist, as the "Xeric and Mesic Mixed Grass Prairie." In the "Triangle" good water and wood were scarce; precipitation was very limited, and many of the few lakes were alkaline. Much of the soil was either clay that baked hard in the hot sun or a sandy waste. Except in a few places, this semi-arid land was not suitable for cultivation. The problem of prairie drought in the past two years seems to bear out this judgement, as did the "Dirty Thirties," despite the splendid crops of grain that have been grown, for example, on the Regina Plains, in sufficiently wet years. Then, as the explorers pointed out, most of what precipitation fell, usually came in the growing season.

(4) Enclosing this triangle to the east, north, and west lay what Palliser (and Henry Youle Hind, of the Canadian expedition) called "The Fertile Belt." This consisted of the "Fescue Prairie" and the Aspen Parkland where bluffs of small trees provided wood and shelter. This was a region of good soil and rich pasture, eminently suited for agriculture, stock raising, and settlement. Despite intense cold, cattle and horses could graze outside all winter, needing only a little hay at the end of winter. There was plenty of natural hay, and cattle thrived on the lush grasses and vetches in the summer. On the treeless plains and on the parklands, settlers would not have to clear away dense forests before they could plough and plant crops. Trees along river banks and coulées, on the northern slopes of such eminences as Moose and Turtle Mountains, and in the adjacent forest area would provide materials for building, fencing, and fuel.

(5) The Boreal Forest, which bordered the Fertile Belt, offered not only timber resources, but also fur-bearing animals and a variety of game, from rabbits to moose and woodland caribou. Its lakes and rivers swarmed with fish and wildfowl.

(6) White settlers would certainly come into Rupert's Land to occupy the Fertile Belt. Palliser had no hesitation in expressing his

> conviction that it is impossible for the Hudson's Bay Company to provide a government to meet the exigencies of a growing colony. Indians they can govern well through the medium of the trading shop; but the interests of a commercial community, which at all events must be adverse to their own, would not be likely to prosper under their rule. (524)

In addition, there might be trouble with the Indians. Even the friendly Cree and other Indians who were accustomed to white traders, missionaries, and visitors might steal the settlers' horses, while the tribes of the Blackfoot Confederacy were likely to be hostile to strangers. The Indians should be prepared for the culture shock of white immigration. They should be educated. Palliser suggested that the funds for this purpose should be obtained from a reorganized fur trade, since the revenues accruing from that trade were *"Indian earnings"* (Palliser's emphasis).

Palliser "emphatically" denied

> incapacity and want of intellect in Indians and half breeds, or their incapacity for instruction, and a settled life - But this will not come in one day - nor be produced without an effort - Why not make an effort of the Kind? (517)

The Indians should also be prepared for the impending disappearance of the buffalo. They should be given agricultural implements and be introduced to the art of farming. The expedition had found that at least some Indians were anxious to learn how to produce a means of subsistence by cultivation (137). Moreover, "it would be a policy pregnant with no earthly good, that Indian tribes, should have no ulterior object, than that of hunting furs, for civilized communities" (515).

The expedition had also had considerable experience with the Indians' cousins of mixed white and Indian ancestry. The men who worked for the expedition were Red River Scottish and French "half-breeds" and Lac Ste Anne Métis. Hector wrote that the habits of the Métis

> differ very little from those of the natives [Indians] except that their dress is all of European manufacture. Many of the men could talk French, but all prefer to talk the Cree language. The men are generally handsome, well-made fellows, but very few of the women are even comely. They were very hospitable, and we had many feasts of the finest buffalo meat. (222)

As they travelled across the country, the explorers met freemen (Rupert's Landers who were not HBC *engagés*) and free traders. Palliser was certain that "free trade" (i.e., trade in furs carried on in defiance of the HBC claim to monopoly rights under its 1670 charter) could not be stopped, short of "extirpating" all the traders (516). Many of the freemen were people of ability and energy. Palliser mentioned the determination of the

> English and Scotch half-breeds in carrying out what they once undertake; and there is little doubt, if their energies were only rightly directed in pursuit of agriculture, commerce, and trade, they would progress as rapidly as any Anglo-Saxon communities.

He went on to observe:

> There is a very remarkable difference between the Scotch half-breed and the Canadian or French half-breed; the former is essentially Scotch, he trades, speculates, works, reads, inquires after and endeavours to obtain the information, and to profit by the advance of civilization in the old country as well as he can. Should his mother or his wife be Indian women, he is kind to them, but they are not his companions.

On the other hand:

> The Canadian or French half-breed, probably on account of an indolent disposition, allied to sociable habits, becomes more and more Indian. If he has energy he is a hunter, and able to beat the Indian in every department of hunting, tracking, running and shooting. But there his energy ends, his sympathies are all towards his Indian mother, squaw, and especially his (*belle-mère*) mother-in-law. (169)

The excuse given by the expedition's old hunter, Paul Cahen, for refusing to go into Blackfoot territory, was that his *belle-mère* had forbidden him to do so (409).

Palliser was impressed not only with the importance and influence of the Métis *belle-mère* but also with that of Indian women. In the great Blackfoot ceremonial, it was the woman chosen by the other women in camp as the most virtuous who selected the tree that was to be the centrepiece of the sacred medicine lodge (244). Palliser also reported that Indian women encountered near the site of modern Regina expressed surprise that the explorers' wives were not with them (139). No doubt their surprise was occasioned by the problem of how they could manage without women, whose role was essential to survival. Hector wrote that when his party, worn out by struggling through the Kicking Horse Pass, arrived at a Stoney Indian camp on the east side of the Rockies,

> the squaws took the whole management of our affairs, - unpacked the horses, put up the tent, lined it beautifully with pine foliage, lighted a fire, and cut wood into most conveniently sized billets,

and piled them up ready to hand. They then set about cooking us all sorts of Indian delicacies, - moose nose and entrails, boiled blood and roast kidneys, &c. (314)

The expedition made a rough census of the numbers of Indians and Métis they had met in those parts of the country in which they had travelled, and Hector compiled rudimentary vocabularies of four Indian languages.[23] Later, with one of Palliser's friends at the British Museum, W.S.W. Vaux, he prepared a paper about the Indians of western British North America, which they presented in 1860 at a meeting of the Ethnological Society of London, England.[24]

A most important asset of the expedition was that its members had no axes to grind in making their observations of Rupert's Land and in writing their report about it.[25] They had, of course, their personal biases, but they were not seeking to make a profit from the resources of the country, either by trading in furs or prospecting for gold. Nor were they trying to make converts to a particular denomination. They attempted, at least, to record objectively what they saw. They carefully described the country's fauna and flora; its topograhy, geology, soils, and climate; its inhabitants and resources. They were essentially detached observers trying to discover with scientific accuracy such facts about Rupert's Land and possible access to it as might be identified in a quick, three-season survey of that immense domain. Even the help and hospitality given to them by Simpson and other HBC officers does not seem to have swayed their judgement unduly as to the possible future role of the Company.[26]

Their findings were extraordinarily perceptive and shrewd. Their descriptions of landscapes are most vivid. To this day one may come over the edge of their "Grand Coulée" (near Unity, Saskatchewan) and see precisely the scene described in the *Report*,[27] or over the rim of the valley of Battle Creek, flowing through the Cypress Hills, and there see exactly that lovely oasis, where there was wood, water, and pasture for a party worn out with long travel on desolate, arid plains (421).

Another asset the explorers enjoyed was their zest for discovery, travel, sport, and adventure. Hector proved himself to be such a hardy traveller that he became almost a legendary figure in a country of tough travellers.[28] His journeys were exciting as well as strenuous. He waded a river when it was so cold that the men's clothes froze solid,[29] he got lost in a snow storm (387-88), and he was kicked by his horse after he had helped to haul a packhorse out of a river. He was given up for dead. His men were sadly burying him when — still unable to speak — he managed to wink! This was the origin of the modern name of Kicking Horse Pass.[30]

Little Bourgeau was so fascinated by plants and excited by new specimens that he inspired not only his colleagues, but also the voyageurs in the party, with his dedicated interest in the flora of the plains and mountains. Discovery of a new plant was for him an adventure (xxvii-xxviii).

Sullivan — when not engaged in mathematical calculations or in quarrelling with Blakiston — had his testing moments, too. Taking the horses to Fort Colville, while Palliser made a canoe trip through Lake Kootenay, he and his men ran out of food (479). While trying to effect a connection north of the 49th parallel between Fort Shepherd and the junction of the Kananaskis Pass and the Kootenay Valley, he had to send back the horses, which could not force a way through the fallen timber, and continue on foot with a volunteer companion, Mr. Margary of the HBC service. They carried all their equipment and camping gear on their backs (481-82).

Even Blakiston, an exceedingly correct military man, gave way to excitement on occasion:

> We were now on the watershed of the mountains, the great axis of America; a few steps farther and I gave a loud shout as I caught the first glimpse in a deep valley, as it were at my feet, of a feeder of the Pacific Ocean. It was the Flathead River, a tributary of the Columbia. At the same moment the shots of my men's guns echoing among the rocks announced the passage of the first white man over the Kootanie Pass. (566)

To Palliser, the expedition was not only a matter of serious exploration but also (as he wrote of his two sporting friends) a journey "in search of adventure and heavy game" (lxxxvi). He certainly had his adventures. Apart from running buffalo and shooting grizzly bears, he had to cope with mutinous voyageurs, who refused to travel into Blackfoot country, and with "troublesome" young "scarmps" among the Indians in that territory.[31] They were intent on stealing the expedition's horses and on killing their hunter, Nimrod, who was a Mountain Stoney, and so a tribal enemy (402, 420-21). These adventures, the sport, the travel in wild country — all added up to enjoyment for Palliser. As a niece was to write many years later, the months he spent in the wilds of Rupert's Land were among the happiest of his life.[32]

Notes

1. For the sources of data concerning Palliser's family and friends, and social and educational background, see Irene M. Spry, ed., *The Papers of the Palliser Expedition* (Toronto: Champlain Society, 1968, xv-xx). Evidence for most of the statements made in this paper is to be found in this Champlain Society volume, hereafter cited as Spry, ed., *Palliser Papers*. Subsequent page references to this volume are given in parentheses in the text.

2. Local tradition has it that he did so. Though there seems to be no mention of him in the relevant file in the PRO, Kew, England, it does contain a letter that appears to be in Palliser's rather distinctive hand-writing.

3. John Palliser, *Solitary Rambles and Adventures of a Hunter in the Prairies* (London: John Murray, 1853 and subsequent editions, including a reprint, Edmonton: Hurtig, 1969); for Palliser's Arctic voyages see Irene M. Spry, "The Pallisers' Voyage to the Kara Sea, 1869," *The Musk-Ox*, 26 (1980), 13-20.

4. Oral communication by the son of one of those tenants. The County Longford property had to be sold and the entail on the other estates broken to allow them to be mortgaged (cxxxviii).

5. Frederick Palliser's correspondence while he was in Ceylon (now Sri Lanka) in the possession of a granddaughter, Mrs. Anne Gelius of Copenhagen. Copies in the author's possession.

6. Spry, ed., *Palliser Papers*, xxiii-xxv and intermittently thereafter.

7. For preparations for the expedition and its personnel see *ibid.*, xxiv-xli and lvii and Appendix 11.

8. For the explorers' journeys see the expedition's daily journal reprinted from the *Report* of 1863 in Spry, ed., *Palliser Papers*.

9. For the explorers' sojourn in Red River Settlement see, Spry, ed., *Palliser Papers*, 85-94.

10. For a biography of James McKay see Allan Turner, *DCB*, Vol. X, 473-75, and N. Jaye Goossen, "'A wearer of mocassins:' The Honourable James McKay of Deer Lodge," *The Beaver* (Autumn 1978): 44-53.

11. See Spry, ed., *Palliser Papers*, Appendix V.

12. For an illustrated discussion of which of the Kananaskis Passes he traversed, see Irene M. Spry, "Prairies and Passes: Retracing the Route of Palliser's British North American Exploring Expedition 1857-1860," *Journal of the Royal Society for the Encouragement of Arts, Manufactures and Commerce*, September 1965, 807-27.

13. Spry, ed., *Palliser Papers*, Appendix V.

14. For Blakiston's quarrel with Sullivan and Palliser see Spry, ed., *Palliser Papers*, lxxii-lxxv and lxxx-lxxi.

15. These friends were Captain Arthur Brisco, late of the 11th Hussars, and William Roland Mitchell, who wrote voluminous letters describing this adventure. Copies of these letters are to be found in the Regina holdings of the Saskatchewan Archives Board (SAB(R)). Another set is in the author's possession. The originals are in the possession of the Mitchell family in Dorset, England. See also Spry, ed., *Palliser Papers*, lxxxv-lxxxvi, 502, and 603.

16. Spry, ed., *Palliser Papers*, lxxxviii and Charles Gay, "Le Capitaine Palliser et l'Exploration des Montagnes Rocheuses, 1857-1859," *Le Tour du Monde*, 1861, 290.

17. For an analysis of this aspect of the expedition's work see Spry, ed., *Palliser Papers*, xcvi-ci.

18. Spry, ed., *Palliser Papers*, 14-19 and the daily journal.

19. Hector's geological observations are scattered through the journal (see Spry, ed., *Palliser Papers*) and consolidated in his Geological Report in the 1863 *Report*, 210-45. A series of drawings of geological sections is included in the fourth Blue Book of 1865. For Hector's other publications on the structure and geology of the country see the *Palliser Papers*, 617. For a comment on resources of iron ore see, for example, 17.

20. Spry, ed., *Palliser Papers*, 30-31 and Appendix III.

21. Spry, ed., *Palliser Papers*, 524 and Palliser to Sir William Hooker from Lachine, December 11, 1857, in Royal Botanical Gardens, Archives, W.J.H., N. American Letters, 1851-58, LXIV, item 330, cited in Spry, ed., *Palliser Papers*, cxxi.

22. See Spry, ed., *Palliser Papers*, cviii-cxv, cxxxiii, 9, 18-19, and 255.

23. Hector's report on "Indian Tribes and Vocabularies" in the expedition's 1863 *Report*, 199-215. The vocabularies include those of the Gros Ventres, Sarcee, Mountain Stoneys, and Blackfoot.

24. James Hector and W.S.W. Vaux, "Notice of the Indians Seen by the Exploring Expedition under the Command of Captain Palliser," *Transactions* of the Ethnological Society of London, Vol. I, 245-61.

25. John Ball had stressed the importance of this detachment (x)i and 501), and Palliser had mentioned it in his confidential despatch (519).

26. See, especially, Palliser's confidential despatch in Appendix III of the *Palliser Papers*.

27. Spry, ed., *Palliser Papers*, 237 and especially footnote 7 on this and the following page.

28. Peter Erasmus, *Buffalo Days and Nights*, Irene M. Spry, ed. (Calgary: Glenbow-Alberta Institute, 1976), 73.

29. Spry, ed., *Palliser Papers*, 368-69, and Erasmus, *Buffalo Days and Nights*, 92-93.

30. Spry, ed., *Palliser Papers*, 309, especially footnote 1.

31. These twin problems are described in the expedition's journal for June and July of 1859.

32. Letters from Miss Caroline Fairholme, Palliser's heir, to H.S. Patterson, Q.C., in the possession of his son, Judge Patterson, Calgary.

Chapter 9

THE CHURCH IN THE NORTH

Fred Crabb

The Historical Evidence

The first recorded meeting of the Church and Rupert's Land took place long before the name "Rupert's Land" was given to that part of the continent that drained into Hudson Bay. In 1577, on his second journey in search of the Northwest Passage to the Indies, Martin Frobisher stopped at a bay that would later bear his name on Baffin Island, near the entrance to a huge bay to which Henry Hudson would give both his name and his bones. There, on land, his chaplain solemnly celebrated the Holy Communion according to the rites of the Church of England, "there being present also certain natives of the area."[1] It is generally conceded that this is the earliest record of an Anglican — and possibly Christian — service on the shores of North America.

However, nothing further came of this brush between the Church and these unknown and unnamed territories, although not for the lack of will and motivation, as the narrative of Dionise Settle, a member of Frobisher's expedition, reveals in the entry for July 20, 1577. Speaking of this event and its immediate purpose, Settle wrote "that by our Christian study and endeavour these barbarous people, trained up in paganry and infidelity, might be reduced to the knowledge of true religion, and to the hope of salvation in Christ our Redeemer."[2] That expression of purpose and motivation in 1577 should be borne in mind, for it was the same purpose and motivation that moved the Church in Europe, and, more than two centuries later, in Upper and Lower Canada. In 1827 the Rev. John West, chaplain to the Hudson's Bay Company and the Selkirk settlers, writes of his mandate, which includes "to seek the instruction and seek to ameliorate conditions of the Native Indians."[3] Notwithstanding advice or criticism from sources today, this remained the driving motivation of most of those hardy men and women who left the comforts of home to serve the people of this new and mysterious Canadian frontier.

There is some evidence in the Hudson's Bay Company's records that chaplains for Company staff were in place by 1683.[4] If so, then their efforts, although confined to the staff, would have reached numerous native people in the Company's employ. The next firm evidence of this mandate being served, however, does not appear until the early decades of the nineteenth century.

Meanwhile, two events of first importance took place:

1. The Charter of 1670 and the territorial authority bestowed by it on the Trading Company commonly known as the Hudson's Bay Company.
2. The arrival of the first Scottish settlers under the 5th Earl of Selkirk at York Factory, September 24, 1811.

A third less noted but perhaps not less notable event was the penetration of the Roman Catholic missionaries from New France to the area of Hudson Bay and Lake of the Woods around 1660. However, New France was on the decline and Old France had no stomach for ventures of this kind. Not until 1820 did the Holy See establish the Vicariate Apostolic of the Northwest, under Bishop Norbert Provencer, at Saint Boniface on the Red River, with vicariate jurisdiction over the whole of western British North America to the Pacific and Arctic oceans. This Bishop Provencer petitioned New France and Old France for missionaries; the French, under the Oblates of Mary Immaculate (O.M.I.), responded about 1844, together with the Grey Nuns, now with a Mother House in Montreal.[5] Their combined labours and zeal founded a series of missions — together with the inevitable schools — across the prairies and west and north down the Mackenzie Valley. It is estimated that perhaps ninety percent of the Indians along the Mackenzie today are adherents of the Roman Catholic Church.[6] Of the many names of Roman Catholic missionaries that grace the pages of the history of Western Canada, none is better known than that of Albert Lacombe, himself half Indian. And a string of place names across this territory attests the influence of members of O.M.I. In northern Alberta alone, for example, the villages of Breynat, Grouard, St. Albert, and Lacombe all bear the mark of the Oblates of Mary Immaculate. As we shall note, the four main Christian Churches first to penetrate this "Great Lone Land" — as it was referred to in Britain — were the Roman Catholic, the Anglican, the Methodist, and the Presbyterian. All except the Roman Catholic began their work after 1820, and all began or established administrative roots in the area of modern Winnipeg. Bishop William Bompas, first Anglican Bishop of Athabasca, wrote in his journal around 1870 that the Hudson's Bay Company was the "true handmaid of the gospel," and noted further that the Company was indeed the first church agent, and that the Bay posts were the sites of most of the early Christian congregations and schools.[7]

Although records are limited, we must suppose that the staunch agents of the Hudson's Bay Company—most of them God-fearing Presbyterians with orders to serve the native peoples and consciences that would impel this service—had considerable influence on the native peoples with whom they traded, many of whom came to settle at the trading posts, and with many of whom they had faithful conjugal relationships. The fruits of such relationships often remained at the trading posts after the fathers returned to the Old Country, forming a substantial sub-culture and bearing such names as Louis Riel and Gabriel Dumont. Perhaps the most important agency for the spread of the Christian gospel in the Northwest was the existence of this Métis group, and many of the church's own leaders sprung from its midst. A remaining tragedy is that this widespread sub-culture of half breeds never found a true identity in either of the cultures it shared, and to this day are a people largely in suspension.

Lord Selkirk had promised chaplains and school teachers to his settlers—largely Presbyterian like himself—and had deeded land at the confluence of the Red and Assiniboine rivers for a church and school. As fate would have it, when the Company applied to England for a chaplain to its staff and for the settlers, it was an Anglican, the Rev. John West, who came. He first settled at York Factory at the mouth of the Nelson River where from the start he worked with the "heathen" (not necessarily a perjorative word then, but descriptive of anyone to whom the Christian gospel was unknown) as well as with the whites. In fact, it is important here to point out that John West was a member of a newly-formed British missionary society—the Church Missionary Society—whose commitment was exclusively to the preachings of the gospel to the heathen, not to chaplaincy work with expatriate Christians. Like the Roman Catholic O.M.I., here lay their mission.

John West immediately established a school, and among his first pupils were the Crees Henry Budd and James and John Hope, who, with others, were destined to become missionaries to their own people. Budd was the first Indian to be ordained to the Anglican priesthood, and he set a pattern for many others who followed.[8] A notable lay Indian missionary at this time was Chief Pegwys. The almost spectacular advance of Christian missionary work from this point rests largely on the existence and quality of native Christian leadership.

John West also sowed the seeds of residential schools by bringing a few young men and women into Selkirk for residential training. Because of the current controversy over residential schools, we shall return to this subject. This same clergyman established a multi-racial local congregation and school where Lord Selkirk had set aside land for the purpose. West called the congregation St. John's (precursor of the present Anglican Cathedral of St. Johns in Winnipeg), and the school St. John's (precursor of the now famous St. John's Schools and of St. John's College, Winnipeg, itself the forerunner of the University of Manitoba).

Of the four church denominations to work in Rupert's Land and beyond, the Methodists arrived last. In 1840 the HBC agreed to support three Methodist missionaries as chaplains to the Company and as missionaries to the Indians. Robert Rundle (Rundle Mountain) is perhaps the best known. Another was the Rev. James Evans, who was appointed superintendant at the same time and who invented the syllabic script that became the foundation tool for committing Canadian native languages to writing; that was used by the first Anglican Bishop John Horden of Moosonee in preparing a Cree grammar still used today; and that enabled Anglican James Peck to reduce the language of Baffin Island Inuit to writing. Other Methodists include the McDougalls, George (1854) and son John, to whom the Stoney Indians of Alberta owe their Christian conversion and an abiding allegiance.

As I have noted, the Roman Catholic missionary work expanded strongly to the northwest and down the Mackenzie Valley. Anglican work was more evident in the Hudson Bay area, and later particularly in the High Arctic among the Inuit, of whom about eighty percent are Anglicans. As European settlements increased, and while adherents of churches grew especially in the South, native membership in white areas decreased. Apart from Morley (Stoney Indians), where Methodism (now United Church) retained its hold, non-episcopal missions declined among native communities; they were unknown among the Inuit until recent years, when Pentecostal missions opened.

It is necessary here to point out that the church's impact on Western Canada is probably much more significant in its influence on the continually growing immigrants than on the aboriginal people, particularly across the prairies. A record from the 1850s suggests that by this time over fifty separate national representatives could be identified in the population that poured through the Red River Settlement, and adds that most of them brought their own brand of Christian institution.[9] We are still familiar with the multiplicity of church buildings, representing competing church allegiances, in any prairie town.

Notwithstanding this diversity, the West became a deeply religious community (or tangle of communities), and Christian faith and dogma and ethics have had a profound effect on how this land has developed, though this took place mostly after 1870. The story of this development has yet to be written. But it is perhaps titillating to reflect, for example, on the political and economic influence of such hard-line churchmen as Aberhart and Manning in Alberta and Tommy Douglas and Stanley Knowles (both ordained ministers) as founding fathers of the Co-operative Commonwealth Federation, now the New Democratic Party; or reflect on the influence of deeply sincere Christian lay people, represented by Irene Parlby (1868-1965) of Alix, Alberta, a leader for women's rights, agricultural reform, education, and public health, and the first Canadian woman to become a Cabinet Minister.[10] A lifelong devout Anglican layperson, she, at least, had no doubt about the source and inspiration of her work. And there are a host of others, many of them women. Although this story is still to be told, reference to such Christian influence must not go unremarked even in this short essay.

It would seem fair to conclude from this brief survey that the evidence of history points to the fact that people, not institutions, exerted the impact and set the directions that would shape the quality of life for the mixed peoples of Rupert's Land. Many of these had precise church affiliations; some were Christian converts from the aboriginal tribes. To attempt to list them would be both invidious and out of place in an essay such as this. But it is a fair judgement that, in order to trace the events and to estimate and evaluate (as we must attempt) the motivation and achievements of the church in Rupert's Land, we must study people rather than institutions.

Schools

The driving motivation of the early missionaries, whatever their church affiliations, was to convert the "heathen", "pagan", "savage" – all these appellations were used – native peoples to Christ. They were perhaps more successful initially than they were in the long run.[11] Indian and later Inuit Christian congregations were established everywhere, and to this day most of Canada's western aboriginal peoples claim membership of a Christian church.

The second motivation was the desire and intention to bring the native peoples of Western Canada as soon as possible into a partnership that would allow them to benefit fully from European culture, values, and knowledge. This ambition was founded on imperialist Europe's apparently unassailable confidence in its own traditions and institutions, and on a compulsive drive to share this "Divine" treasure with others, particularly the "pagan" peoples they subjugated – the self-styled "white man's Burden". The churches and missionaries by and large shared this mind set. In Rupert's Land, as in Africa and wherever else the sun of Empire rose, they felt the compulsion not only to convert the "heathen" to Christ, but to bring them, by all means and as quickly as possible, into the white man's concept of the kingdom of heaven – the European way of life. We may today assess the whole approach as arrogant, mistaken, and injurious; we may not question the sincerity and motives of those who worked within the system.

The tool most generally and effectively used was education through schools, and although the Hudson's Bay Company, and, subsequently, governments espoused the idea and the objectives of schools, the missionaries were initially responsible for establishing them, staffing them, and for setting up the curricula and style. The residential schools, especially, were conscious copies of the so-called "Public School" system of the Old Country.

Allow me to illustrate from examples of early Anglican work with education, although similar examples can be given from Methodist and, especially, Roman Catholic missionary work. Mention has already been made of John West's work in establishing schools alongside congregations. In 1844 the English Church appointed a Scot, David Anderson, the first Anglican Bishop of Rupert's Land, with his seat at St. John's on the Red River, and his territory all that was encompassed by the term "Rupert's Land."[12] Anderson established an academy that he called St. John's College, and under his successor, Robert Machray, that academy became the foundation institution for the University of Manitoba after Confederation. St. John's College remains a federated Arts and Theology College of the University of Manitoba.

Bishop (later Archbishop) Robert Machray became the first Metropolitan of Rupert's Land, with other bishops sharing diocesan jurisdiction under his presidency, and later still the first Primate of the Anglican Church of Canada. Robert Machray made it a linchpin of his work that every Anglican parish had also a school.

When the Hudson's Bay Company surrendered jurisdictional power to government in 1870 and government took an increasing interest in education, the churches continued to play a major part at all levels. For example, the government of Manitoba appointed the Anglican Bishop Machray to the post of Chairman of the Board of School Management, a position he occupied with distinction to his death in 1904. Similarly, upon the foundation of the Provincial University of Manitoba in 1877, not only did St. John's College remain as a full liberal arts college, but Archbishop Machray was appointed Chancellor, also until his death.

Mention should be made of school curricula, as modern critics of the church's school system in these years often attack its relevance to the needs of the people. Certainly a strong emphasis fell on the English language and on skills and custom that would assist native peoples to adjust to the dominant white culture. But this emphasis must be seen against the conviction that to survive in the new white world, native peoples must be assisted to come quickly to terms with the white man's society. Persuasion to hasten this process, not least in the residential schools, may seem to modern minds to have been cruel, unnatural and barbarous; nonetheless, the same methods were used back home in the Public School system. Nothing was racist about the system. The aim was to fashion out of these aboriginal peoples men, women and children who could take their places as soon as possible in the white cultural system.

There is abundant evidence that the curricula also included such relevant subjects as health and, in particular, agriculture. The missionaries were the pioneers of health services throughout the region, and the schools provided essential training in agricultural pursuits. Bishop Bompas's far northern work at Old Crow and Coppermine, for example, made practical agriculture an important element in the curriculum. John McLean, first Anglican Bishop of Saskatchewan (at that time, "Saskatchewan" included territory that would later become the provinces of Saskatchewan and Alberta), established a school in Prince Albert in 1879 that taught the three "R"s, theology and agriculture. In 1883 McLean was granted a charter by the Dominion Parliament establishing his Prince Albert school as "The University of Saskatchewan." When, at the beginning of the twentieth century, the fledgling Province of Saskatchewan decided to set up its own provincial university at Saskatoon, the old dominion university in Prince Albert surrendered to the new provincial university its title and its right to give general education and to award degrees. At the same time, the Dominion Parliament granted charter to the old dominion university to continue as the "University of Emmanuel College," with degree-granting powers in religion, and with the governor general of Canada as perpetual "Visitor." Also at the same time, the church college transferred to the campus of the new provincially administered University of Saskatchewan at Saskatoon, thus becoming the first of the federated colleges of that university. Significantly, the University of Saskatchewan retained agriculture as its primary faculty.[13]

One other example might be given as supporting evidence: the Rev. John Gough Brick, first Anglican missionary to the Beaver at Dunvegan, carried out a successful campaign for a farming colonization of the Peace Country at Shaftesbury, where he later continued his mission work. The first to demonstrate that wheat could be grown in this northern latitude, Brick won awards for his wheat (precursor of the famous No. One Northern) in American farm shows. A national historical plaque to his achievements graces the walls of the Federal Building in the town of Peace River.

Passing reference has been made to the residential schools, of which there were over seventy across Canada by the 1920s, most of them in the present Ecclesiastical Province of Rupert's Land, materially the same territory as that ceded to the Hudson's Bay Company in 1670. These began with a handful of students, both male and female, generally on the site of a trading post, where there was already a nucleus of more or less residential people. But the itinerant tradition of native peoples made any serious attempt at education impossible. The residential school system, however, did establish the school population and provided for the largely orphan or semi-orphan population of abandoned children of mixed parentage.

The fruits of these schools in terms of their effects on the growth of Christianity and the Christian churches, and to native Christian leadership, are a large part of the story of Rupert's Land through the second half of the nineteenth century and the first half of the twentieth. For example, by 1864 there were thirty-two Anglican clergy in the territory, of whom eight were Indian or Métis, and two of them were Archdeacons. In 1870 the prestigious parish of St. Andrews on the Red was in the charge of a full-blood Saulteaux Indian, Henry Cochrane, who later established the church in Portage la Prairie, and who along with his followers, became a pioneer farmer in the area.

Such events and developments illustrate some of the achievements of education, notably through residential schools. However, numerous recent attacks on both the system and the people who planned and managed it demand that these achievements be reassessed.

The Modern Assessment

In the light of present day conditions among western Canadian native peoples, penetrating and often harsh questions are being asked, both about the motives of the churches and of their policies and practices especially in the area of education. Some anthropologists have accused the churches in particular of cultural genocide.

When the psychology of defeatism began to overcome western Canadian aboriginals is not clear; what caused it is debated and debatable. Some anthropologists and social historians trace the seeds of this decline to the cumulative erosion of traditional cultural values and practices, and they blame the churches for this erosion by their almost total rejection of native religious and social values and by their insistence on conversion into not only the Gospel, but into the whole alien cultural package of European Christendom. Charles Hendry, former Director of the School of Social Work, University of Toronto, claims that missionaries played a Jekyll and Hyde role: "On the one hand they smashed native culture: on the other hand they picked up the pieces of an indigenous way of life which had been smashed by other Europeans." Hendry concludes: "Missionaries have been both a disruptive and an integrative force."[14] It seems no one reminded the missionary of the words of the great Pope Gregory to the monk Augustine, charged to convert the English to Christianity in 597 A.D., to "take the customs of the people, and baptise them into Christ."[15]

A close examination of some of the original writings and records of the early missionaries to Rupert's Land provides insight into their motivations, and clearly their motives, as much as their methods, are assailed today. Without doubt, these varied from person to person, as would be expected in a primitive and immense land where most achievements were by individual effort.

Several of these motives are revealed by common threads that run through the records. Basic to them all is a compelling conviction in everyone's need for the saving grace of the gospel of Jesus Christ, with a driving compulsion to go and tell. Of equal centrality is a genuine and loving concern for the people to whom they went, and a readiness to give up everything else to their missions. A silent witness to the measure of one such sacrifice by the Rev. Arthur Garrioch and his wife is a lonely grave marker in a thick grove of poplar on the banks of the Peace River where the Dunvegan Bridge crosses. There lie human remains of their only child, dead at nine months old. Another unifying thread is a readiness — often transformed into action — to defend their people against the predatory advances of other white people. The records also reveal a naive, almost triumphal, belief in the power of the gospel and of its western cultural context (the western way of life) to raise up the people from heathen darkness and sin. Confidence in a European model of education as a sure way to achieve this is unquestioned. It has been said that the Hudson's Bay Company's absolute rule of behaviour was "autocratic and benevolent".[16] So, by and large, was that of the missionaries, even though Sir Alexander Mackenzie once severely criticized missionaries for not exercising this attitude.[17]

In common with the HBC bosses and government authorities in Britain (and, after 1867, in Ottawa and then in the individual provinces), the church leaders faced the decision as to how the native people could best be helped to grow to share the life of the white invaders. Only two options seemed possible: either integration as soon as possible into the dominant white culture, or some form of separate development—in effect, apartheid. A third option hinted at today simply did not exist, and it does not today—complete isolation, or "self-determination."

Only the first option was seen to be viable and useful; the educational system—including the now decried immersion policy of permitting only English to be spoken in residential schools on pain of corporal punishment—was designed and geared to this end. The overriding objective was to educate the Indian to be at home in and to function fully in the white man's world. That such an objective has not been met, except in some few cases, is the real judgement on a policy that was sincere and altruistic, but that failed to understand the power and significance of tradition and culture, the human need for self-expression, and the necessity of selfhood. With notable exception—for example, Bishop Bompas—little consideration was given to native cultural values and customs. Hindsight now enables us to see that the very policies designed to give native peoples a real place in the white man's world served instead to rob them of a place in their own world.

In due course, governments fumbled toward a partial reversal of earlier policies by establishing reservations, essentially modified forms of modern South Africa Homelands. Today, few see this as having reversed anything substantially, and this consensus is even stronger among native groups.

Some advocate a return to "primitivism," the third option mentioned above—a radical turning back the clock to the days before the whites came. Even if such a plan were viable, few native peoples would opt for it. Here and there experiments along this line have been made, such as the attempt by Chief Robert Small Boy and some members of his Hobbema Band in central Alberta.

Some modern idealists have tried to paint a picture of idyllic harmony and beauty before the arrival of the depredating white man—the "gentle Savage" syndrome of Negley Farson. Little we can read substantiates this myth; illustrations to the contrary are profuse. In his autobiography, Bishop William Bompas refers at length to the records of a journey made over the same territory as his own journey by a

Hudson's Bay Company agent, Samuel Hearne, more than one hundred years earlier to the Coppermine people. Hearne, in his journal, writes of his distress and frustration at being unable to prevent his travelling companions, mainly Chipewyans, from massacring a whole family of Coppermine Inuit, apparently for no other reason that that they were different; that is, they spoke a different language. Just over one hundred years later Bishop William Bompas tells of the Coppermine Inuit's readiness to receive the gospel because of the changes it had made in the Chipewyan on their southern border, who no longer regarded the Inuit as prey to be slaughtered. Bombas's autobiography *Diocese of Mackenzie River* (1888) is a fund of carefully collected material about developments from about 1775 to 1875. He speaks highly of the influence of Company factors and agents, traces the growth of Christian congregations, and chronicles the tragic decrease in native population, brought about through the abuse of firearms and alcohol, but mainly resulting from contact with European diseases to which they had no immunity—diphtheria, measles, even the common cold, and smallpox. (In 1781 nine out of ten Chipewyans died by small-pox.)[18]

A major frustration and confusion that native people came up against in the missionary credo was that, although fighting with neighbours was a sin and love for all was the Christian virtue, the missionaries taught bitter opposition to, even hatred for, other creeds and even other missionaries. The seeds of European Christian division were avidly sown and nurtured in the Canadian West; nor was there any voice to say—as have native Christian leaders in India—"We need the gospel: we don't want your past wars." Edmund Morris, best known for his painting of Blackfoot people, wrote of the evils brought to native people by the divisions among white Christians who carried the gospel, and when he compared the spiritual values and practices of the "pagan" Indians to those introduced by the missionaries, the latter were put in a poor light.[19] A modern United Church historian comments of his own ecclesiastical antecedents: "Methodists did not quite say, 'we must save the prairies for God and the Methodist Church, or the devil (and the Presbyterians and the Anglicans and the Baptists) will get there first,' but...."[20]

It seems reasonable to conclude, then, that the main failure of the missionaries (as of white society in general) lies in the failure to recognize the value of the traditional beliefs and life styles of native people, and to accommodate these to the gospel or the gospel to these. One notable consequence of this failure is that Western Canada has nowhere a truly indigenous Church, although here and there, particularly in northen

British Columbia, encouraging signs can be found.[21]   Another consequence is to be seen in the tragic mark of a people robbed of their old traditions and frozen in limbo between the old way of life and the new European way.

For these reasons, if society is to profit from the mistakes of history, we must realize that the way to restoration and restitution is not the perpetration of the patronage/tutelage syndrome (which, it seems, continues to be the attitude of many white do-gooders, in and out of the church) but the provision of assistance, space, and support as it is requested. Only in this way will native peoples be free to take their own action, at their own pace, in accordance with their own wisdom — either to rediscover and re-embrace past tribal values and customs or to seek their own way towards accommodation to the dominant white culture.

In the past decade or so, the churches have consciously tried to follow this direction, from the World Council of Churches to local Christian communities as they seek to support, for example, Haida on Lyell Island, Crees of the Lubicon Band in northern Alberta, or Dogrib in the Mackenzie Valley. The conscious motive is to assist native peoples to find the time and space to work at their own solutions. Nor should it be overlooked in what has become the popular sport of denigrating churches that just as Father Albert Lacombe helped both white and Indian to hammer out treaties with the white government in the nineteenth century — something he achieved because both sides trusted him (the poor man cannot have rested well in his grave in light of subsequent white betrayal of those treaty conditions!) — so in recent days the Indians and Inuit of the Far North have demanded the active presence there of the Anglican and Roman Catholic Bishops as a guarantee of the integrity of their political referenda.

Mistakes there have been — bad mistakes and plenty of them. Many have arisen from racial arrogance and greed. But where the church is at fault, it is the contention of this paper that the errors have been more in method than in motivation.

If all sides can learn the lessons of these mistakes and take adequate and intelligent steps to redress them, then there is hope that what began three hundred years ago in this "Great Lone Land" of Rupert's Land as a partnership of races, old and new, and so sadly degenerated to first and second class citizens, will emerge into a land, a sizeable part of Canada, where all peoples and races are equal in law and tradition, in opportunity and self-determination, as they are equal in the sight of God.

Notes

1. Thomas Charles B. Boon, *The Anglican Church from the Bay to the Rockies* (Toronto: Ryerson Press, 1962).

2. Quoted in Boon, *Anglican Church*, xi.

3. Eugene Stock, *The History of the Church Missionary Society: Its Environment, Its Men, and Its Work* (London: Church Missionary Society, 1899-1916), vol. 4.

4. William Carpenter Bompas, *Diocese of Mackenzie River* (London: Society for Promoting Christian Knowledge, 1888).

5. Robert Handy, *A History of the Churches in the United States and Canada*, Oxford History of the Christian Church (Oxford: Clarendon Press, 1976), 254.

6. These statistics are based on estimates made by church and civil authorities.

7. Bompas, *Diocese of Mackenzie River*.

8. Boon, *Anglican Church*, 6.

9. Boon, *Anglican Church*.

10. See *The Sower*, diocesan paper of the Anglican Diocese of Calgary, January, 1986.

11. Today, in all the mainline churches there are relatively fewer ordained Métis and Indian clergy than even fifty years ago. Among the Inuit the reverse is true.

12. At the time, the Anglican Church used the term to refer to the original territories ceded to the "Governor and Company of Adventurers trading into Hudson's Bay." More than one hundred years later, John McLean, first Anglican Bishop of Saskatchewan (a diocese carved out of the originial Diocese of Rupert's Land, and comprising what would later be the civil provinces of Alberta and Saskatchewan and the Northwest Territories and Alaska), describes his diocesan borders as reaching "to the Aurora Borealis, and world without end." Even the original borders referred to in the Royal Charter of 1670 were vague. In modern

times, it is the Anglican Church that has preserved the term, and to some degree the geographical shape, of "Rupert's Land." The Ecclesiastical Province of Rupert's Land today embraces the three prairie provinces, part of northwestern Ontario, the Northwest Territories, and arctic Quebec.

13.   Boon, *Anglican Church*.

14.   Charles E. Hendry, *Beyond Traplines* (Toronto: Anglican Church of Canada, 1969), 21.

15.   *A History of the Church of England* (London: A. & C. Black)

16.   Bompas, *Diocese of Mackenzie River*.

17.   Bompas, *Diocese of Mackenzie River*.

18.   Bompas, *Diocese of Mackenzie River*.

19.   See Jean Gill, "The Indian Portraits of Edmund Morris," *The Beaver* 310 (Summer 1979): 34-41.

20.   *Historic Sites Committee Report, 1985* (Calgary Presbytery of the U.C.C.)

21.   See Records of the Anglican Diocese of Caledonia, Prince Rupert, British Columbia. Prominent among the evidence that the church here is becoming indigenous is the rise of a grass-roots movement called the "Church Army," in which entire native communities — including non-natives where present — have accepted enthusiastic and active involvement under largely native leadership in church life, with the incorporation of many native customs and rites in worship and community celebrations.

Chapter 10

IMAGE OF TRANSITION:
PHOTOGRAPHY IN RUPERT'S LAND

Edward Cavell

Rupert's Land was slowly introduced to the ways of European civilization in carefully measured, self-serving portions by its Lord and Master the Hudson's Bay Company. In 1858, one of the manifestations of the impending rush of civilization into this artificially preserved museum of the fur trade was the presence of a photographer on the western plains. The art born of science was there to record the entry into the modern age of a society caught halfway between tradition and the future. The carefully nurtured image of the cold colony was giving way to the pressures of European and Canadian expansionism. The subject of this paper is the photographic document that was created of this land in transition. Most photographs made in Rupert's Land were of the western plains, a fact reflected in this paper. The period of the survey has been kept between 1858 and 1880 and does not include any material from the arctic islands.

The Victorian Age was a wonder of invention and investigation. With the introduction of photography in 1839, European society was given a new ability to see and record the minutia that had become the essence of life. The natural world had become a continuum; everything was interrelated. Theories of the origins of life and the structure of the earth were actively pursued and hotly contested. Society was overwhelmed with a passion for codification and exactitude. As British art historian Michael Bartram put it, "The Gate of Heaven was no longer a great arch in the sky, but the eye of a needle."[1] Photography was perceived as the handmaiden to truth; except for colour, it was the perfect rendering of reality. It took many years for non-photographers to become aware of what every photographer knew from the moment of the first exposure — that photographs are a subjective reality, a two-dimensional abstraction guided by the mind of a man, and involving all the inherent bias and cultural imperatives of any art form or historical document.

The general fascination with travel in an ever-expanding world created an obvious use for the new medium of photography. Within weeks of the invention of the first photographic process, daguerreotypists were travelling to the Holy Land to document the reality of the most fabled place on earth. Tired of the often romanticized or excessive renderings of topographical artists, the armchair travellers of Victorian England relished the words "from a photograph" printed under the wood engravings that appeared in the new illustrated newspapers and travel books. This, at last, was the world as it really was.

The use of the initial photographic processes on expeditions to very remote places was not immediately practical. The processes were awkward, time-consuming, and limited. It would be almost fifteen years before photography developed to the point where it could be a practical tool on extended expeditions to unpopulated areas without roads and without access to supplies. Daguerreotypes were made with limited success on several expeditions in the American West in the mid-1850s, but few have survived. The calotype, a paper negative-to-positive process invented at the same time as daguerreotype, was not widely used in North America because of patent restrictions. In 1851, Frederick Scott Archer's collodion process revolutionized photography. Known also as the wet-plate process, the clear, sharp, collodion negatives were made on glass and could be used to generate multiple prints on the equally new albumen silver printing paper. This negative/positive system is basically photography as we know it today, and the process remained virtually unchanged until the 1880s when dry emulsions and flexible film bases would, once again, simplify photography.

This is not the occasion for a detailed description of the collodion process, but since the technique was used to produce virtually all of the images we are discussing, and its limitations affected the nature of the document, a general understanding is essential. In brief, all aspects of the process had to happen on the spot. Once the view was determined, the photographer and assistant would position the camera, frame the image, and focus. A dark tent or portable darkroom was then set up. Because enlarging photographs was not practical at the time, a negative the size of the desired print had to be made. The size for most of the pictures we are concerned with is 6 x 8 inches (known as a full plate) or smaller. Occasionally 10 x 12 inch plates were used, and by the 1860s 20 x 24 inch plates were quite common in the United States. A glass plate was coated with the syruplike collodion (a mixture of guncotton, ether, and alcohol); then it was sensitized in a bath of silver nitrate. The plate was then put in a light-tight holder, carried quickly to the camera, exposed, returned to the dark tent and developed — all before the collodion dried. Then the plate was washed, dried, and coated with varnish.[2]

An experienced photographer with a well-trained assistant, under ideal circumstances, could produce a negative in about fifteen minutes, but they had to be exceptionally well organized and motivated. The usual time was somewhat longer — about forty-five minutes. This does not include the time spent waiting for the light on the scene to be correct. In order to maximize the time available to them, the photographers would, if possible, make several views close to the established dark tent. Four to six images would be considered a good day's work in most cases. American frontier photographer William Henry Jackson was famed for making up to thirty-two plates in a day[3] (Fig. 1).

Depending on the amount of light and the type of equipment, exposure times in the 1850s and 1860s were often in the five minute to twenty second range. By the 1870s, most pictures would have been exposed from two to twenty seconds. The collodion negatives were susceptible to uneven coating, crystallization in cold weather, bad water, dust, breakage, imbedded insects, and fingerprints. Frederick Dally, an early photographer in British Columbia, once had a rattlesnake lick the emulsion off a plate left to dry in the sun![4] The total photographic supplies for a season's work in a remote area could range in weight from several hundred pounds to a ton and could be rendered useless by a faulty batch of silver nitrate. On an expedition that required many weeks of travel away from sources of glass or chemicals, photographers were in constant fear of damage to their negatives or equipment. A canoe accident, an uncooperative packhorse, or the carelessness of an assistant could instantly destroy an entire season's work.

Because of the nature of the beast, photographs in the nineteenth century could only be taken at certain times. Anything that happened at night, took place inside a tent or house, involved even slow movement, or happened spontaneously could not be recorded. Landscape photographs could not be made on windy days and were difficult in the rain or cold. Portraits demanded that the subject be cooperative and remain perfectly still for as long as two or three minutes. The process demanded that every image be carefully considered, and the results were usually rather static.

Humphrey Lloyd Hime was the photographer attached to the Assiniboine and Saskatchewan Exploring Expedition during its second year of activity in 1858. The expedition, under the leadership of Henry Youle Hind, explored the area to the west of Red River Settlement for the Canadian government. This was the first successful use of the wet-plate process on an expedition in North America.[5] But the success was limited. With several hundred pounds of equipment and chemicals and over two hundred glass plates, Hime only managed to take eight poor-quality photographs while in the field. Hind was not amused. Hime did, however, take over three dozen excellent pictures later that fall in the more controlled environment of Red River Settlement. These remain as the earliest photographic record of the Canadian Plains and are a truly unique achievement.

Exactly why Hime had such a hard time making pictures during the expedition is unclear. His ability as a photographer is proven by the work he did later in the fall. He had not used the collodion process in the field before, but he was well acquainted with it and did have time to experiment on the journey to Red River (Fig. 2). West of the settlement, following a gruelling travel schedule, expedition encountered bad weather and alkali water. Hime also had to carry out additional duties as a surveyor. There is also the suspicion, based on later arguments between Hime and Hind, that the two men did not get along and that Hime did not pursue photography in the field with as much zeal as he could have. His failure to make any pictures of the native peoples outside the civilized confines of the settlement stemmed perhaps from the attitude they first encountered in the Fort Francis area. Here the Indians were convinced that "evil medicine" would be made over the photographs and that the "Indians who were drawn would all perish."[6] The poor results and extra work caused Hind, like many expedition leaders who attempted to use photography at that time, to recommend that the medium not be used in the future. Fortunately, he was ignored.

The photograph *The Prairies Looking West* (Fig. 3) was probably made as Hime's final comment on the summer's activity. He must have smiled with self-satisfaction as he placed a human skull in the foreground of the world's most minimalist landscape.

Hime's images illustrate well the fact that the demands of the process create their own aesthetic. The common blank sky is due to the excessive blue sensitivity of the plates, which made the capturing of the atmospheric effects virtually impossible. The fact that Hime included as much sky as he did (usually one-half to two-thirds of the image) to emphasize the flat landscape is unique for that period. The convention, in photography, was to show as little of the sky as possible in order to minimize what was perceived as a flaw in the process. Hime's portraits are reminiscent of the photographs made a decade earlier in Scotland by David Octavius Hill and Robert Adamson. This arises, in part, from a shared visual heritage and the norms of Victorian portraiture. It also arises from the shared problem of long exposures: subjects had to be braced against something to prevent movement, creating a stiffness common to all mid-Victorian photographs (Fig. 4). The fact that the settlement appears to be a very quiet place is also, in part, a function of exposure, since anything that moved faster than a plant growing would not register on the plate.

Apart from his emphasis on the flat landscape, Hime recorded what he saw using compositional devices based on traditional European art. He, like the other photographers we will be discussing, responded instinctively to what can only be defined as the "picturesque," and many of his Red River photographs are disturbingly reminiscent of rural scenes in eastern Canada or Europe.

It is difficult to attempt to describe photographs using terminology created to define painting. Both are visual documents and both are considered art forms, but terms such as romantic, classical, and picturesque were created to describe the intent of the artist. The photographer tries to select that portion of reality that best forms an image. Then, as now, this is usually defined as "having a good eye," which means being able to recognize a good, or familiar, composition when you trip over one. As Michael Bartram stated, the photographer "was never happier than when the landscape arranged itself according to the traditional formulae."[7] Although some consistency of vision does develop, virtually every photographer will make images that will fall into any of the formal categories.

Although it lies outside the literal boundaries of Rupert's Land, one picture that raises a few interesting points about the photographic document warrants our attention. This image of three Spokane Indians was taken by the Royal Engineers at the Hudson's Bay Company's Fort Colville in 1862 (Fig. 5). John Keast Lord, the naturalist on the International Boundary Commission, noted that the rifle held by the centre Indian was borrowed from the Chief Factor for "the occasion." Lord proceeded to purchase the stone celt and the bow and arrow from the other two. (They now rest somewhere in the British Museum.)[8] All the other pictures taken that season of the Indians at Colville have them in the common semi-European dress, leading one to suspect that these fellows may have been asked to strip down for effect (Fig. 6). In one picture we have the accepted view of European society towards the Indians as naked savages, and, because the rifle was introduced, we have the creation of a visual myth. Lord, walking off with their real weapons, turns this into something of a visual record of cultural imperialism.

The 1860s witnessed the development of what was to be the world's most unique camera club. Between about 1865 and 1870, a group of Hudson's Bay Company employees dabbled with the new art form at

Rupert House and Moose Factory on James Bay. The group consisted of Chief Factor James L. Cotter; the accountant, Charles Horetzky; the surgeon, Dr. William Malloch; George Simpson McTavish; and the Chief Trader at Rupert House, Bernard Rogan Ross (Fig. 7). They made most of their photographs near the posts, but occasionally they did venture out and photographed as far north as the Little Whale River near Richmond Gulf (Fig. 8). Apart from providing us with a unique view of life in a Company depot, they produced what may be the first photographs of the Inuit in North America. Since they were enthusiastic amateurs (photographing their homes and friends), their pictures tended to be more informal and relaxed than the professional photographs made on expeditions (Fig. 9). The group was obviously influenced by the style of imagery popular with the British camera clubs of the day, and again, we have a very pastoral image of frontier life.

One member of the group, Charles Horetzky, went on to become one of the most important and colourful photographers of the Western Plains. After leaving the Hudson's Bay Company in 1869, he was hired in 1871 as a photographer for the Canadian Pacific Railway surveys. As part of Frank Moberly's exploration party, he travelled west from Fort Garry to Fort Edmonton, and then on to Jasper House during the 1871-72 season. His photographs made on this one extended trip are the single best photographic record of the main western forts and the traditional fur-trade route west. Horetzky's photograph of the *Camp at the Elbow of the North Saskatchewan River* has become the Canadian visual cliché of western travel (Fig. 10). Surprisingly, Horetzky used one of the new, prepared dry plate processes that eliminated the use of the portable dark tent. This type of plate was not in common use until later in the decade, and the quality of his photographs belie the poor reputation of the earliest prepared plates.

Horetzky was the first of the western photographers to succeed in making a true topographical record. He was less encumbered with equipment, and the process had evolved enough to permit more casual poses and to allow the photographer to respond to situations with more spontaneity. During that first season he made a considerable number of technically perfect, well-composed pictures that not only satisfy the topographical requirements but show the influence of the James Bay group in his casual, very pictorial renderings (Fig. 11).

In 1872 Horetzky acted as guide for Sandford Fleming's cross-country trip. From Fort Edmonton, he and the naturalist John Macoun headed through the Peace River Pass while the rest of the group crossed the Rockies via the Yellowhead. Horetzky and Macoun parted company when they reached Fort St. James. An interesting assessment of Horetzky's personality and merit as a travel companion can be gained from Macoun's observation that he was happy to get away from Horetzky with his life. After his first year of service, Horetzky considered himself an exploring engineer, and he regarded being a photographer as demeaning; the quality and quantity of his photographs decreased rapidly. After a few more exploration trips in northern British Columbia, he spent the rest of his life in an embittered dispute with the powers-that-be over the choice of route for the Canadian Pacific Railway.

In 1872, the Royal Engineers began to mark the international boundary west from the Lake of the Woods, completing the project that was started in 1858 on the west coast. By this time, photography had established itself as a viable tool on expeditions and was being used by the Royal Engineers around the world. It was also employed extensively on numerous surveys of the western United States. Despite Horetzky's success with the dry plate, the collodion wet-plate technique was still the most popular; the demands of the process were outweighed by the ensured quality of the photographs. Four sappers, trained in photography by Captain William Abney of the Royal Engineers, were assigned to the boundary survey party. The well-trained, well-equipped photographers, operating independently from the main survey party, produced the first comprehensive document of the southern part of Rupert's Land.

A new influence had entered photography during the 1860s. The use of photography to document the American Civil War and improvements in the process had initiated the concept that photographs could record the human condition as well as the picturesque. There was a surge of interest, particularly in England, in documenting the horrid conditions endured by the poor. It became fashionable to portray life as it was rather than how it should be (Fig. 12). The sapper/photographers working along the forty-ninth parallel responded to the native inhabitants in a new, far more egalitarian way than had any of the previous photographers in the Canadian West. Their voluminous document of Plains society is exceptional in the quantity of images that are pure social document.

Hime's photographs — and to a certain extent the images by the James Bay group and Horetzky — are strongly romantic views of a land and people conforming to European influences. The Royal Engineers' photographs, however, describe the encounter between very different societies. Their pictures of the Indians are informally posed and show the native environment rather than the walls of the dominant fort, which was common in the earlier photographs (Fig. 13). We have, for the first time, a visual hint of social problems and the image of pathos. The original peoples are recorded as human with a distinct society, rather than as the savage inhabitants of a wasteland (Fig. 14).

By the mid-1870s, Rupert's Land was no longer remote. Going through the United States, a traveller could get to Montreal from the Red River in a matter of days, rather than weeks. The railway was coming, and European society was living on the Canadian plains in clapboard houses and towns, rather than log and stone forts. Colonel Wolseley had shown the West the might of the Empire. Rather than being considered a threat, the Indians were thought of as a poor race doomed to eventual extinction. The inevitable demise of the Indian was reflected on in many mid-nineteenth-century accounts, typified in William Francis Butler's statement that "...the red man of America is passing away beneath our eyes into the infinite solitude."[9]

By the late 1870s, photography was simplified again with the introduction of the commercially prepared, dry, gelatin emulsions that we use today. Cameras became standard equipment, and the photographic document proliferated. It became routine practice for members of the Geological Survey, like Robert Bell (Fig. 15) and George Dawson (who used a camera with some success in the early part of the decade), to use photography to document their explorations. Commercial photographers took up permanent residence in Red River Settlement, and the more western territories were visited by a number of itinerant photographers. One, an ex-Mountie named George Anderton, made and sold stereo views at the various police posts and Company forts (Fig. 16).

Prior to the construction of the railroad, photography had little direct effect on the inhabitants of Rupert's Land. Few of them would have even seen the resulting prints. What these pictures did, however, was give a new vision to the civilized world of what was considered a hostile, almost mythical land. Most of the photographs taken in Rupert's Land in this period were sponsored by the Canadian or British governments and were used to illustrate limited edition, official reports. Unlike their American counterparts, which were actively sold as prints to help finance the expeditions, the Canadian photographs were not readily available to the public. The images would mainly have been seen as wood engravings in the popular illustrated press or in the many published accounts of travels on the western plains. The finely detailed photographs were reduced to lines of black ink. Often the rendering was truthful and more accurate than the earlier topographical sketches, but occasionally artistic licence was employed with the addition of some trees or a figure to aid the composition of the image.

The bane and boon of photography is that it is ultimately dependent on reality. Photographers then, as now, have struggled against this truth and have eventually succumbed to its inevitability. The selective vision of the photographer and the limitations of the process have filtered our view of the past, but no more so than any other form of historical document. The process demands that all photographs contain at least some version of reality. The romantic vision of Hime or the James Bay group, the topographic record of Horetzky, or the social documentary style of the Royal Engineers were all formed from the same land, the same people. Along with their "civilized" view of Rupert's Land, the photographers have left us another truth. Those natives Humphrey Lloyd Hime had encountered in the Fort Francis area were right: Photography can capture the soul—not to kill, as the Indians had feared—but rather to allow them to live on in our vision forever.

Notes

1. Michael Bartram, *The Pre-Raphaelite Camera: Aspects of Victorian Photography* (Boston: Little, Brown and Company, 1985), 15.

2. The most accurate and detailed description of the collodion process is by Doug Muson, "The practice of wet-plate photography," *The Documentary Photograph as Work of Art: American Photographs, 1860-1876* (The David and Alfred Smart Gallery, University of Chicago, 1976), 33-38.

3. Robert Taft, *Photography and the American Scene* (New York, 1938), 309.

4. Joan Schwartz, "Frederick Dally," 1979, unpublished manuscript.

5. Richard J. Hayda, *Camera in the Interior: 1858 H.L. Hime Photographer* (Toronto: The Coach House Press, 1975).

6. Ibid., 22.

7. Bartram, *Pre-Raphaelite Camera*, 58.

8. John Keast Lord, *A Naturalist in Vancouver Island and British Columbia Vol. II* (London: Richard Bentley, 1866), 252.

9. William Francis Butler, *The Great Lone Land*, 17th ed. (Toronto: Macmillan Company of Canada, 1910), 243.

FIGURE 1

Royal Engineers: Photographers Camp, North American Boundary
Commission, 1873
Glenbow Alberta Institute

Figure 2

Humphrey Lloyd Hime: Assiniboine and Saskatchewan Exploring Expedition,
by the Red River, 1858
Public Archives of Canada C4572

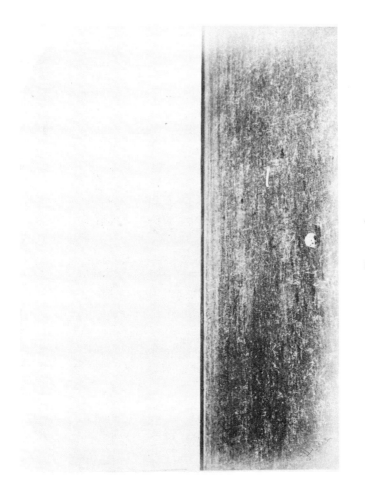

FIGURE 3

Humphrey Lloyd Hime: The Prairies, Looking West near Red River Settlement,
September-October 1858
Public Archives of Canada C17443

FIGURE 4

Humphrey Lloyd Hime: Laetita Bird, a Cree Halfbreed, Red River Settlement, 1858

FIGURE 5

Royal Engineers: Spokane Indians at Fort Colville, Washington Territory, 1860-61
Beinecke Rare Book Library

FIGURE 6

Royal Engineers: Flathead Indians at Fort Colville, 1860-61
Public Archives of Canada C78999

FIGURE 7

Bernard Rogan Ross: Rupert's House, Salt Store and Forge, 1865-68
Public Archives of Canada C15041

FIGURE 8

George Simpson McTavish: Inuk at Little Whale River, 1865-75
Public Archives of Canada C8160

FIGURE 9

Bernard Rogan Ross: Rupert's River; Shooting a White Bear, 1865-68
Public Archives of Canada C8158

FIGURE 10

Charles Horetzky: Railway Survey Camp at the Elbow of the North
Saskatchewan River, 1871
Public Archives of Canada PA9170

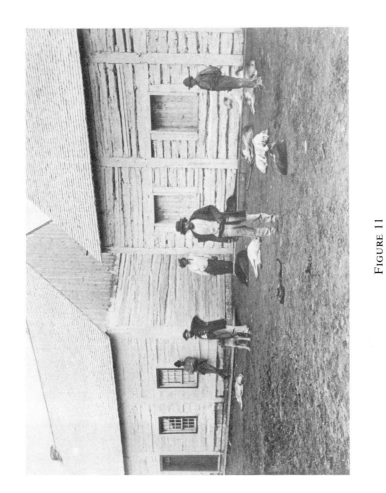

FIGURE 11

Charles Horetzky: Interior View of Carlton House, 1871
Public Archives of Canada
Glenbow Alberta Institute

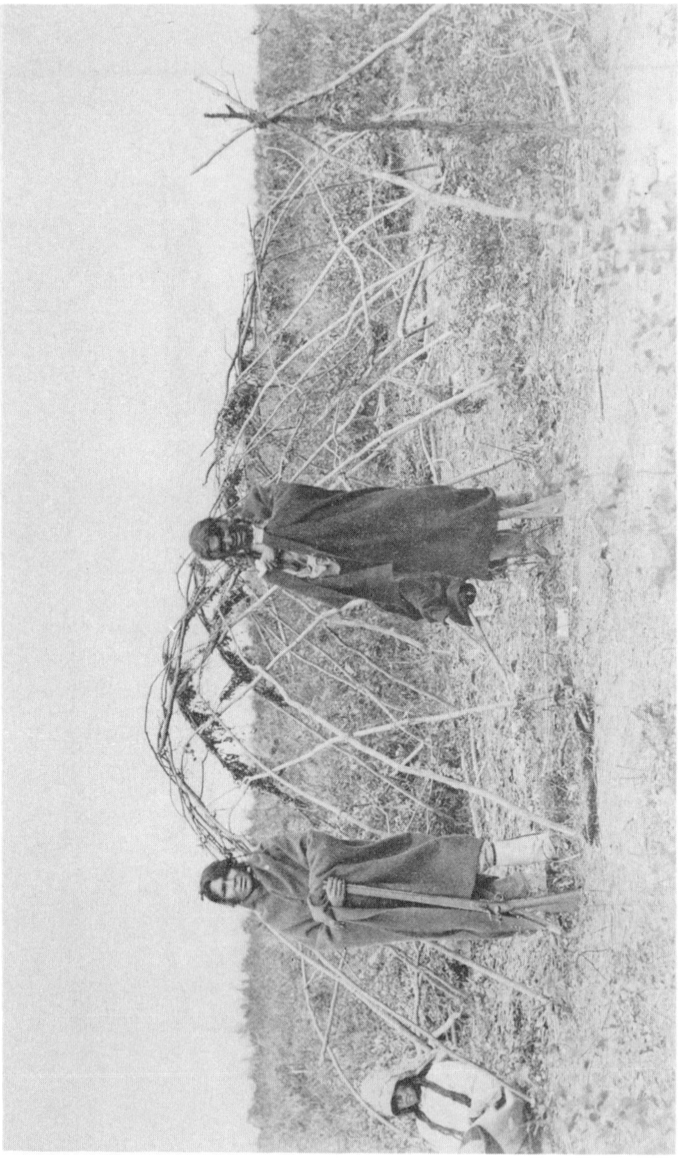

FIGURE 12

Royal Engineers: Chipewyan Indians at Dufferin, 1873-74
Public Archives of Canada C79636

FIGURE 13
Royal Engineers: Chipewyan Indians near Dufferin, 1873
Public Archives of Canada C79638

FIGURE 14

Royal Engineers: Chipewyan Indian Graves and Mourners near Dufferin, c. 1873
Manitoba Archives

FIGURE 15

Dr. Robert Bell: Main Street looking south, Winnipeg, Manitoba, 1879
Public Archives of Canada C33881

FIGURE 16

George Anderton: Sioux Chief Long Dog and George Wells (NWMP), Fort Walsh, 1879
R.C.M.P. Museum

Chapter 11

THE IDEAL AND THE REAL:
THE IMAGE OF THE CANADIAN WEST
IN THE SETTLEMENT PERIOD

R. Douglas Francis

Widespread settlement of Rupert's Land did not occur until after the region ceased to be known as "Rupert's Land." As long as the area was under the control of the Hudson's Bay Company, settlement was minimal. Indeed, the Hudson's Bay Company actively discouraged settlement, seeing it as a threat to its fur-trading activities. Agriculture and fur trading were antithetical activities, and so long as Rupert's Land remained a fur-trading empire, agriculture did not flourish. Once the Canadian government purchased the area in 1869-70 from the British government (which in turn had acquired it from the Hudson's Bay Company) for purposes of making it an agricultural hinterland for the commercial centres of central Canada, the shift from fur trade to agriculture was dramatic. Within half a century, most of the good agricultural land — and much of the marginal land too — had been claimed and settled. The population of the West went from a mere 73,000 in 1871 to 1,956,000 by 1921. The West had become a prosperous region whose settlers and agricultural economy had become the backbone of the national economy and the basis of national prosperity. This paper will explore the transition from fur trade to agricultural settlement and the response of settlers to the region through an examination of the changing images of the West (Rupert's Land) in the middle and later years of the nineteenth century.

Settlement in the West in the pre-1870 period was restricted to small enclaves of people clustered around the fur-trade posts and mission stations.[1] These people provided food supplies for fur traders and for permanent staff at the posts through growing gardens and tending livestock. But these agricultural enterprises were limited in size and in production, and could be seen as evidence of the inability of the West to sustain an agricultural economy as much as evidence that agriculture could succeed here. For these gardens fell prey to natural hazards — frost, drought, floods, and grasshoppers. The only major agricultural settlement in the area was the Red River colony at the junction of the Red and Assiniboine rivers, begun by Lord Selkirk in 1811-12 as an experimental farming community. Despite incredible hardships in getting established, the colony did grow to become an agricultural centre by midcentury. Here seemed to be evidence of the possibility of large-scale agricultural settlement on the prairies.

Yet prior to the 1860s, the Red River colony was seen as an anomaly, the exception to the rule. Thomas Simpson, the nephew of George Simpson, governor of Rupert's Land from 1820 to 1860, described Red River Settlement in his *Narrative of the Discoveries of the North Coast of America* (1843) as "a comfortable retreat . . . for such of the retired officers and servants as prefer spending the evenings of life with their native families in this oasis of the desert."[2] Captain Henry Warre, commissioned by the government of the Canadas to make a military reconnaissance of the Oregon Territory in case of war between Britain and the United States, described the Red River colony as a successful agricultural settlement but only to contrast it with the "flat and swampy" country around it. The territory offered "little to attract the eye, or tempt the industry, of even the most persevering husbandman."[3] So the Red River colony was seen as the exception to the rule rather than as evidence of the agricultural potential of Rupert's Land. And, indeed, the struggle of the settlement to survive and its limited agricultural success, which at no time replaced fur trading or the buffalo hunt as the colony's dominant economic activity, only reinforced the difficulty of agricultural settlement in the West and discouraged the idea of other settlements beginning in the area.[4]

What accounts for this negative view of the settlement potential of Rupert's Land in the pre-1870 era? One major factor was the negative image of the area in the minds of Europeans, the British, the Americans, and the British North Americans. Up until the mid-nineteenth century, the North West was perceived as a cold, desolate, barren wasteland, inhabited by hostile Indians and unfit for agricultural settlement.[5] Henry Kelsey first projected this image in his reports, prefaced by ninety lines of doggerel, to the Hudson's Bay Company about his trip from York Factory on the Bay into the western interior between 1690 and 1692. In his verse, Kelsey introduced many of the descriptive terms for the region that reappeared in later fur-trading reports. He called the southern grasslands a "plain," first used the term "desert" to describe the lonely empty spaces, and termed the general terrain "barren ground" because of the lack of trees. Throughout he stressed "the Emynent Dangers that did often me attend"[6] in this *terra incognita*, this land where no white man had previously been.

Later fur traders reinforced this negative image of the West. In 1783 Alexander Mackenzie, an employee of the Montreal-based North

West Company, made his great exploratory journeys from Montreal to the Arctic Ocean down the river that bears his name and later to the Pacific. He recorded his impressions of the area in his *Voyages from Montreal*. Mackenzie was optimistic about the fur-trade potential of the area, but voiced pessimism about settlement possibilities. "The proportion of the region that is fit for cultivation is very small, and is still less in the interior parts; it is also very difficult of access; and whilst any land remains uncultivated to the South of it, there will be no temptation to settle it. Besides, its climate is not in general sufficiently genial to bring the fruits of the earth to maturity."[7] David Thompson, another North West Company trader (a former employee of the Hudson's Bay Company) and an expert cartographer, made a similarly sweeping indictment of the North West. He concluded in his *Journal* that although distinct regions within this vast territory had their own unique geography, resources, assets, and liabilities, overall the North West territories "appear to be given by Providence to the Red Man for ever."[8]

The fur traders and explorers naturally pictured the territory as a wasteland in terms of settlement potential. After all, as employees of the fur-trading companies, they were predisposed to observe the area in terms of its fur-trade potential and therefore downplay its agricultural potential since the two activities were seen as being incompatible. Furthermore, these early explorers and traders pursued their exploits in the northern regions where the fur-trading potential was best. The most popular fur-trade brigade route, for example, ran from York Factory, up the Nelson River to Norway House and Cumberland House, and north to the Churchill River, thus never leaving the rugged Canadian Shield. Their generalizations about the region were based often only on their exposure to such northern locales. Even those European explorers and travellers who did reach the more southerly prairie lands quickly gained a negative image of the North West. Whether from Britain or France, they came from heavily forested areas of the world where successful agriculture was associated with abundant vegetation, trees, and a moist climate. They came upon the grasslands, devoid of trees and lush vegetation, and could only conclude, based on their own experience, that the land was ill-suited for settlement. As the historical geographer, Wreford Watson, notes: "There developed in the minds of Europeans an equation that went as follows: bareness equals barrenness equals infertility equals uselessness for agriculture."[9]

The American fur traders and explorers also fostered a negative image of the North West. As Americans began exploring the area west of the Mississippi River in the early 1800s, they were struck by the arid, sterile landscape. Zebulon Pike, in his exploration of the area along the Arkansas River in 1806-07, referred to the region as a "sandy sterile desert." But to Stephen H. Long—or more precisely the chronicler of his expedition, Dr. Edwin James—belonged the decisive condemnatory view of the region. On the map that accompanied his report of his 1819-20 expedition was written in bold letters: "Great Desert." The term was applied to a region that extended from the Mississippi to the Rockies and from the Gulf of Mexico to the Parkland belt. "In regard to this extensive section of the country," Edwin James wrote, "we do not hesitate in giving the opinion that it is almost wholly unfit for cultivation and, of course, uninhabitable by a people depending on agriculture for their subsistence." It was this image of a desert badland that influenced John Palliser in his perception of the southern grasslands of Rupert's Land, although Palliser would also stress the existence of a "fertile belt" north of this region.[10]

Thus, prior to the 1860s the Canadian West—as it was viewed from both northern and southern perspectives—held little potential for agricultural settlement. For northern fur traders, it was a wilderness, full of danger and terror, where the climate was forever cold and the land barren. For southern travellers, it was a desert, lacking trees and water essential to agriculture and having a monotonous, dreary landscape unappealling to human eyes. In both cases, the area was considered unsuited for agriculture and best left as a fur-trading area under the aegis of the Hudson's Bay Company.

The amazing thing is that this same dreary, desertlike, bleak, cold, inhospitable wasteland that was ill-suited for agriculture and settlement was purchased by the Canadian government in 1869-70 in expectation of turning this area into an agricultural hinterland. Furthermore, half a century after these negative prognostications of the area, the West had become the greatest agricultural and settlement region of North American—the "last best West" where a settler was almost guaranteed success simply by choosing to live there. A number of factors went into altering the region from fur-trade empire to settlement frontier. The one on which I will concentrate in this paper is the role the Canadian government and early western Canadian writers played in altering the perception of the West through extensive immigration propaganda and early western Canadian literature designed to attract settlers to the West. Then I want to examine how that image corresponded with reality as expressed by early western settlers, and finally to suggest how the incongruity between the ideal and the real might have affected the development of the West.

As soon as the Canadian government purchased Rupert's Land, it undertook to integrate it into the existing nation. This was accomplished by means of a national policy that required creating some means of linking this isolated region to the rest of Canada and encouraging east-west trade, and by populating this territory with white settlers to ensure the success of the first two components. By 1885, the West was linked to the East with the completion of the Canadian Pacific Railway; in 1879 a policy of protection was established by means of a high tariff on trade goods from outside the country to foster east-west trade. What was needed were settlers. The Canadian government made preparations for these settlers by surveying the land, placing Indians on reserves, and ensuring law and order through the establishment of the North West Mounted Police. Then it embarked on an ambitious immigration propaganda scheme, the success of which would not reach its peak until the Laurier era at the turn of the century. The government used a variety of techniques to lure immigrants to the West, including giving bonuses to shipping companies that brought immigrants to Canada, and sending agents to selected countries to persuade hesitant but interested individuals to immigrate.[11] But by far the most successful technique was the distribution of thousands and eventually millions of immigration pamphlets that extolled the virtues of the West and explained why immigrants were wise to consider settling in the West. By 1896, the Department of the Interior, under the able management of Clifford Sifton, possibly the most powerful individual in the Laurier cabinet, sent out sixty-five thousand pamphlets; by 1900 the number reached one million.

These immigration pamphlets presented a decidedly utopian image of the Canadian West.[12] In these pamphlets, the West was "the land of opportunity" where every hard working and committed immigrant had a chance to succeed and indeed was almost assured of success. Nicholas Flood Davin, editor of the *Regina Leader* and a pamphleteer for the Canadian Pacific Railway Company, captured the utopian image of the Canadian West in the following quotation:

> All the fabled mutations of wand and enchantment sink into insignificance before the change which this free world works on the serfs of Europe. Toil, combined with freedom and equality — and you have a more marvelous as well as nobler force than the fabled secret of the philosopher's stone. What they are weaving here for humanity Time will show; there is magic in the web of it; something better anyway than the tear-drenched, blood-stained tapestry of the old world's past.[13]

Pamphleteers extolled the numerous virtues of the West often in superlative terms, implying that with such abundant assets at his disposal, a settler had every reason to succeed. Nowhere did the pamphlets acknowledge that some failed to make a go of it or that others regretted coming and wanted to return home if they could. Anyone, they claimed, stood to gain if he was willing to apply himself. Europeans already struggling to eke out a living could not help but be attracted by an official government or CPR pamphlet that offered assurance of success for one's toils in this "promised land." "It is no Utopian dream," one pamphleteer wrote, "to look forward and see these endless plains thickly populated with millions to whom Western Canada has given happy homes, larger opportunities in life, and the assurance of a prosperous future."[14] The reader wanted to believe what he read and so read his dreams into the pamphlet. As one author notes: "Imagine what the words 'The West' suggested to the desk-tethered clerk, the factory-weary British workman, the mortgage-burdened Ontario farmer, or the landless Galician peasant? It offered a new chance, a new life, a new freedom."[15] To every immigrant the West was "the promised land." Their motives for migration might differ—persecution, slum conditions, poverty, lack of opportunity for themselves and better opportunities for their children, or even adventure—but all had a common image of the West as a better place. In this sense, the West was a utopia.

The pamphlets followed a standard format. They contained an introductory section describing the West as a "land of opportunity" — followed by sections on climate, soil, crops, the means to locate a homestead, advice on how to get started, transportation facilities, and social and cultural facilities. Such matter-of-fact information was embellished to exaggerate its importance. Pamphlets described the climate, for example, in terms of its positive effect on farming and on people's well-being. Sifton wanted to ban the daily publication of Manitoba's temperature so as to disassociate the North West—which he wished to promote—from Rupert's Land, which conjured up images of furs, frost, and snow. Fearing this might have a greater negative effect, he and his pamphleteers simply eliminated certain negative words like "snow" and "cold" and used instead such positive terms as "bracing" and "invigorating."[16] One description showed the impact of climate on the soil of Western Canada: "In Canada there are not just thousands, but millions of arable hectares of land waiting for the industrious hand to liberate them from the wild bush and tree cover, from the dry woody prairie grasses. The soil must come in contact with the air, bringing to it the marvelous nitrogen which causes the grain kernel to germinate and magically transforms it into a mighty heavy bending grain stalk!"[17] Others dwelt on the positive effect of climate on character. Thomas Spence, "the father of Western immigration pamphlets," believed the "climate gives quality to the blood, strength to the muscles, power to the brain. Indolence is characteristic of people living in the tropics, and energy of those in temperate zones."[18] Living in the *North* West was an asset, not a liability. Another pamphleteer proclaimed that "the climate of Western Canada does more than make wheat—it breeds a hardy race."[19] The effervescent poet of the West, Charles Mair, was more explicit as to how climate affected character:

> A peculiar feature of the climate [of the North West] is its lightness and sparkle. There is a dryness and a relish in its pure ether akin to those rare vintages which quicken the circulation without impairing the system. The atmosphere is highly purified, joyous and clear, and charged with ozone—that element which is mysteriously associated with the soundness of mind and body and at war with their morbid phenomena. Surrounded by this invisible influence, one lives a fuller and healthier life than in the denser atmosphere of the east. The cares of manhood press less heavily on the brain, and the severest toil or exposure finds increased capacity to endure it.[20]

Ebullient descriptions of the land matched those of the climate. The image of the prairies as ideal farm land—"the last best West"—was popular in immigration literature. A delegation visiting the West recorded their impressions in one of the pamphlets: "Altogether the whole district is very encouraging and hopeful to us. It is a nice prairie, covered with beautiful grass, and dotted here and there with little poplar forests which gives the whole a very romantic appearance. The settlers whom we visited look forward to a very happy and contented future." Here was the myth of the "one hundred and sixty acre homestead," where a man with his wife and children could enjoy a comfortable and rewarding life. A popular technique in many immigration pamphlets was to contrast a farmer's progress in his first five or six years of operation through a succession of annual pictures that showed a homestead transformed from a humble dwelling on unimproved land to a large frame two-storey house surrounded by trees, livestock, and cultivated fields of wheat. The photographs or illustrations depicted a diversified farm of dairy, grain, and fruit farming, implying that each farmer could be self-sufficient. The emphasis was on economic success based on the assumption that material comfort was a necessary prerequisite to spiritual well-being.

It was left to the early western Canadian writers and artists — Charles Gordon (Ralph Connor), Robert Stead, Nellie McClung, Emily Murphy (Janey Canuck), Washington Lynn, James Henderson, Augustus Kenderdine, and C.W. Jefferys — to capture in print and on canvas the quality of this new western society, to show to what extent the ideal presented in the propaganda literature had become real. Believing that they were only describing the West, these individuals actually created their own mythical West that was as utopian as that depicted in the propaganda literature. By setting their romantic stories in the physical locale of western Canada, and by painting lifelike yet idyllic scenes of the prairies, these writers and artists made people believe that the West they depicted was the "real" West. The ideal became real; the pastoral West was removed from literature to history, from form to reality, from the imagination to an actual physical setting.

Western Canadian artists depicted an opulent West through the effective use of European painting techniques combined with selective prairie scenes.[21] Using dark rich tones, restrained colours, and soft outlines, these artists set the mood of a peaceful scene. Then they chose familiar landscape settings — farmsteads, valleys, and trails — to convey a sense of the prairies as a pastoral land reminiscent of an English countryside or a northern French landscape.

James Henderson's depictions of the Qu'Appelle Valley in his *Summer in the Valley* and *Autumn Hillsides* are good examples. Quiet prairie homesteads nestled in the valley convey the same utopian image of the land as that created by western novelists. Augustus Kenderdine's paintings of the Qu'Appelle region have a similar effect. Tranquil scenes, rich in trees and presented in subdued colour tones, present an image of the prairies that is remarkably distant from the wind-swept, drought-stricken prairies many prairie farmers experienced. Charles Comfort commented on Kenderdine's selective view of the prairies: "He interprets the Western landscape more imaginatively than circumstances would require, and a preference for softly modulated tones and colours in his composition suggests that of the quiet solitude of the French paysage rather than the breeze-swept plains of the Canadian prairie." Edward Roper, a writer of travel books on Canada, crossed Canada in 1887 by CPR and recorded his impressions in *By Track and Trail*. The trip also afforded him an opportunity to paint prairie scenes. The two records, his verbal account and his paintings, contrast greatly. His travel book conveys a desolate and lonely land, while his paintings present a picturesque land where settlers are successfully turning virgin land into settlement. He concentrated on farmsteads and ploughed fields to convey a land of promise, contentment, and personal fulfilment. C.W. Jefferys, a Canadian prairie artist, pointed out the popularity of these familiar scenes to settlers in a new country like western Canada at the turn of the century: "In a new country like this, where life in general is crude, and regardless of little beyond material things, it is natural that the first conception of art should be that of the sheltered garden, where the finer spirits may dream awhile and forget the hurly burly."[22]

Western writers believed, like the immigration propagandists, that this "garden of the West" would be the home of a new and better society, one more egalitarian, democratic, free-spirited, and co-operative than that which existed elsewhere.[23] They delighted in contrasting this new land with older societies, particularly that of eastern Canada: it was young, not old; free, not restrained by tradition; egalitarian, not class-bound; virile, not weak; and pastoral, not urbanized. Here in the new West, anything and everything seemed possible, if not today at least tomorrow in "next year's country." Optimism was the finest quality that westerners possessed. Emily Murphy observed "with what joy I ride over the land this morning! In God's great blue all things are possible, and all things are fair."

Their image was of a West full of romance and adventure where daily a life and death drama of good versus evil was acted out on a majestic stage by heroic individuals. Young, virile men and modest, maidenly women struggled to conquer the forces of evil so as to create the perfect society here in the golden West. Emily Murphy epitomized the virile westerner in her *Janey Canuck in the West*: "The real Westerner is well proportioned. He is tall, deep-chested, and lean in the flank. His body betrays, in every poise and motion, a daily life of activity in the open air. His glances are full of wit and warmth. There is an air of business about his off-hand way of settling a matter that is very assuring. Every mother's son is a compendium of worldly wisdom and a marvel of human experience. What more does any country want?" Again she notes: "It is a great place this Canadian West—the country of strong men, strong women, straight living, and hard riding. Tut! Who wants to go to heaven?"[24]

Western writers and artists believed, like the immigration pamphleteers, in the magical quality of the West to turn ordinary individuals into superior beings. "How wonderful the power of this country of yours to transform men,"[25] proclaimed one of Ralph Connor's characters. In *The Sky Pilot*, Connor describes the impact of the environment on British immigrant cowboys in the Alberta foothills: "These young lads, freed from the restraints of custom and surroundings, soon shed all that was superficial in their make-up and stood forth in the naked simplicity of their native manhood. The West discovered and revealed the man in them."[26]

There is no doubt that these propaganda pamphlets with their glowing depictions of this utopian West and reinforced by the existing popular literature, which was widely read—and believed—at the time (Ralph Connor's novels sold in the millions), had a tremendous influence in luring thousands of immigrants from Europe, Britain, the United States, and eastern Canada to the "last best West." A number of immigrants who have recorded their homesteading experience talk about their initial interest in coming to western Canada because of their romantic and utopian image of the West based on what they had read or had heard from others who had read the immigration literature. A substantial number of these early settlers were members of explicitly utopian communities organized by people who believed that here in the virgin lands of western Canada lay the possibility of translating their dreams into reality.[27] Others were simple folk who were in search of a better livelihood, a new adventure, or a new land where they might create the idyllic conditions that were a part of every man's and woman's dreams.

Immigrants wanted to believe that here, in this isolated wilderness, the conditions were perhaps right for the creation of a perfect society. They came with high expectations and hopes. According to one ethnic historian, many immigrants saw themselves "as characters in a Zane Grey or Oliver Curwood romance trekking across the limitless prairie, living a life free of cares and worries and dedicated to novelty. They would have echoed the plaintive cry of one of their fellow emigrants: 'I wanted to see strange people, Indians, Chinese, Arabs and Hottentots, so long as they were different from the people who crossed my path everyday.'"[28] An emigrant recalled being elated when told as a young boy that he would be going to America. His introduction to Canada was through the romantic novels of James Fenimore Cooper. "My brother read me stories such as *The Pathfinder* and *The Deerslayer*; in fact, anything he could get hold of that was written by James Fenimore Cooper and others of that period. America was a big, faraway place where there were thrills one after another without end. We would start preparations even now, by learning about it and keeping alert."[29] Stephen Leacock once explained: "Going West, to a Canadian, is like going after the Holy Grail to a knight of King Arthur. All Canadian families have had, like mine, their Western Odyssey."[30] Wilfred Eggleston, recounting his family's "Western Odyssey," recalled having a "bi-focal image" of homesteading: "I made my acquaintance with the old homestead first through the imagination and later on through the eyes of a sensitive boy. And after sixty-five years those early impressions still dominate. So I see the experience through a romantic veil. There is still an element of dream or fantasy in my memories. I was a precocious reader and had been raised on such fare as *King Arthur and his Knights of the Round Table, Robin Hood and his Merry Men*, on *Swiss Family Robinson*, on the novels of Henty and Ballantyne, on *Coral Island* and *Treasure Island*, and *Lorna Doone* and all the rest. It was more than two years after my father's struggle through the blizzard before we children actually saw the homestead, and this period of delay only heightened the suspense and enhanced the glamour. It became a sort of Promised Land, the Garden of Eden, or Shangri-La. The grimmer realities of course had to be faced by my father from the beginning."[31]

How did the image correspond to reality? That question is difficult to answer since so little research has been done on early settlers' experiences. But what work has been done suggests a wide gap naturally existed between what immigrants expected to find and what they found. For some, the West seemed to approximate all that they had hoped for, and they were contented. But for many more, reality was a far cry from the fantasies they had woven in their minds. Let me cite a few examples. One immigrant who began a book on "My Four Years Experienced in the North West of America: Roughing It in the Far West" explained in the preface to his manuscript why he was writing: "This book is not written for the purposes of running down America but for the purposes of letting any who are thinking of immigrating to America know what they *may* have to go through." He then begins his first chapter:

> So many books, pamphlets etc. (mostly untrue) have been written about the charms and beautiful climate of the North-West of Canada and none about the hardships that have to be endured there that I think it high time someone should let the public know the true state of affairs in that region of the world. Having been frequently asked both by friends in England and America to write both my own experiences in Canada and also my opinion of that country as a field of immigration, I shall attempt in the following pages to comply with their wishes. I know perfectly well that this is not the sort of book that pleases the Canadian Pacific Railway Company and I have no doubt if I ever got into their clutches they would like to make short work both of me and the book, however

I don't intend to give them any such chance. I have before me the latest pamphlets on Manitoba and the North West and all I can say is that the ones that are not a pack of lies are a pack of rubbish, but rubbish or no rubbish I know perfectly well that they have been and in future will be the means of enticing people to immigrate to the North West.[32]

In the remainder of the manuscript he went on to recount the misfortunes that befell him from the moment that he arrived until he decided to leave.

This immigrant's experience was characteristic of many. In the 1920s, the *Grain Growers' Guide*, the newspaper of the Grain Growers' Association of western farmers, asked homesteaders to contribute to a special issue of the newspaper on their "Homesteading Experiences." The best were printed in the paper while the remainder were copied by A.S. Morton of the University of Saskatchewan's history department, and later deposited in the archives. One is struck, in reading over these reminiscences of settlers' firsthand experiences at homesteading, by the difficulty they had adjusting to their new "home" and by the realization that a large part of the adjustment came about as a result of the high expectations with which they had come to the West. One account began:

I was born in Yorkshire England my home being one of the fashionable English inland watering places which are scattered through the country. Whilst away from home I met the man who now is my husband, often like myself read the literature which was distributed wholesale especially in rural parts of England describing the beauties of Canada, showing pictures of cattle knee deep in prairie grass, miles of golden grain all just waiting for some one to take possession....We arrived at Estevan, Saskatchewan about the first week of April 1907, any one who remembers that winter and spring will surely feel sorry for the immigrant who left their own country of green hedges, green fields, primroses, snow drops out [sic] and found here huge banks of snow the likes of which we had never seen before, and zero weather, people muffled up to the eyes in furs certainly by the pamphets we read on Canada did not describe that side of the country to us....[She then goes on to say] I was very lonely that summer as my husband had got his crop in he took some breaking to do quite a few miles away. He would camp in a wagon coming home Saturday to spend Sunday with us and get fresh supplies of food which I would have ready....The harvest that year was very poor owing to the late spring. A lot of grain was never cut the frost getting it before it was ripe. That was another thing that pamphlets in England did not tell us about.[33]

Another woman also recalled the loneliness of homesteading for women: "There was always a ceaseless longing for the home land and old familiar faces, and it took many a long years [sic] to overcome that lonesome feeling."[34]

Another man recalled his decision to go to western Canada and his escapades to find a suitable homestead site:

> Early in 1903 one of my school friends gave me a Canadian Government pamphlet which pictured the great chance of getting a farm in three years! I hunted up all the information available until the present I felt [sic] the great Canadian west calling for me. She became a land to be explored. In the firment [sic] I beheld a great rainbow and adventure was calling. I decided to lay by the testtube and microscope for three years to get titles to one of Canada's new farms. I had little idea that I was leaving the halls of learning for the last time....In 1903 [my brother and I] crossed the U.S. line into Manitoba with $80 between us and a return ticket to Saskatoon. The immigration department at Winnipeg advised us to look up some country north of Fort Quappelle (it was 20 miles north of the railroad then)....Not finding suitable land we proceeded to Saskatoon. We landed in a drizzly misty day and slept under one of the elevators that night. There were few homesteads available near Saskatoon it having been effectively blanketed by the reality dealers [sic]....We heard from a homesteader that he had found a wonderful township where the pea vine grew four feet high, where the soil was black and underlaid with a wonderful chocolate clay, so we hired a team of broncos and a democrat, did our own driving, and followed the rainbow once more....This time I arrived. But oh the great silence and the loneliness. It was where I asked myself was it worthwhile. I guess it was the stubborn old spirit of one of my great grandfathers who fought the forests and the red Indians that commanded me to stay with the game and to endure.[35]

One final excerpt will suffice:

> When I look back over our homesteading days in Saskatchewan I have to laugh and cry at the same time. And I think all others who were among the first settlers on the prairies have the same feelings. When you think of how strange and different everything would be to one reared in a city, in the central

[United] States, where there is very little snow and ice, where the thermometer never reaches the zero mark, where the grass is greener in the winter than it is here in summer (on account of the dead grass that is still on the prairie).... [My husband] came to Davidson in 1905. I did not come for a few weeks after Frank did, as we had three little girls, the youngest only three months old. So I could not come till the shack was built.... The country around Davidson did not look too bad for me, but the further north and east we came it got pretty rough and the knolls got steeper til they became hills. My heart sank. I could not image why anyone wanted to live in such a place for.[36]

The few firsthand accounts can be supplemented by numerous others, some published in books or in local histories, some still lost in the archives, still others stored up only in the memories of family members whose parents or grandparents had first immigrated to western Canada to homestead.

How typical are these accounts? The cold statistical figures available on the successes and failures of homesteading testify to the large number of people who did *not* fulfill their dreams in the "last best West," who did *not* find "the promised land." The rate of attrition — the failure of the homesteader to "prove up" and thus obtain a patent for his quarter section — was extraordinary.[37] Chester Martin once calculated that four in ten prairie homestead applications were never fulfilled, and concluded rather sardonically that "'free' homesteads had been costly beyond computation." V.C. Fowke, a noted western Canadian author and economist, described the attrition rate as "little less than shocking."[38] Almost half of those who tried to bring their dreams into reality had their dreams shattered in a nightmare of failure. For them, the prairie west was *not* "next year's country." This says nothing about those who stayed — "weathered the storm," so to speak — and eked out a marginal living.

This striking contrast of dream and reality, the ideal and the real, is not surprising to anyone who has read extensively about immigration experiences (although the tendency is to dwell on the successes more than the failures) or who has talked to old-timers who have pioneered. But I do not think enough has been made of the impact that such adjustment from ideal to real had on the history of the prairie West. Let me present a few conjectural conclusions.

Douglas Owram in his splendid study *Promise of Eden: The Canadian Expansionist Movement and the Idea of the West 1856-1900* links the bust in Winnipeg in 1883 to the rise of disillusionment in western Canada. "The depression," he writes, "had a profound effect on those who had gone west on the premise that expansionist optimism was justified."[39] As Charles Mair, an exponent of that expansionism, wrote George Denison in 1885: "Matters instead of improving in the North West are getting worse. To use an old phrase the bottom seems to have fallen out."[40] Mair's disillusionment, however, was only a small part of a much greater disillusionment that befell thousands of immigrants when they found a reality that scarcely resembled the ideal they had created in their minds. A natural reaction was to lash out at those "image makers" — the federal government and the Canadian Pacific Railway Company — that had deceived them. Underlying western Canadian discontent, therefore, was a dissatisfaction with those in authority and command who were seen to be at the root of the West's plight. As Lewis G. Thomas noted in his Canadian Historical Society Presidential Address of 1973:

> The complaints of the western farmer about his exploitation by eastern business stem ultimately from the hard fact that he was attempting what was next to impossible even on the best of western farm land and under the most favourable of prairie climatic conditions. None but the most exceptionally fortunate and the most exceptionally provident could make the quarter section family farm a continuing financial success; the unit was too small to begin with and it could not generate sufficient additional capital to permit its enlargement to an economic size by consolidation with adjacent small properties. The farmer's grievances against the grain trade, the elevator companies, the railways, the banks and the federal government that maintained what was to him an iniquitous tariff structure were real grievances but behind them lay the fact that he had been permitted and indeed encouraged to place himself in an impossible situation.
>
> Western alienation is rooted in this colossal national blunder. The settler himself entered all too willingly into what he saw as the road to new opportunities for himself and his family. The politicians failed to find a means of shaping policies that would have given the pressure for development more creative direction.[41]

Since these institutions and politicians tended to be in the East, western protest took on an anti-Eastern bias. Part of western regional consciousness was an attempt to vindicate the West by projecting the blame for the limitations of the West on those who distorted it. This took the form of a utopian spirit, as W.L. Morton notes, which ironically turned upon the very institutions that had created that spirit.[42]

The gap between the ideal and the real was also, I would suggest, a motivating force behind the agrarian reform movement in the early twentieth century. When the initial idealistic utopias were inevitably unfulfilled in the harsh economic and physical realities of western Canada, western farmers turned to reform in hopes of bridging the gap between their hopes and their unfulfilled expectations. They did so with equally naive utopian assumptions that "God Made the Country, Man Made the Town" — that farmers were God's Chosen People and that the family farm was the ideal social unit. Agrarian reform, then, was an attempt by western farmers to create that utopian society that seemed to be out of tune with the everyday reality they experienced but that remained as their elusive goal. Ultimately westerners believed, as W.L. Morton points out, that they could bring the nation around to their regional perspective. This was the extreme form of utopianism which grew out of the incongruity of the ideal and the real.[43]

Finally, I would like to suggest that the disillusionment that inevitably accompanied the settlement process led to the demise of the utopian literature of early western Canadian writers. These early exponents of western Canada were simply expressing the same utopian imagery so evident in the immigration propaganda. As this ideal failed to match reality, the utopian literature it spurned also seemed inappropriate and was, therefore, replaced by a more realistic literature of the interwar years. Robert Stead's *Grain*, Martha Ostenso's *Wild Geese*, and Frederick Philip Grove's *Settlers of the Marsh* are cited as the best examples of this new realistic literature, which depicted the West in terms of its harsh environment, its feeling of isolation, and its unfulfilled expectations in a land that extracted a heavy price from those who tried to conquer it and bring it under the plow.[44] This realistic image was in many respects not unlike that of the earlier negative image of the West in the pre-1850 era. The perception of the West — of Rupert's Land — had come full circle, and the utopian image had, ironically, turned on itself.

In conclusion, the Canadian West underwent a dramatic shift in imagery in the late nineteenth century from a negative one of a wasteland to a positive one of a utopian agricultural society. Yet the utopian image was a far cry from the reality that westerners found when they began homesteading, and led in turn to a western Canadian consciousness that was a peculiar mixture of utopianism and realism. This ambivalent perspective has remained a characteristic of the region ever since.

Notes

I wish to thank Irene Spry for pointing out errors in an earlier draft of this paper, and John Allen, whose comments on a related paper of mine helped refine some erroneous generalizations in this paper. What errors, omissions, and limitations remain are, of course, my own responsibility. I also want to acknowledge the assistance of a Killam Resident Fellowship from the University of Calgary that contributed to the completion of this paper.

1.   On agricultural settlement in Rupert's Land during the era of the Hudson's Bay Company's rule, see Grant MacEwan, *Illustrated History of Western Canadian Agriculture* (Saskatoon: Western Producer Prairie Books, 1980); A.S. Morton, *History of Prairie Settlement* (Toronto: Macmillan, 1938); F.G. Roe, "Early Agriculture in Western Canada in Relation to Climatic Stability," *Agricultural History*, 26 (July 1952): 104-23; and Lewis H. Thomas, "A History of Agriculture on the Prairies to 1914," *Prairie Forum*, 1 (April 1976): 31-45, reprinted in R. Douglas Francis and Howard Palmer, eds., *The Prairie West: Historical Readings* (Edmonton: University of Alberta Press, 1985), 221-36.

2.   Thomas Simpson, *Narrative of the Discoveries on the North Coast of America* (London: R. Bentley, 1843), 15-16.

3.   Captain Henry Warre, *Sketches in North America and the Oregon Territory* (London, 1848), 16.

4.   On the limitations of agriculture in the Red River colony, see W.L. Morton, "Agriculture in the Red River Colony," *Canadian Historical Review*, 30 (December 1945): 305-21; and Grant MacEwan, *Cornerstone Colony* (Saskatoon: Western Producer Prairie Books, 1977).

5.   On images of the North West, see Douglas Owram, *Promise of Eden: The Canadian Expansionist Movement and the Idea of the West, 1856-1900* (Toronto: University of Toronto Press, 1980); and R. Douglas Francis, "Changing Images of the West," *Journal of Canadian Studies*, 17 (Fall 1982): 5-19.

6.   *The Kelsey Papers*, intro. by A.G. Doughty and C. Martin (Ottawa: Public Archives of Canada, 1929), 1.

7.	Sir Alexander Mackenzie, *Voyages from Montreal* (London: T. Cadell, 1801) quoted in J. Warkentin, ed., *The Western Interior of Canada* (Toronto: McClelland and Stewart, 1964), 89.

8.	*David Thompson's Narrative of His Explorations in Western America 1784-1812*, ed. J.B. Tyrrell (Toronto: Champlain Society, 1916), 241. See as well J. Warkentin, "Steppe, Desert and Empire," in A.W. Rasporich and H.C. Klassen, eds., *Prairie Perspectives 2* (Toronto: Holt, Rinehart and Winston, 1973), 102-136.

9.	W. Watson, "The Role of Illusion in North American Geography: A Note on the Geography of North American Settlement," *The Canadian Geographer*, 13 (Spring 1969): 16.

10.	See John Warkentin, "The Desert Goes North," in Brian Blouet and M. Lawson, eds., *Images of the Plains: The Role of Human Nature in Settlement* (Lincoln: University of Nebraska Press, 1975), 149-63. On John Palliser see Irene Spry, Introduction to *The Papers of the Palliser Expedition, 1857-1860* (Toronto: Champlain Society, 1968).

11.	For a general discussion of immigration propaganda see Norman Macdonald, *Canadian Immigration and Colonization: 1841-1903* (Toronto: Macmillan, 1934); Harold M. Troper, *Only Farmers Need Apply* (Toronto: Griffin House, 1972); and Klaus Peter Stich, "'Canada's Century': The Rhetoric of Propaganda," *Prairie Forum*, 1 (April 1976): 19-30.

12.	I have dealt with the utopian image of the Canadian West in relation to other images of the West in the nineteenth century in "From Wasteland to Utopia: Changing Images of the Canadian West in the Nineteenth Century," *Great Plains Quarterly*, 7 (Summer 1987): 178-94. This present paper uses some of the same material to develop a different argument.

	It should be kept in mind that this utopian imagery was important in influencing others to settle in the Canadian West, but did not, of course, necessarily reflect the writers' own images of the area since they were paid to present such imagery.

13.	Nicholas Flood Davin, ed., *Homes for Millions: The Great Canadian North-West; Its Resources Fully Described* (Ottawa: B. Chamberlin, 1891), 6.

14. Canada. Department of the Interior, *Canada West* (Ottawa, 1913), 4.

15. Bruce Peel, "The Lure of the West," *Papers of the Bibliographical Society of Canada*, 5 (1966), 29.

16. Pierre Berton, *The Promised Land: Settling the West 1896-1914* (Toronto: McClelland and Stewart, 1984), 15.

17. Letter from Frans Van Waeterstadt to *Leeuwarder Courant*, 4 April 1927 in H. Ganzevoort, *Canada: The Last Illusion* (unpublished manuscript). I am indebted to Professor Ganzevoort for the use of this quotation.

18. Thomas Spence, *The Prairie Lands of Canada: Presented to the World as a New and Inviting Field of Enterprise for the Capitalist and the New Superior Attractions and Advantages as a Home for Immigrants* (Montreal: Gazette Printing, 1880), 6.

19. Canada. Department of the Interior, *Canada West: Ranching, Dairying, Grain Raising, Fruit Growing, Mixed Farming* (Ottawa, 1913), 4.

20. Charles Mair, "General Description of the North-West," in N.F. Davin, ed., *Homes for Millions*, 11.

21. For a discussion of prairie painters, see Ronald Rees, *Land of Earth and Sky: Landscape Painting of Western Canada* (Saskatoon: Western Producer Prairie Books, 1984).

22. Rees, *Earth and Sky*, 35 and 37.

23. For a discussion of imagery in western Canadian literature see Gerald Friesen, "Three Generations of Fiction: An Introduction to Prairie Cultural History," in D.J. Bercuson and P. Buckner, eds., *Eastern and Western Perspectives* (Toronto: University of Toronto Press, 1981), 183-96; and R. Douglas Francis, "Changing Images of the West," 5-19 passim. Both articles have been reprinted in Francis and Palmer, eds., *The Prairie West: Historical Readings*.

24. Emily Murphy, *Janey Canuck in the West* (Toronto: McClelland and Stewart, 1975), 114, 211, and 213.

25. Ralph Connor [C.W. Gordon], *The Foreigner: A Tale of Saskatchewan* (Toronto: Westminister, 1909), 378.

26. Ralph Connor [C.W. Gordon], *The Sky Pilot: A Tale of the Foothills* (1899; reprint, Lexington: University of Kentucky Press, 1970), 27.

27. See Anthony Rasporich, "Utopian Ideals and Community Settlements in Western Canada 1880-1914," in H. Klassen, ed., *The Canadian West: Social Change and Economic Development* (Calgary: Comprint Publishing Company, 1977).

28. Quoted in H. Ganzevoort, "The Land of Champagne Air," (unpublished paper), 12.

29. Klaas de Jong, *Cauliflower Crown* (Saskatoon: Western Producer Prairie Books, 1973), 10.

30. Stephen Leacock, "Preface" to *My Discovery of the West* (London: The Bodley Head, 1937).

31. Wilfred Eggleston, "The Old Homestead: Romance and Reality," in H. Palmer, ed., *The Settlement of the West* (Calgary: Comprint Publishing, 1977), 116-17.

32. Public Archives of Canada [PAC], MG 29 C 38 "My Four Years Experience in the North West of America: Roughing it in the Far West," (unpublished manuscript), 1-2. In the following quotations I have left the texts in their original form despite grammatical errors.

33. PAC, MG 30, C 16, vol. 2, 397. No author or title listed.

34. Ibid., "Pioneer Days," 459.

35. Ibid., "Homesteading Twenty Years Ago," 553-59 (passim).

36. Ibid., "Homesteading Days," 626-28.

37. For a discussion of this subject, see Gerald Friesen, *The Canadian Prairies: A History* (Toronto: University of Toronto Press, 1984), 308 ff.

38. Chester Martin and Vernon Fowke quoted in ibid.

39. Owram, *The Promise of Eden*, 171.

40. Quoted in ibid.

41. Lewis G. Thomas, "Associations and Communications," Presidential Address, Canadian Historical Assocation *Historical Papers* (1973), 8.

42. W.L. Morton, "The Bias of Prairie Politics," *Transactions of the Royal Society of Canada*, Series III, vol. 49 (June 1955), pp. 57-66. Reprinted in B. McKillop, ed., *Contexts of Canada's Past: Selected Essays of W.L. Morton* (Toronto: Macmillan for the Carleton Library Series, 1980), 149-60.

43. Ibid. On agrarianism and social reform see also R. Allen, "The Social Gospel as the Religion of the Agrarian Revolt," in C. Berger and R. Cook, eds., *The West and the Nation: Essays in Honour of W.L. Morton* (Toronto: McClelland and Stewart, 1976), 174-86.

44. On realism in western Canadian literature, see Dick Harrison, *Unnamed Country: The Struggle for a Canadian Prairie Fiction* (Edmonton: University of Alberta Press, 1977).

Chapter 12

AFTER-IMAGES OF RUPERT'S LAND FROM THE JOURNALS OF ERNEST OBERHOLTZER (1912) AND P.G. DOWNES (1939)

R.H. Cockburn

During the London winter of 1910-11, a young American named Ernest Oberholtzer spent long hours in the British Museum, reading accounts of far northern exploration and travel. A canoeman himself, he had journeyed extensively through the Rainy Lake watershed along the Minnesota-Ontario border, where he had developed a consuming passion for the rigorous satisfactions of canoe travel itself, for the Shield country, and for the companionship of Ojibwa Indians, whose culture fascinated him. "Above all," he reminisced many years later, "I met Billy Magee...the most wonderful Ojibway or any Indian I have ever known." The two men canoed prodigious distances into what was then the Quetico Provincial Forest Reserve, "and I saw that Billy was extremely intelligent, well-informed, industrious, and willing to do almost anything to please." Oberholtzer, a Harvard graduate and sometime newspaperman, found these experiences "as wonderful if not more so than I had ever dreamed [and] my whole interest in the far north was tremendously stimulated."[1]

Now, in the reading room of the British Museum, Oberholtzer discovered J.B. Tyrrell's Geological Survey reports of his Barren Ground explorations of 1893 and 1894[2] and determined to follow Tyrrell's 1894 Kazan River route to Chesterfield Inlet. "The two things that meant more to me than anything else," he recalled as an old man, "were seeing all those caribou and seeing these Eskimos [Caribou Inuit] that nobody had ever known. And my imagination was at work. I thought, well, there are probably other groups of those Eskimos up there. What that would mean, what a delight to be the first one ever to find them!"[3] He had to wait for one more year; short of money, he accepted an offer to serve as United States vice-consul in Hanover, Germany, during 1911. Then he translated his dreams into action.

On June 26, 1912, in an eighteen-foot Chestnut Guide Special canoe, Oberholtzer and Magee embarked from The Pas, their intention being to trace Tyrrell's 1894 Kazan route as far as Yathkyed Lake, whence he had portaged east to the Ferguson, and to then continue down the Kazan to Baker Lake and the recently established HBC post at

Chesterfield Inlet. Neither man had ever canoed north of the Rainy Lake watershed. To those who saw them off—"pessimistic predictions of the inhabitants about our trip"[4]—they must have looked a doomed pair. Oberholtzer, twenty-eight, stood 5' 4" and weighed 137 pounds, and Magee, although strongly built and 20 pounds heavier, was fifty-one years old; the Ojibwa, who had agreed readily to the trip during the winter, was now becoming uneasy at the prospect of strange Indians, far stranger Inuit, and the treeless regions for which they were bound.

However, this paper must not become an account of Oberholtzer and Magee's epic voyage as such. Rather, emphasis must fall upon those parts of the Harvard man's journal that illuminate traditional and enduring characteristics of that part of the North. That such after-images of Rupert's Land are numerous is unsurprising, for the two men were setting forth into country that had seen few changes in the forty-two years since the Company had surrendered its charter to the Dominion. Although Revillon Frères had begun to make its presence felt, it did not yet threaten the Company's supremacy along the waterways stretching northward from The Pas to Brochet. Nor would Oberholtzer encounter any agent of government until he reached Fort Churchill in mid-September. In this part of the North, timeless patterns and rhythms endured: the natives were on the land or in the employ of the Company; settlements remained as isolated as ever from the outside; and along the old trade routes, freight canoes and York boats passed, the sounds of paddle shaft on gunwale, creaking cordage, and displaced water absorbed by and inseparable from the wilderness itself. Maps of this territory bordered by the Churchill, Reindeer Lake, the Kazan, and the Bay were dominated by vast white blanks and the dotted lines of uncertainty.[5]

Abrupt, revolutionary transformations lay only a decade ahead. But as Oberholtzer and Magee set out from The Pas, leaning into their strokes, they entered a region that could still have been known as Rupert's Land.

On June 30, at Cumberland House, they were welcomed by H.M.S. Cotter, who had been born into the Company: he and his family had reached this new posting by canoe a few weeks earlier.[6] The only man met en route who believed Oberholtzer might succeed in his audacious venture, Cotter entrusted him with a letter to deliver to Solomon Ford, the sole occupant of the Company's post at Chesterfield Inlet.

Leaving Cumberland House, the Rainy Lake men found themselves following two Revillon freight canoes. "These men,"

Oberholtzer noted, "have a way of paddling that is new to me. It consists of a very rhythmical forceful stroke with a pause in between during which the paddlers frequently change sides. The top hand lets go entirely; the lower one slips to the top; and the paddle is swung deftly across the gunwales." Years afterward, P.G. Downes would find this technique still in vogue.[7] Breakfasting at the mouth of the Sturgeon-Weir on July 4, Oberholtzer wondered "why so many long bark shavings are lying on the ground." Then the Revillon crew arrived, came ashore, and "pretty soon [the leader] comes back with a number of poles and begins shaving the bark. Then I understood this is the junction for the upriver trip where poles are needed."

On the evening of July 11 the adventurers had just made camp when several southbound canoes appeared, under the command of James Christie, HBC manager at Pelican Narrows. With him were the two sons of R.H. Hall, the Fur Trade Commissioner. Gordon Hall explained to Oberholtzer that his brother Herbert, "who was passing in a canoe with a sail out in the middle of the lake, was just returning from a stay of four years at Ennadai Lake....[8] It had taken him 26 days to come down as far as Pelican Narrows; the route was bad, and there were no men to be had [to serve as guides]. When this young man had done all he could to dissuade me from attempting the trip to Chesterfield, he paddled on. The next moment we heard a loud, ominous swish repeated at regular intervals, and there, rapidly approaching, appeared a York boat."

What follows exemplifies Oberholtzer's observant and articulate journal at its best. "It was full of halfbreeds. They landed in the bay beyond our canoe; one man jumped over the prow; two oars were tied together as a gangway; and down came the whole crew—some twenty men and a squaw with two children. All the men filed past us to shake hands and they stood about examining our fire, our food, and our tent. Then they went over into the bushes, lighted a fire, and began gambling with cards and matches. One old fellow, who Billy thought was a Sioux and who told a funny story about squaws, was squatted in front of the fire with a bent pan in his lap and kept beating it in two-four rhythm and wailing a queer, wild, monotonous dance. When I went over to see him, he was wrapped in a blanket, his head bobbing time and his face drawn with lines of pleasure that stood out black in the firelight.... Ten of the other men were sitting close together with their cards and matches spread out on a white, black-edged H.B. blanket drawn taut across their knees. The cook...told me that the men had had a fine dance at the Narrows the day before....One man sat in the stern of the boat strumming a fiddle. Only a few of these people spoke any English. The last thing I heard was a low sort of chanting like a prayer."

In the morning, Oberholtzer was awakened "by a voice shouting 'Wee-chow'—'Get up!' When I came out, I found the York boatmen straggling down to the boat with their personal packs, usually in flour sacks. Some were washing their faces. The cook hastily distributed tea and the bannocks which he had been cooking all night, and then carried his whole kitchen pantry off in a box to the boat. The squaw took her seat in the stern; the steersman manned his oar; two men shoved off with poles; a third on shore put his shoulder to the prow and crawled aboard just as the boat moved off, like a Greek argosy. A man at each oar and one over, for this boat had two crews returning to Cumberland House. The usual crew consists of eight oarsmen (sometimes nine, four on one side, five on the other), a steersman, a bowman, a guide, and lately (to save waste) a cook. As the boat moved out upon the calm lake, her great oars washing like the slow beat of a funeral drum, she was magnificent. We heard the rub of her oars for half an hour afterwards."

Reaching Pelican Narrows later that morning, the travellers first pulled in to the still new "French Company" post, then "paddled round the next two points beyond the HBC store and came ashore beside an old York boat painted white." Here the assistant manager told Oberholtzer that Christie's brigade was bound for Cumberland House and that two more York boats were about to embark for Amisk Lake. "Some of their best workers," Louis Thwaites remarked, "were boys of eighteen. All of them were in the store buying [large, brightly coloured] handkerchiefs, mouth harps, candies, and other delicacies. They seemed a very high spirited lot; and Thwaites said they were the best boatmen in the north." Oberholtzer photographed the departing vessels, their great sails making a brave show as they picked up the breeze and surged out of sight down the Narrows. These craft would be only a memory by Downes's day, but he would meet the priest Oberholtzer now sought out, Father Nicholas Guilloux. This Oblate missionary, who had been posted to Pelican in 1906, was to serve there until the 1950s.[9] Oberholtzer, who had never imagined making his voyage unguided, had been unable to find a guide at Cumberland House. Now he negotiated through Guilloux for a Cree to lead him as far as Lac du Brochet, but the native in question both drove a hard bargain and was indecisive, causing Oberholtzer to decide "to go alone in spite of everybody's warnings."

From Pelican Narrows, the American and the Ojibwa pushed on to Frog Portage and the Churchill, then worked up the Reindeer River's "wonderfully clear green water" to South End, the small HBC post at the foot of Reindeer Lake. There followed the arduous 170-mile paddle north to Brochet along the lake's convoluted eastern shore; the two got lost in blind bays, ran into some stiff weather, and could not put their sail to much use, but, fortified by Magee's balsam tea and by a growing confidence in their fitness and ability, they made good time. When, 116 years before, David Thompson, bound for Athabaska, explored the western shore of Reindeer, the territory east and north of the great lake had elicited these observations from him: "That these countries are unknown, even to the natives, can excite no surprise.... It is a pity that the Hudson's Bay Company do not have these countries explored; by their charter they hold these extensive countries to the exclusion of all other persons."[10] Tyrrell's explorations apart, however, no penetrations of significance into this enormous, harsh transitional zone had been accomplished since Thompson's day.

On the afternoon of July 27, some five hundred miles out from The Pas, Oberholtzer and Magee "could discern four or five gleaming patches on a hillside across the lake.... We found an Indian encampment—the best one I have ever seen. One of the men...could answer a few words in English. They were all glad to have their pictures taken. Long fish that looked like herring [tullibee] hung from a pole to dry. Half a dozen new paddles, their blades painted red, were also drying against a screen of boughs.... The bark canoes—those on the beach and the unfinished one above—were narrower, flatter, and at the ends straighter and sharper than any I had seen before.... I tried to talk Cree from my book. The Indian leader, whose name turned out to be El Laurent, took me to the top of the hill to show me the fort, and, when I was ready to go, he got in his canoe and took us all the way across."

Lac du Brochet, as it was then misleadingly called, was an HBC post and Oblate mission remote from major trade routes and a place seldom visited by outsiders. Founded by the Company either in 1859 or 1861—the evidence is uncertain—it had been important until the turn of the century not as a fur post but as a meat post. The Chipewyans who traded there, the Barren Land and the Hatchet Lake bands, whose existence centred on the caribou, had been employed in drying the meat they slaughtered and making pemmican, which was freighted south and west to supply other posts and to fuel the crews of the York boat brigades. That heyday was past, and for the next thirty-five years Brochet, drowsing in its isolation, would remain one of the least changed posts in all the North.[11] But Oberholtzer was glad to have reached it, for this settlement was the last he could hope to see for many weeks to come and offered his final chance to obtain a guide.

At first sight, "Du Brochet, with its picketed cemetery and church and numerous clay-covered houses on the south side of a sand ridge, looked a considerable village. On closer inspection, however, most of the buildings, especially the HBC store, which had a pair of caribou antlers on the gable, proved pretty dilapidated. I gave Laurent half a dollar and some tobacco and went where he pointed out the Company's dwelling house. Allan Nunn, the assistant factor, introduced me to Andrew Flett, a halfbreed,[12] and a red-head named Roland, with whom he was playing pool. They listened in astonishment to my plans. Then all of them, together with [an] Indian named Alphonse Chipewyan, and several others, carried my outfit up into the kitchen. Alphonse was the man [who] had taken Father [Arsène] Turquetil down to Churchill by dog team and returned up the Little Seal [in 1911]. He looked a good man." Soon, Oberholtzer met Father Joseph Egenolf, who was to become a well-known northern figure. A first-rate Chipewyan linguist, an able traveller, and a stern, unyielding shepherd to his Indians, this German-born Oblate had been sent to Brochet in 1905; he was never to leave, and would die there in 1957.[13]

Oberholtzer has left us a rare vignette of a far northern Catholic service, which he attended the following morning: "Father Egenolf brought me a special chair and a prayer table to kneel on and I sat at the back of the church, where I could see all of the Indians at worship. The women and children sat on benches or on the floor to the left. The men in their wrinkled clothes and with their heads of black straight hair bowed sat to the right.... Nearly all the women seemed to have colds and some kept spitting.... [They] all wore shawls on their heads, black, striped-red, and gray; several wore dresses with neat tucks of green or blue round the skirts. When all the people had come in and crossed themselves with holy water from a conker shell at the door, the service began. Two altar boys, tinkling of bells, censers. An intermittent wheezing turned out to be an organ, with Alphonse presiding.... Service books in syllabic Chipewyan and illustrated. The thud of the flat moccasined feet when the Indians were leaving after they had taken communion. The rude equipment and decorations of the church. Stations of the cross, bunting, paper stained-glass, crucifix."

The next day's entry reveals how uncertain Oberholtzer was as to his route and destination but also how determined he was to take his chances. Alphonse Chipewyan could not go — his wife put her foot down — nor could El Laurent, who "said he was not well enough." And so, wrote Oberholtzer, "I made up my mind that...I would start north with Billy either for Ennadai [on the Kazan] or for Churchill via Nueltin. Billy said he thought we could find our way. I was [of] half a mind to go straight through to Chesterfield." Nunn, who, to his credit, had insisted that Magee sleep in the HBC dwelling with himself and Oberholtzer, "had afternoon tea and made us presents of gloves, moccasins, a deer skin, a skin bag, some dried meat that looked like leather, and a *pie*. He also helped carry down our outfit. I said good-bye to the priest...and then at nearly six o'clock on a beautiful clear evening, Billy and I set out for the [Cochrane] river."

Before following Oberholtzer up the Cochrane and into *terra incognita*, a further, clarifying, explanation of his audacity is in order. That nearly everyone he met thought him mad to persist with his plan — such as it was — is hardly surprising. The territory reaching north from the 59th parallel to the Kazan was almost entirely unexplored, was unpredictable in its weather and in the whereabouts of its only major game, the caribou, was but thinly populated by nomadic natives, and, with its rapids, windswept river expansions and lakes, and inevitable portages, presented a constant menace to two men travelling alone. A mere handful of white men had preceded Oberholtzer. The first of these explorers was of course Samuel Hearne, who was not followed until more than a century later, by Tyrrell. Though no explorer, Fr. Alphonse Gasté, OMI, had stolen a march on Tyrrell by travelling overland from Brochet to Ennadai in quest of Ahiarmiut souls in 1868.[14] In 1896, Joseph Lofthouse, the Anglican missionary at Fort Churchill, had canoed with two Indians from Hudson Bay up the Tha-anne River as far as South Henik Lake, where ice forced him to turn back.[15] We have caught a glimpse of the next such figure, Herbert Hall, on his way south from Ennadai Lake. And in 1908 J.P. Ault and C.C. Stewart of the Carnegie Institute of Washington's Land Magnetic Observations survey, guided by Indians from Brochet, had followed in Hall's path as far north as what was known as "Canoe Limit" on Putahow Lake, the spot at which canoe freight bound for Ennadai was unloaded and stored to await the winter dog teams.[16]

Of Nueltin Lake, almost nothing was known. In 1912 the likenesses of *Nu-thel-tin-tu-eh*, or Sleeping Island Lake, that appeared on maps were based solely on Hearne's experience, native reports, and conjectures. Hearne had crossed it in the winter of 1770-71, but his representations of "Island Lake" in both his MS map of 1772 and his published map of 1795 owed next to nothing to actual observation or surveying.[17] Tyrrell, who had journeyed far to the west of it, showed it on his 1896 map as a crude shape in dotted lines.[18] What Oberholtzer had been able to learn about the lake and routes to and from it derived simply from what the Caribou-Eaters and the Caribou Eskimos had passed on in the course of trading at Brochet and Ennadai. Distant, immense, and mysterious, it would, if he succeeded in finding it and its northern outlet, provide him with an opportunity to reach Hudson Bay in time to get south before being marooned, and almost surely killed, by winter weather. As he headed up the Cochrane, however, he still entertained the slim hope of going all the way to Chesterfield Inlet, where even if marooned, he and Billy could somehow pass the winter at the HBC post.

The route from the mouth of the Cochrane to Kasmere Lake has become well known to northern travellers in late years, and so can be dealt with sparingly. Caribou were met with in plenty, as were signs of their slaughter: "Caribou bones everywhere from Reindeer Lake up." August 7th found the companions sailing down the upper section of Tyrrell's Thanout Lake. On the eastern heights above the first narrows, "at the top-most point, some Indian has built a new conical lookout of spruce trees, from which he can see the surrounding country for miles." The Indian, then in his prime, was Casmir (variously spelled Kasimir, Kasmir, and Kasmere), who for five decades was the dominating personality and sometime chief of the Barren Land Band; in 1940 he would be buried on this commanding site, where the wooden cross that marks his grave still stands.[19] The partners kept going, "until at last on the west shore near the end, we saw the several well built log-hewn houses of the Red Head family." There here occurs what at first appears to be an unaccountable omission in the journal, for Oberholtzer says nothing about seeing Fort Hall. According to the Company's records, this outpost was built in 1910 by Herbert, who, it is thought, named it for his father, R.H. Hall, who had been appointed Fur Trade Commissioner that year. Yet when Ault went through in 1908 he spent three days taking observations at the "new loghouse residence...known as Husky Post or Fort Hall." How to make sense of this confusion? Oberholtzer was following Tyrrell's 1896 map, on which the Red Head place is shown, and had with him the G.S.C. explorer's report, in which he would have read that "a mile above the north end of the lake [on the NW shore], Red Head, the chief of the band of Chippewyan Indians trading at Reindeer Lake, has a comfortable little house where he spends the winter." The answer would seem to be that Oberholtzer somehow failed to hear of the existence of Fort Hall, which the indefatigable Herbert must have established in 1907 or 1908 on the Red Head site, presumably following the latter's death.[20] In the event, Oberholtzer did not stop, and saw only "a nondescript bushy dog with a cheerful curl in his tail" who followed them along the shore for a distance toward the portage that leads to Kasmere, or Theitaga, Lake.

On the 8th, on Kasmere Lake, Oberholtzer made up his mind to depart from Tyrrell's map and strike northeast for Nueltin, in the hope of thereby reaching the Bay and Churchill before freeze-up. Late that afternoon, at the northeast end of the lake where the southern part of the Thlewiaza River begins in earnest, they came upon a Chipewyan encampment consisting "entirely of squaws and children," one of the latter of whom, like the women, "indicated his inability to understand by exclaiming and putting his fingers in his ears. I first shook hands with two dirty old squaws, the older of whom had filth caked on her naked breasts." Having photographed them and given them a bit of tobacco, Oberholtzer was presented with a can of deer fat and a red handkerchief full of powdered deer meat; then he traded "a young squaw with a suckling" four plugs of tobacco for a pair of moccasins. "Everywhere," he recorded, "meat was hanging to dry and a number of fat skin bags showed how it was stored...in powdered form. A number of skins were in the lake soaking for the tanning and others stretched tight on the ground had been rubbed with caribou brains, which looked like brown moss or clay.... The dogs, as usual, were having fights and being belabored by the squaws. One squaw with a hideous twisted face and exposed teeth charged upon me with a stick as if to break the camera, but as everyone laughed, I did not move. Perhaps she was only claiming to be a witch, which she fully looked."

Moving on in the twilight, Oberholtzer and Magee found the river banks thick with dead caribou. "We counted 25 in the first 15 minutes of paddling and from there on saw them all the way down... sometimes whole, sometimes only the blue decaying meat, nearly always the white antlers. While we were getting supper an Indian named Null-get Josay, who was camped [close by] came over in his bark canoe to see us. He had one of the long, shallow kyack-like canoes used for deer hunting with a skin in the middle for a seat, a long bloody-headed spear, and a single and a double [bladed] paddle.[21] We gave him some supper, matches, and a smoke, for which he seemed grateful. He could not understand Cree but knew some Eskimo words for which he gave us the equivalents in Chipewyan." Early the next morning the travellers were treated generously at Null-get's camp, being given moccasins and "a pair of bloody skin gloves." Then, with half-understood directions for the course to Nueltin, they moved on downriver, and soon left the route to Putahow, the last known to white men, behind.

Here we must leave Oberholtzer and Billy Magee. They were not to meet another human being until they reached Hudson Bay thirty-four days later. During those weeks they explored, and Oberholtzer mapped, the southern Thlewiaza, the eastern shore of Nueltin—which Father Egenolf had taught him to pronounce "Nu-thel-tin"—and the northern Thlewiaza, from Sealhole Lake to the Bay. Inuit whom they providentially found at the river's mouth saw them safely to Fort Churchill, by whaleboat, after which they resumed their sagalike exploits, canoeing from Churchill to York Factory, then up the Hayes to Norway House, then, in bitter snow-filled weather, the length of Lake Winnipeg to Gimli, where they took out on November 5th.

That winter Oberholtzer sent a report on his canoe route from Kasmere Lake to the Bay and a blueprint of his three miles to the inch reconnaissance map to J.E. Chalifour, the Dominion's chief geographer in Ottawa, who acknowledged them with polite indifference. Earlier, only days after getting home, Oberholtzer had written to his exemplar, Tyrrell, who answered, "It was a hazardous undertaking for you to go through that northern country with one Indian who knew nothing of it...and I heartily congratulate you on having made a good adventurous journey which will add materially to our knowledge of that portion of northern Canada."[22] But Tyrrell's expectations came to nothing. As Oberholtzer explained in a letter to Downes in 1939, "I have never published anything about this trip. It was my ambition at the time to return to the general locality for five years, but that could never be carried out and my life has been very crowded ever since."[23]

*   *   *

Prentice Downes, like Oberholtzer an American and a Harvard man, resembled his predecessor in other particulars. He too found northern exploration and travel literature absorbing, was an able outdoorsman, and had developed a deep and lasting interest both in Indian cultures and the lore and history of the North. By 1939 he had four summers of northern travel behind him, two of which had been spent in the Pelican Narrows and Reindeer Lake countries.[24] But he had yet to venture north of Brochet. Whereas Oberholtzer had been inspired by Tyrrell, Downes was first stimulated with visions of the Barrens and the Caribou Eskimos by William Brooks Cabot, a redoubtable Labrador traveller, who had himself begun such a trip in 1918.[25] Since meeting Cabot in 1936, Downes's desire to canoe to Nueltin had been strengthened by what he heard of the lake and the way to it from traders, trappers, Indians, and Father Egenolf. Among these men was Del Simons, who had guided Thierry Mallet of Revillon Frères to the Kazan in 1926 and who was renowned throughout the region for his feats of hard travel.[26]

However, Simons, Egenolf, and others like them were a dying breed. The old North so irresistible to Downes – "the north," to use his words, "of no time, of game, of Indians, Eskimos, of unlimited space and freedom,"[27] had dwindled and was in its final few years. The transformations that followed the Great War had been dramatic, had altered many seemingly timeless features of the northern way of life and brought to a virtual end much that had been indigenous in the lives of both natives and whites. The bushplane was now a fixture; outboard motors propelled freight canoes that only a few years earlier would have been paddled by men; great mining operations had been established, as had commercial fisheries; the Company's former far-reaching monopoly had been crippled by rivals and by a proliferation of free traders; and the tentacles of bureaucracy, both federal and provincial, had reached to many a spot that hitherto had known only the authority of the Hudson's Bay Company, a missionary or two, and an infrequent Mounted Policeman.

Yet for all the changes the postwar years had brought in, there remained much that appeared everlasting. Indians, Christianized though nearly all of them were, and despite the weakening of their cultures, held to their immemorial myths and skills. Among white trappers, traders, prospectors, missionaries, and policemen, feats of wilderness travel, by canoe in summer or with dogs in winter, were celebrated and remembered, and a man could still make his name by the distance he could run in thirty-below weather or by the weight of the load he could carry on a portage. The demands and hardships of climatic extremes, isolation, and tremendous physical challenges were still common, and created among true northerners an attitude almost contemptuous toward those from "outside" who were strangers to such experience. These characteristics were still pronounced in the Reindeer Lake country and in the back-of-beyond reaching north and east from it, a region which in 1939 remained all but unmapped and would stay so until aerial mapping came fully into its own after 1945.

Downes, bound for the Barrens, was a romantic, of course. But he was more honest and astute about his escapism than most outsiders. In 1936, returning to Boston by train after canoeing to Reindeer Lake with a Cree, he had made this entry in his journal: "Several people have said, 'Now you can write up a wonderful account of your sights, etc.' But how can you write about it. One way, you see the romantic North no longer romantic; you see people working and starving for a precarious living, you see Indians losing everything hundreds of years have handed down to them—losing it through missionaries and [other] whites so that they are but poor imitations of both whites and Indians. You see them dying of t.b. everywhere. You see country burned [deliberately, by prospectors], and game pushed out and trapped out.... The real people of the North...cling to that complex in themselves which is satisfied by their situation—by the freedom of being their own boss, or any of the other set-ups which the North may offer—to make money, or the illusion of a strike, or the wandering irresponsibility of it all." On the same page, he added, "I know I will always go north again."[28]

Now, three summers later, arriving in Pelican Narrows by air on June 23, Downes found that the abandoned Revillon Frères store had become a government day school for Cree children. Having got his grubstake for Brochet, he played bridge with none other than Father Guilloux, "a curious old creature. It is a wonder to me that such as he keep as much sanity as they do.... One has...to bear in mind that many of these creatures [Oblate missionaries] are not human in a sense which would include tolerance and a breadth of view—they are fanatics—and human values are of small account to fanatics."[29] The evening before he pulled out, he, the HBC men, and assorted Crees listened to the Louis-Gallento heavyweight title fight on the radio. One familiar with Downes's journals is here reminded of the Cree with whom he travelled in 1936, who was so impressed by news of the former heavyweight champion Max Baer that he told Downes: "That Baer, I bet he was trained [for portaging], he pack 600 pounds."[30]

The first leg of the journey, from Pelican to South End, was by outboard-powered freight canoe. Downes found his Cree companions, the sons of those York boatmen Thwaites had bragged about to Oberholtzer, skilful, hard working, and cheerful. At South End, he was able to take passage aboard the Company's motor vessel *Lac du Brochet*, which had been in service on Reindeer since 1924. "There was a good deal of chat on illegal fur—marten & beaver.... The fur trader who tries to deal strictly within the law is apparently handicapping himself badly. Personally, I see little excuse for the existence of so much illegal traffic if there was any real law enforcement at all. After all, it centers down to a very few well known trippers or buyers. If no one will buy up illegal furs, obviously no Indian is going to go out of his way to trap it. If the police, instead of [undertaking] tremendous, heroic patrols which do no particular good would busy themselves in an aggressive manner in more domestic affairs, they could stamp it out."

Another development that would have taken Oberholtzer and Magee aback was a commercial fishery at Halfway Island. "It is," Downes noted, "quite a business, with the cook shack, ice house, etc. 'Wings' is flying out the fish for them. We had a fine lunch at the camp—with *pie*. I never thought the day would come when I would have *pie* in the middle of Reindeer Lake."

Father Egenolf was aboard, and Downes found him "as gay and voluble as ever." In 1937 he had written that the missionary "is a remarkable linguist, one of the very few [whites] who can really speak Chipewyan.... His insight into the Chip mind is profound and he is a marvelous dialectician. He frankly admits that he has but one real hold on the Indians and that is fear. He says, 'I cannot make them Christians. I am beginning to believe that our Lord did not intend that they be lifted up. They are so independent. They do what they please. As soon as they leave me and go back into the bush—whish! Back to their old beliefs and ways again. They never tell the truth, never, if it suits their convenience not to, and they will not learn.' He told me a tale which made me smile a bit. While the Indians are in here [in Brochet] in the summer, he runs a daily catechism class for the children. Day after day he drills them, pounds in the questions and answers. There is one long passage which asks, 'What is the most beautiful thing our Lord has created?' The automatic answer according to the Catechism is, 'The angels & man.' Time and again when he went through this formula, all the children could mumble it correctly—all but one little girl, who insisted on replying each time, 'Idthen'—the caribou. 'So you see,' he concluded, 'they will not, they are not able to learn.'... He went on: 'When I left Prince Albert 32 years ago, my friends waved to me and said, "When will you be back?" I raised my fingers: "Three years!" I said. It has been almost 33 years now. I am old. I am done. In that time, in all those years, travel, travel, dog-team, snowshoes, canoe ... I have done what with these people? —*nothing*!' Personally," Downes continued, "I hate the very sight of these black-robed wretches. But honor is due where honor is earned; old Father Egenolf is a remarkable man and far, far superior to any of his calling whom I have known. If only I could handle [the Chipewyans'] impossible tongue, [they, he says,] would tell me stories all day long."[31]

As the vessel made her way north, Egenolf informed Downes that "the Barren Land Band is not yet in and I will no doubt meet them on the Cochrane. He warned me against giving away my grub supply: 'For they are just like children — terrible beggars.'... He told me of a time, the first winter he spent with the Chips, when he wrote out to a fellow colleague: 'Thank our dear Lord you were not born a Chip. That is something you can always thank him for.'"

They arrived at Brochet on July 2nd, and Downes, a pemmican enthusiast, purchased some for his trip. That evening he heard more tales about the locally famous Del Simons, stories of the sort that were to lead him to write this passage in his classic book, *Sleeping Island*:

> I sat enthralled in the lamplight. The big and small men crowded into the little low-roofed room caused a grotesquerie of light and shadow, and through it all rose and fell the conversation and comment. There was no intrusion of "outside" in this world. And though the conversation was all of the North, it was not the North of any circumscribed small spot. Names mentioned brought other names, and reminiscences wandered with the fluidity of the shadows from the Arctic Ocean to Winnipeg and from the Yukon to Hudson Bay. Time, too, in these conversations seems to lose all importance; twenty years or yesterday live alike in this timeless land. The geographical immensity of the country is staggering, yet so few are its white people, that among those who have spent any real time in the country there is an invisible bond and connecting web of acquaintance all over the North.[32]

Although now linked by aircraft with the outside, Brochet had changed little since 1912. During the twenties it had become the jumping-off place for Nueltin Lake when Revillon, the HBC, and free traders established outposts there. The other development of interest occurred from 1931 to 1936, when the HBC, unable to compete with the combined opposition of Revillon Frères and independent traders, temporarily surrendered the post to the French Company.[33] "It is," Downes had written in 1937, "one of the true gateways into the Barrens. It was not many years ago when the ... Caribou Eskimos used to occasionally come down from the Kazan River to trade at this post. But today, with the various coastal posts on Hudson Bay, and particularly the inland post, Padlei [established in 1925 on the Maguse River], they no longer do this." Now he recorded that "there has been a good deal of flying north of here to Padlei, where the H.B. Mining & Smelting has prospectors in the field.... North of Nueltin the pilot reports ice — ice everywhere, and snow."

Downes enjoyed no better luck than Oberholtzer had in obtaining an Indian guide: "Solomon Cook refuses to go at the price of $50 a month [plus] something for his canoe and grub. He'd rather sit around and starve. I'll be goddammed if I will be held up for some ridiculous price by any of these chaps. Particularly as it is no freighting job." Downes visited Father Egenolf "to see about the route & also some meat. He has never been to Nueltin (properly Nu-thel-tin-tua: Lake-with-the-island-lying down) by the water route, so was [of] little assistance ... although he was cheering and also promised me some dried meat. He also advised me that Solomon Cook has fits." Fortunately for Downes, a German trapper in from Wollaston Lake agreed to join him, but the prospect was not pleasing: "I do not want a white man, but an Indian. It is most discouraging.... However, I shall go on—even though neither one of us knows one foot of the route. It is a departure for me—the first time I have ever travelled with a white man." On July 6, having been given "8 caribou tongues & a bit of pemmican" by Father Egenolf, and having bought an additional five pounds of pemmican from the Company, Downes and his partner, John Albrecht, embarked, about to follow, unbeknownst to Downes, the selfsame route taken by Oberholtzer and Magee twenty-seven years before.

Five days into the trip, at Misty Lake on the Cochrane River, "we spotted tents on a point, a big encampment. As we approached, another canoe pulled in, but from the north.... The other canoe—which had an engine—held old Casmir ... and a bunch of others.... It was the northern, or Barren Land Band of Chipewyans on their way down to Brochet. We shook hands all around.... It was a rather nerve-racking business, as the crowd just stood and stared—not smiling ... quite as ill at ease as we were.... Eventually I got out my [all but useless] map and went over the route with Casmir and Edzanni.... They were a wild-looking outfit. A surprising number of cross-eyed children & men—the children very Mongol-looking. The tension lessened after a while. Old Casmir had the most curious rig, a peaked sort of bonnet & a 10 lb. flour sack around his neck. He is a powerfully built chap, & the granddaddy of the northern band. He looked like some ancient gnome."

Downes and Albrecht moved on. Late that day, as they dined on a jackfish at the foot of a portage, "two men came upon us so silently [that] they were standing by the fire before we realised it. One of them, Pierre, knew about 10 words of English. We gave them each a smoke and some tea and Pierre became quite affable. Relieved of the pressure of a crowd, I managed to get along much better.... It developed that there were a lot of Chips on the way down.... There [is] also a band at the mouth of the Putahow River [on the southwestern shore of Nueltin].... He understood when I said I was an American (Beschaw), but could not figure out where I came from, as I said 'no' to both Fond du Lac &

Churchill. He said in 2 Sundays there would be lots of caribou at Nueltin Lake. We really, by using English, Cree, & Chip, got along very well."

Two days later, still working upriver on the Cochrane, and just finishing breakfast, Downes "saw a canoe sailing down upon us.... The newcomers were two more of the band who had been hunting.... The older was Louis Néglé. He had one eye. They [drank] some tea ... & the one-eyed gentleman was most informative, though he knew not a word of English, [only] some Cree. He drew a map for me of the route to Nueltin Lake & I expect it is much more accurate than the sketch which I possess....[34] Out of our 'conversation' it developed that there are lots of Chips at the mouth of the Putahow; that Eskimo Charlie is at Putahow Lake;[35] that the mosquitos are very, very bad & even the Huskies' eyes swell up so they can hardly see – and as for me – big laugh. The Eskimos trade in at Windy [River HBC post] in the winter.... We will not see deer until [we reach] Nueltin. He first went to Nueltin when he was five years old [and] a stick flew up & put his eye out.... He was well acquainted with the route to Churchill via Caribou Lake post....[36] In fact he had a wealth of information he was quite willing to impart but which I could not [understand]."

July 15th found the canoemen traversing the Esker Lakes between the Cochrane and Fort Hall Lake, and here they encountered two more groups of Brochet-bound Chipewyans. "Paddling through a narrows," Downes wrote, "we abruptly came upon two big canoes loaded with men & one woman.... They were straight down from the north – had bags & bags of dried meat.... We gave them a smoke. Finally one of the men dragged out a piece of dried meat for us. The woman was very vague and very reticent. She had a baby in a moss bag.... I wonder how many white men have ever really seen this...migration of the *Idthen-Eldeli* down out of the Barrens, actually in progress." Downes was one of the last to do so, as within a few years this way of life would be finished.

On what had long since become known as Fort Hall Lake, Downes and Albrecht passed the narrows where Oberholtzer and Magee had noticed Casmir's "new conical lookout of spruce trees." In the following summer of 1940, returning this way from an unsuccessful attempt to reach the Kazan, and having by then learned more about Casmir, Downes recorded that "we went ashore at the first narrows. On the east side...on the high cut-bank knoll, is the grave of old Kasmere, who died last spring. It is a fine spot. There he stands (if they accorded him his last request), looking down the lake so – as he said – he could watch for [his] people coming and wish them good luck; so that he could watch the deer for them and see them as they passed by."[37]

Fort Hall itself "had quite fallen to rack and ruin. There were many signs of more recent occupancy—some very large deerskins lying about, a big set of horns and head upon the porch roof. Everywhere caribou bones. Up in back was a little graveyard with eleven graves." Farther along, at the head of the carry to Kasmere Lake, the men passed the wreck of what had, in the 1920s, been a Revillon Frères outpost.

On July 19th, at the northeast extremity of Kasmere Lake, on the site where years before Oberholtzer and Magee had visited the encampment of Chipewyan women and children, Downes found only "a fenced enclosure—graves.... there were wolverine tracks leading from...some twenty-five old graves. One, that of a child, had just been dug out by a fox. On some of the rickety little crosses were hung the victims' rosaries."

As we left Oberholtzer near here, so we leave Downes. How he reached Nueltin, found the rest of the Barren Land Band at the mouth of the Putahow, and was guided by two of them to the HBC's remote Windy River post, where a party of Kazan River Inuit had come in to trade, is told in *Sleeping Island*.

The great lake was not much better known than it had been in 1912. White trappers had moved into the country by the end of the Great War, and in 1924 one of them, "Husky" Harris, found a cairn on the summit at Nueltin Narrows, and in it a tin can with a note left by Oberholtzer. He took the note but left the can in place. Revillon Frères, the HBC, and a handful of free traders established outposts on the northwestern reaches of the lake during the 1920s, but the activity of that decade soon ebbed, as did familiarity with the canoe route from Brochet, and by the late 1930s Nueltin was, for white men, nearly as isolated from the outside as it had been in Oberholtzer's day.[38] Downes's reconnaissance mapping of the lake and its approaches from Kasmere proved helpful, but accurate, aerial maps of the region would not appear until the 1950s.

From Windy, Downes managed to fly out to Churchill, where he met Cecil "Husky" Harris.[39] "Harris tells me," he wrote in his journal, "that Oberhauser or Obenhauser made his trip through in 1911." This was the first Downes learned of his predecessor's feat. It was now late August, but Downes had time in hand and so made his way back to Pelican Narrows, where he and the schoolteacher "talked of the war news. That is all I have heard since coming out. It sickens and disgusts me.... Better to be back in the Barrens among civilised people—Chips and Huskies."

From Pelican, at summer's end, Downes retraced most of what had been the first stage of Oberholtzer's route. In order to travel yet again with the Crees he so admired, he joined a freighting crew that carried empty gasoline drums out to Amisk Lake and returned to the Narrows with twenty-five hundred pounds of freight in their two canoes. At Dog Rapids Downes saw, "washed up on [a] ledge ... a gigantic oar — an old York boat oar — what tremendous sweeps these are!" In 1947, on his last canoe trip, he was to find it still there, serving as a route marker.

Before 1939 was out, Downes, having learned that Oberholtzer was still living, wrote to him, and the now distinguished conservationist replied enthusiastically to what he described as "your amazing letter." He remembered Father Egenolf as "a rare personality and... the best informed man I met." And he remarked that he would like nothing better than to revisit Nutheltin — he had not forgotten the correct pronunciation taught him by the missionary — but feared the expense. "What you tell me about yourself," he added, "though very little and modest, is [most] intriguing. You are to be congratulated on your spirit and good taste in the choice of a pastime."[40]

Downes eventually visited Oberholtzer at Rainy Lake, and the two corresponded until Downes's death in 1959. In 1963, Oberholtzer, in his eightieth year, returned to Nueltin. Accompanied by a young friend, he flew in to a commercial fish camp on the 60th parallel, was given the loan of a steel boat, and set forth. "With my own map made 51 years before," he later wrote, "we had not the slightest difficulty finding our way." Below Hawkes Summit, where Hearne Bay stretches southeast to the horizon, Oberholtzer, who had injured himself, crawled ashore; painfully, he dragged himself uphill among the boulders. And there, on the summit, "we located the cairn and the very same tin container in which I had left a note all that time ago.... I have the can here now and the wonder is that it is so little rusted."[41]

In his final years, Oberholtzer was brought to reminisce about his great voyage with Billy Magee,[42] and in his mind's eye saw again the flash of approaching paddles across sunlit water, York boats under sail, the clay-sided houses of Brochet, the Chipewyans' bloody gifts, and the far-distant, island-mazed lake he had found. But the last vestiges of that world had been seen by Downes, and the old man, as he looked north in memory, was recalling images that had vanished forever.

Notes

1.   Interview with Ernest C. Oberholtzer, 1963; Acc. #9430, Reel 1, Minnesota Historical Society, St. Paul.

2.   J. Burr Tyrrell, "Report on the Dubaunt, Kazan and Ferguson Rivers and the North-West Coast of Hudson Bay," in Geological Survey of Canada *Report* for 1896, vol. 9 (Ottawa: Queen's Printer, 1897).

3.   Interview with Oberholtzer. For a fuller account of both the 1912 trip and Oberholtzer's life, see R.H. Cockburn, "Voyage to Nutheltin," *The Beaver* 66 (January/February 1986): 4-27.

4.   Ernest C. Oberholtzer, Journal of Trip to Nutheltin Lake, 1912, Ernest C. Oberholtzer Foundation, Chicago. MS and typescript. All subsequent unnumbered quotations in the first part of this paper come from this source.

5.   See, for example, William McInnes, Map 58A, "Explored Routes in the lower parts of the drainage area of Churchill and Nelson Rivers, Manitoba and Saskatchewan," Department of Mines Geological Survey (Ottawa, 1914).

6   Mrs. Frances Adair, née Cotter, letter to author, 24 July 1985. And see Robert Watson, "Captain Cotter of Cumberland," *The Beaver* 260 (September 1929): 260-61.

7.   R.H. Cockburn, ed., "To Reindeer's Far Waters: P.G. Downes's Journal of Travels in Northern Saskatchewan, 1936," *Fram: The Journal of Polar Studies* 1 (Winter 1984): 144. See also H.S.M. Kemp, *Northern Trader* (London: Jarrolds, 1957), 36; and L. Donovan Clark, *Raisins in the Rice* (Renfrew, Ontario: Juniper, 1983), 42.

8.   Herbert H. Hall (1880-1938) was the toughest and most venturesome Barren Lands traveller of his generation. In 1906 he established an outpost at Ennadai Lake for the HBC. See both "Trader Hall Recounts Experiences in Arctic," *Prince Albert Herald*, 10 Dec. 1932; and "Hall, Herbert Hanley," in Employees: HBC vertical file, HBC Library, Winnipeg.

9.   Father A. Chamberland, OMI, letter to author, 9 August 1984.

10. *David Thompson's Narrative 1784-1812*, ed. Richard Glover (Toronto: Champlain Society, 1962), 113-14.

11. See P.G. Downes, *Sleeping Island* (New York: Coward-McCann, 1943), 75-89; and J.A. Rodgers, "Lac du Brochet," *The Beaver* 275 (March 1945): 11-13.

12. Flett, like many another obscure northerner, lived a full life. By 1912 he had driven dogs for the Mounted Police during the Klondike Rush and had served as a sharpshooter with Canadian troops in the Boer War (Dr. R.M. MacCharles, letter to author, undated, February 1985); Downes was to meet him at Amisk Lake, Saskatchewan, in 1939. See R.H. Cockburn, "'Like Words of Fire:' Lore of the Woodland Cree from the Journals of P.G. Downes," *The Beaver* 315 (Winter 1984/85): 39.

13. Father A. Chamberland, OMI, letter to author, 10 March 1984.

14. See "Father Gasté Meets the Inland Eskimos" and Father G. Mary-Rousselière, "Importance of Father Gasté's Voyage" in *Eskimo* 57 (1960): 3-17. Father Mary-Rousselière offers the dubious assertion that Father Gasté travelled as far as Dubawnt Lake.

15. The Right Reverend Joseph Lofthouse, *A Thousand Miles from a Post Office* (Toronto: The Macmillan Company of Canada, 1922), 156-63.

16. L.A. Bauer, Researches of the Department of Terrestrial Magnetism, *Land Magnetic Observations, 1905-1910*, Pub. 175, vol. 1 (Washington, D.C.: The Carnegie Institution of Washington, 1912), 112, 151, and 153.

17. See Samuel Hearne, *A Journey to the Northern Ocean*, ed. Richard Glover (Toronto: The Macmillan Company of Canada, 1958), 43-46.

18. See map accompanying J. Burr Tyrrell, "Report on the Dubaunt, Kazan and Ferguson Rivers."

19. Robert J. LeBlanc, letter to author, 12 October 1983.

20. Records for this, as for so many of the outposts operated by the HBC, are all but nonexistent. See Hudson's Bay Company Archives [HBCA] standing files on Fort Hall (Manitoba), Herbert

Hall, and The Barrens. Downes's investigations suggest that the "Fort" saw intermittent use as an outpost into the early 1920s. For a good account of place names between the Cochrane and Kasmere Lake, and from Kasmere to northern Nueltin, see P.G. Downes, "Notes on the Place Names Used on Four Sheets Covering a Reconnaissance Map in Northern Manitoba and the Northwest Territories," file 64/18609 (Aeronautical Charts Section, Geographical Services Division, Energy, Mines and Resources Canada, Ottawa, n.d., photocopied).

21. See E.T. Adney and H.I. Chapelle, *The Bark Canoes and Skin Boats of North America* (Washington, D.C.: Smithsonian Institution, 1964), 166-67.

22. J.B. Tyrrell, letter to E.C. Oberholtzer, 16 November 1912. The Ernest C. Oberholtzer Foundation, Chicago.

23. Ernest C. Oberholtzer to P.G. Downes, 7 December 1939. Mrs. E.G. Downes.

24. See "To Reindeer's Far Waters" and R.H. Cockburn, ed., "Distant Summer: P.G. Downes's 1937 Inland Journal," *Fram: The Journal of Polar Studies*, 2 (1986): 31-119.

25. See Stephen Loring, *O Darkly Bright: The Labrador Journeys of William Brooks Cabot, 1899-1910* (Middlebury, Vermont: Johnson Memorial Gallery, Middlebury College, 1985), 5. Stephen Loring, letter to author, 12 April 1986.

26. See "Distant Summer," 74, 84, and 99-102.

27. P.G. Downes, *Prentice G. Downes: Selections From His Writings* (Belmont, Massachusetts: Belmont Hill School, 1960), 6.

28. "To Reindeer's Far Waters," 174.

29. P.G. Downes, "Sleeping Island" journal, 1939. Mrs. E.G. Downes. MS. All subsequent unnumbered quotations come from this source.

30. "To Reindeer's Far Waters," 151.

31. "Distant Summer," 67.

32. *Sleeping Island*, 60-61.

33. From Annual Report, Outfit 261 (1930-31), Saskatchewan District; HBCA: "...last year no goods were forwarded on account of Lac du Brochet Post, as arrangements had been made for the taking over of the post by R[evillon] F[rères].... Apart from the difficulty in getting information re the fur market to Lac du Brochet, also its Outposts, we have had to contend with very stiff opposition both from R.F., and D.E. Simons, particularly the latter, who not only pays more for his fur but also charters an aeroplane to bring his fur out, and apparently finds it profitable, and yet our returns from Brochet show a loss...."

34. See *Sleeping Island*, 124.

35. For an account of "Eskimo" Charlie Planinshek, see R.H. Cockburn, ed., "North of Reindeer: The 1940 Trip Journal of P.G. Downes," *The Beaver* 313 (Spring 1983): 42-43.

36. The HBC's Caribou Lake post, situated some 130 miles NW from Churchill, had been established in 1930, shortly after the Hudson Bay Railway reached Churchill, in an attempt to keep the Chipewyans "away from the doubtful benefits of civilisation in its pioneering stage." See HBCA standing files on the post itself and The Barrens.

37. P.G. Downes, 1940 journal. Mrs. E.G. Downes. MS. And see *Sleeping Island*, 114-18.

38. See "Floats: A Flying Episode off Eskimo Point, Hudson Bay," *The Beaver*, 264 (June 1933): 48: "From Churchill [in 1932], freight was carried in to Nueltin Lake.... Owing to the inaccuracy of the maps of this region, Nueltin was difficult to locate." Further evidence of Nueltin's "unknown" character can be detected in the Aeronautical Edition of the Nueltin Lake 8:1 Sheet, National Topographic Series, Department of Mines and Resources, 1946.

39. The Company did not find Harris a prepossessing figure: "Mr Harris of Eskimo Post [Ennadai Lake] lives an unclean life and cannot be retained any longer [early months of 1921]" Corres. No. 19, Transfer File 5, HBC Archives.

40. Oberholtzer to Downes, 7 December 1939.

41. Ernest C. Oberholtzer to Francis Harper, 26 June 1964. The Ernest C. Oberholtzer Foundation, Chicago.

42.   Interview with Oberholtzer. Also author's interviews with Ray Anderson, Robert Hilke, and Charles A. Kelly, Rainy Lake, Minnesota, 18-24 August 1985.

INDEX

Abitibi River, 21, 60
Abney, William, 233
Ackermann and Co., 160
Adamson, Robert, 230
aesthetics, 2, 7, 9, 11, 21, 149, 164, 227, 230, 231, 261
agrarian reform, 10, 268
agriculture, 8, 9, 10, 118, 202, 204, 205, 217, 219, 220, 253, 254, 255, 256, 258, 259, 264, 265, 268
Ahiarmiut, 281
airplane, 11, 285, 288, 291
Akaitcho, 104
Alaska, 73
Albany Fort, 67
Alberta, 22, 50, 200, 201, 202, 214, 216, 217, 219, 222, 224, 262
Albrecht, John, 289, 290
alcohol, 100, 101, 104, 105, 123, 125, 223
Alemenipigon, 21
Alexander, 154
Alix, Alberta, 217
all-British route, 201, 203
Allen, John Logan, 94, 95, 96
Altick, Richard, 160
Americae Pars Borealis, Baccalaos, Canada, Corterealis (de Jode), 40
American Civil War, 233
Amisk Lake, 278, 292
ammunition, 62, 100, 101, 104, 105, 108
Anderson, David, 218
Anderton, George, 234, 252
Anglican Bishop: of Athabasca, 214; of Rupert's Land, 218; of Saskatchewan, 219
Anglican Cathedral of St. Johns, 216
Anglican Church, 116, 202, 213, 215, 216, 217-20, 223-24, 281
Annian Regnum, 18
Antarctic, 109
Appalachian Mountains, 81
apartheid, 222
Arcadia, 18
Archbishop of Cashel, 195
Archer, Frederick Scott, 228

Arctic Explorations: The Second Grinnell Expedition (Kane), 161
Arctic Highlanders, 154
Arctic Land Expedition, 1819-22, 4-5, 27, 35, 97, 98, 158, 167; 1825-27, 98, 109, 158, 166
Arctic Regions (Burford), 159
Arrowsmith, Aaron, 3, 4, 26, 27, 44, 47, 79, 80, 84-92
Arrowsmith, John, 27, 48, 50
artists, 1, 7, 21, 151, 152, 154, 157-59, 162-70, 228, 231, 260, 261
Asiatic peoples and New World peoples, 54
Aspen Parkland, 204, 256
assimilation, 4, 8, 69, 217-20, 222, 285, 286
Assiniboine and Saskatchewan Exploring Expedition, 229, 238
Assiniboine Indians, 22, 202
Assiniboine River, 23, 24, 118, 198, 215, 229, 253
astronomical observations, 200-203, 282
Athabasca District, 98, 104
Athabasca Portage, 199
Athabasca River, 102, 199, 201
Athapaskan, Northern, 131
Atkinson, George, Jr., 67
attrition, 66, 258
Ault, J.P., 281, 282
aurora borealis, 151
Austin, H.T., 160
Autumn Hillsides, 260
Ayllon, Lucas Vasquez de, 17

Back, George, 4, 7, 101-103, 105-107, 110, 111, 155, 157, 158, 165-69, 179, 189-93, 195, 196
Back River, 168
Baffin Bay, 13, 97, 153, 154, 156
Baffin Island, 3, 13, 17, 52, 155, 157, 213
Baffin Island Inuit, 216
Baker Lake, 275
Ball, John, 196, 211
Banks Island, 59

banlai, 137
Baptist Church, 223
Barents, William, 156
Barren Grounds, 10, 16, 20, 165,
    254, 275, 284-85, 288, 290-91; *see
    also* tundra
Barren Land band Chipewyan, 279,
    282, 287, 289, 291
Barrow, John, 98, 110, 153
Bartram, Michael, 227, 231
Battle Creek, 207
Battle River, 199
beads, 61, 62
Beads, James, 200
bears, 136, 195, 208, 245
Beaudry (HBC *engagé*), 120
beaver, 63, 65, 67, 68, 136, 142, 286
Beaver Creek, 198
Beaver Hills, 198
Beaver Indians, 219
Beechey, Frederick William, 154
Belcher, Edward, 174
Bell, Robert, 234, 251
belle-mère, 206
Bellin, Nicolas, 24
Bellot, Joseph René, 158
Beothuck Indians, 52
Berg off Cape Melville (Hamilton),
    161
Bergen, 53
Bergi Regio, 18
Bethune, Angus, 120
Big Bend of the Columbia River, 199
Bird, E.J., 160
Birket-Smith, Kaj, 70
bison, 62, 66, 76, 133, 195-99, 202,
    203, 208, 254
Blackfoot Indians, 198, 199, 202,
    205, 206, 208, 210, 223
Blackwood's Edinburgh Magazine,
    162
Blakiston, Thomas W., 197, 198,
    199, 202, 208, 209
Blodget, Lorin, 27
Blood Indians, 202
Board of School Management, 218
Boat Encampment, 199
Boats in a Swell amongst Ice
    (Back), 155
Bompas, Bishop William, 214, 219,
    222, 223

boreal forest, 1, 132, 133, 137, 138,
    141, 152, 204
botany, 3, 197, 199, 202, 204, 207,
    208
Boundary Pass, *see* South Kootenay
    Pass
Bourbon, Fort, *see* York Factory
Bourbon River, *see* Nelson River
Bourgeau, Eugéne, 197, 199, 200,
    208
Bow Pass, 199
Bow River, 196, 199, 200
Bowen, Thomas, 22
Bradford, William, 151, 161
Brazil, 51, 55, 56, 61, 63
Brick, John Gough, 219
Briggs, Henry, 19
Brightman, Robert, 123
Brisco, Arthur, 210
British Admiralty, 4-5, 7, 97, 148,
    154, 158, 160, 162, 166, 167
British Columbia, 16, 224, 229, 233
British Museum, 207, 231, 275
British Treasury, 196
Brochet, 276, 279, 280-82, 284, 286,
    287, 288-92
Brown, Jennifer S.H., 73, 123
Brownie, William H.G., 160, 161,
    177, 185
Buache, Philippe, 25, 42
Buchan, David, 149, 156
Budd, Henry, 215
buffalo, *see* bison
Buffalo Lake, 200
Burford, Robert, 157, 159, 160, 161,
    177, 185
*Burford's Panorama of the Polar
    Regions*, 177, 185
Burke, Edmund, 164
Butler, William Francis, 214, 224,
    234
Button, Thomas, 13, 57, 59
By Track and Trail (Roper), 260
Bylot, Robert, 13
Bylot Island, 153, 155

Cabot, John, 16
Cabot, William Brooks, 284
Cabral, Pedro, 55
Cahen, Paul, 206
calotype, 228

camera, 9, 228, 231, 232, 234, 283
camera lucida, 164
Camp at the Elbow of the North Saskatchewan River, 232
Campbell, Alexander, 120,121
Canada/United States border, 196-201, 203-204, 233
Canadian Historical Society, 267
Canadian literature, 10, 256, 259-62, 268
Canadian Pacific Railway, 203, 232, 233, 257, 258, 260, 263, 267
Canadian Shield, 255, 275
Canadian Wildlife Service, 134
cannibalism, 56, 65, 70, 97, 134, 158
Canoe Limit, 281
Canuck, Janey, *see* Murphy, Emily
Cape Breton, 16
Cape York, 153
caribou, 6-7, 10, 62, 131-36, 138-39, 141-43, 204, 275, 279-83, 287, 290-91
Caribou Eater Chipewyan, 6-7, 11, 131-46, 282
Caribou Inuit, 74, 275, 282, 284, 288
Caribou Lake Post, 290
Carlton, Fort, *see* Carlton House
Carlton House, 103, 197-99, 201, 247
Carlton Trail, 197
Carnegie Institute of Washington, 281
Carpenter, Edmund, 157
Carte de la Nouvelle France (Chatelain), 43
Carte Physique des Terreines ... de la Partie Occidentale du Canada (Buache), 42
Cartier, Jacques, 13, 17, 58
cartography, 2, 3, 4, 7, 13-50, 201, 255
Carver, Jonathan, 82
Casmir (Kasimir, Kasmere, Kasmir), 282, 289, 290
Castel, Father, 25
castor, *see* beaver
catechism, 135-36, 287
Cathay, 16
Catholic Church, 202, 214-16, 218, 224, 280
Cevallos, Pedro, 94
Chalifour, J.E., 284

Champlain, Samuel de, 19
Champlain Society, 128
Charles II, 2, 6, 13
Charles, Fort, 60, 61
Chatelain, H.A., 43
Chesterfield Inlet, 53, 275-77, 282
Chestnut canoe, 275
Chipewyan, Alphonse, 280
Chipewyan, Fort, 102-107, 111
Chipewyan Indians, 6-7, 64-66, 74, 76, 131-46, 222, 248-50, 279-80, 282-83, 287-92; language, 67, 280, 283, 287
Chipewyan Indian graves and mourners near Dufferin, c. 1873, 250
Chipewyan Indians at Dufferin, 1873-74, 248
Chipewyan Indians near Dufferin, 1873, 249
Christian beliefs, 116, 124, 135, 215, 216, 221, 287; values, 117, 121, 122, 124, 216, 221, 223, 287
Christianity, 8, 56, 124, 138, 141, 213-24, 285, 287
Christie, James, 277, 278
Christie, Mrs., 199
Christino, *see* Cree Indians
Church, Frederick Edwin, 151, 161
Church of England, *see* Anglican Church
Church Missionary Society, 215
Churchill Factory, *see* Churchill, Fort
Churchill, Fort, 26, 64, 66-67, 132, 133, 135, 138, 139, 141, 276, 280, 281, 283, 284, 290-91
Churchill River, 20, 21, 59, 255, 276, 278
cinematography, 152
Claesz, Cornelis, 37
Clark, William, 4, 87-92
Claude glass, 164
Clearwater River, 166, 167
Clevely, John II, 159
clergy, 6, 8, 213, 215, 216; *see also* missionaries
climate, 8, 119, 199, 202, 207, 254-56, 258, 259, 263, 281, 285
clothing, 6, 53, 58, 70, 105, 125, 133, 134, 137, 139, 205, 231, 280

Clouston, James, 15, 26
coal, 202
Coats, William, 22
Cochrane, Henry, 220
Cochrane River, 281, 282, 287, 289
Cockburn, R.H., 145, 293
Cocking, Matthew, 66
cold, 9, 119, 137, 204, 227, 229
Cold Lake, 202
Coleridge, Samuel Taylor, 150, 156
Collins, Wilkie, 162
collodion process, 228-30, 233, 236
Colonial Office, 98, 100, 102, 108,
    113, 196-200
colony, 3, 24, 149, 203, 204, 227
Colony of the United Canadas, 8,
    195, 254
Columbia River, 25, 83, 86-90, 92,
    93, 118, 199, 200, 203
Columbus, Christopher, 15, 16
Colville, Fort, 198, 208, 231, 241,
    242
Combe, William, 166
Comfort, Charles, 260
commerce, *see* trade
commercial photography, 234
communications technology, 141
community, sense of, 68
competition, 67, 97-99, 103, 106-107,
    109, 117
Confederation, 149, 218
Conibas Regio, 18
Connor, Ralph, *see* Gordon, Charles
Constable, John, 164
Contarini, 30
Continental Divide, 23, 81-84, 87,
    208
Cook, James, 15, 26, 159
Cook, Solomon, 288, 289
Cooper, James Fenimore, 262
Copper Indians, 104, 105, 137
Copper Inuit, 3, 51, 74
Coppermine Inuit, 223
Coppermine, N.W.T., 219
Coppermine River, 22, 26, 46, 61,
    66, 131, 141, 165
Coronation Gulf, 168
Corps of Discovery, *see* Lewis and
    Clark expedition
Cotman, John Sell, 164

Cotter, H.M.S., 276
Cotter, James L., 232
coulisses, 152
"country people," 56
coureurs-de-bois, 23, 61
Cox, David, 164
Cree Indians, 23, 58, 60, 62-65, 67,
    74, 76, 129, 131, 132, 134, 138,
    139, 202, 205, 215, 216, 224, 240,
    278, 279, 283, 285, 286, 290, 292;
    language, 67, 205, 283
Crimson Cliffs (Ross), 155, 177, 181
Croker Mountains, 153
Crome, John, 164
Crow's Nest Pass, 199
cultural imperialism, 9, 231
cultural relativity, 123
Cumberland House, 23, 104, 106,
    122, 255, 276, 278
Curwood, Oliver, 262
Cuyp, Aelbert, 148
Cypress Hills, 200, 201, 207
cyclorama, 152

daguerreotype, 227, 228
D'Aigular, Martin, 25
Dally, Frederick, 229
Dalrymple, Alexander, 26
Danby, Francis, 164
Danby Island, 59
*David Thompson's Narrative of His
    Explorations in Western America,
    1784-1812*, 270, 294
Davidson, Saskatchewan, 266
Davin, Nicholas Flood, 257, 270
Davis, John, 3, 13, 19, 53, 54, 56, 58
Davis Strait, 13, 19, 57, 73
Dawson, George, 234
Dawson Route, 203
Day and Son, 157
de Crevecoeur, St. John, 95
De Fer, Nicholas, 43
de Fonte, Admiral, 25
de Fuca, Juan, 15
de Jode, Cornelius, 18, 40
de la Cosa, Juan, 15, 16
de Loutherbourg, Philip James, 164
de Vaugondy, Robert Didier, 18
Defoe, Daniel, 115
Del'isle, Guillaume, 21, 25

dẽnẽ, 131
Denison, George, 267
Department of the Interior, 257
Desceliers, Pierre, 17
desert, 9, 204, 254, 256
Devine, Thomas, 27
Dickens, Charles, 162, 163
Diefenbaker Lake, 198
Diocese of Mackenzie River
   (Bombas), 223, 225
diorama, 160
disease, 55, 79, 138, 223, 286
Dobbs, Arthur, 25
Dog Rapids, 292
Dogrib Indians, 131, 137
dogs, 54, 102, 103, 131, 139, 154,
   280-83, 285, 287, 290
Dominion Land Surveyors, 201
Dominion of Canada, 9, 10, 149,
   253, 256-59, 262, 267-68
Dorset culture, 52, 53, 70
Downes, Prentice Gilbert, 10-11,
   135, 277, 278, 284-92
dreams, 136, 138, 258, 261-63, 266
drought, 204, 253, 260
dry emulsion, 228, 232-34
Ducharme, Dominique, 116
Duffield, James, 67
Dumont, Gabriel, 213
Dumont, Gabriel, senior, 198
Dunvegan, Alberta, 219, 221

Eagle Hills, 199
Eastmain House, 64, 67, 74
Eastmain River, 22
Ecclesiastical Province of Rupert's
   Land, 220, 226
Edmonton, Fort, 2, 198-200, 232
Edmonton House, *see* Edmonton,
   Fort
education, 8, 67, 141, 164, 205,
   217-20, 221, 222; *see also* schools
Edzanni, 289
Een coz zy, 60
egalitarian, 10, 261
Egenolf, Father Joseph, 135, 280,
   284, 285, 287, 289, 292
Eggleston, Wilfred, 263
El Laurent, 279, 280
Elbow of the South Saskatchewan
   River, 198, 203

Ellice, Fort, 197, 198, 203
Empress, Alberta, 200
Encyclopédie, 26
engagés, 120, 121, 122, 123, 205
engraving, 158, 159, 161, 166, 168,
   228, 234
Ennadai, 280-82
Ennadai Lake, 277, 281
Enslen, Johann Carl, 155
Enterprise, 160
Enterprise, Fort, 97, 105, 108, 174
Erasmus, Peter, 200, 211
Erebus, 158
Eric the Red, 71
Ermatinger, Charles Oakes, 116
Esker Lakes, 290
Eskimo, *see* Inuit
Eskimo Charlie, *see* Planinshek,
   Charlie
Eskimo Post, *see* Ennadai Lake
Esquawino (Esqua:wee:Noa), 65, 67
Estevan, Saskatchewan, 264
et-Θen-eldili-dẽnẽ, 131
Ethnological Society, 207
European contact: with Indians, 3,
   51, 59, 68, 75, 131; with Inuit, 1,
   3, 51, 57, 58, 59, 68, 70, 157; with
   Skraelings, 3, 52, 53, 58
Evans, James, 216
expansionism, 227, 266, 267
Exploits River, 52

Fairholme, Caroline, 211
Fairholme, William, 195
Farson, Negley, 222
Fauvist, 155
Felix, 158
Feodorovna, Alexandra, 156
Ferguson River, 275
Fertile Belt, 8, 28, 204, 256
Fescue Prairie, 204
Fidler, Peter, 4, 15, 26, 59, 66, 82,
   84, 85, 88, 92
Finden, Edward, 155, 168
firearms, 53, 62, 75, 139, 173, 223,
   231
First Communication with the
   Natives of Prince Regents Bay ...
   Aug.ᵗ 10. 1818 (Sackheuse), 177,
   180
fish, 136, 137, 202, 204, 279, 289

fishing, 11, 64, 119, 120, 136, 140, 285, 287, 292

Flaherty, Robert, 157

Flathead Indians at Fort Colville, 1860-61, 242

Flathead River, 208

Fleming, Sandford, 232

Flett, Andrew, 280

"floating-hotel" school, 151

Fond du Lac, 289

food, 6, 10, 64, 65, 72, 99, 100, 103-105, 108, 119, 120, 125, 131, 133-39, 142, 200, 207, 253, 279, 281, 283, 287-90

Ford, Solomon, 276

Fort Hall Lake, 290

Fort St. James, 233

Fowke, Vernon C., 266

Foxe, Luke, 13, 19, 53, 70, 71, 74, 156

Foxe Channel, 14

Foxe River, 21

France, 23, 24, 80, 87, 214, 255, 260

Francis, Fort, 230, 235

Frankenstein (Shelley), 156, 157

Franklin, Jane, 161

Franklin, John, 4-5, 27, 97-111, 153, 154, 156, 158-63, 166-68, 195

Franklin, Fort, 169

Franquelin, Jean-Baptiste, 21, 22, 41

Fraser River, 25, 200

free trader, 205, 285, 288, 291

freemen, 8, 122, 123, 198, 205

French, 3, 15, 17, 18, 19-20, 21-25, 55, 56, 60, 61, 63, 66, 67, 68, 70, 74, 76, 80, 83, 85, 131, 148, 158, 205, 206, 212

Freuchen, Peter, 157

Friedrich, Kaspar David, 155, 156, 157

Frobisher, Martin, 3, 13, 17, 19, 54-57, 71, 72, 157, 213

Frobisher Bay, 19, 213

Frog Portage, 278

The Frozen Deep (Collins), 162

fur, 7, 53, 59, 62, 67, 68, 135, 137, 141, 142, 202, 204-206, 258, 279, 286

Fur Trade Commissioner, 277, 282

fur-trade/Indian relationships, 5, 6, 7, 123, 125, 126, 130, 137, 138, 141-43, 204, 205, 215, 223

game shortage, 134

Garrioch, Arthur, 221

Garry, Fort, 232

Gasté, Father Alphonse, 281

Gay, Charles, 210

Gelius, Anne, 209

geographical myth, 14, 16, 17, 25, 27

geographical theory, 3, 4, 14, 15, 17, 19, 20, 24, 26, 81-87, 89

Geological Survey of Canada, 201, 234, 275, 282

geology, 3, 8, 197, 198, 199, 200, 202, 203, 207, 209

Germany, 156, 174, 275, 280, 289

Gerritsz, Hessel, 15, 19

Gillam, Zachariah, 63

Gilpin, William, 147, 164, 165

Gimli, Manitoba, 284

Girton, Thomas, 164

Gledstanes, Anne, 195

"Goliah Muff," 159

Gomez, Estevan, 17

Gordon, Charles, 10, 260, 261, 262

Graham, Andrew, 22

Graham, R.B. Cunninghame, 148

Grain (Stead), 268

Grain Growers' Guide, 264

Grand Coulée, 207

Grand Peristrephic Panorama of the Polar Regions (Marshall), 154

Grand Portage, 106, 115, 117

Grand Rapid, *see* Grand Portage

Grand Rapids, 119, 120

grasshoppers, 198, 253

Great American Desert, 204

Great Bear Lake, 165, 169

Great Falls, 89, 90, 92

Great Fish River, *see* Back River

Great Lake River, 86, 89

Great Lakes, 14, 15, 18, 20, 23, 61, 66

Great Lone Land, 214, 224

Great Plains, *see* prairies

Great River of the West, 86

Great Slave Lake, 4, 20, 45, 97, 98, 104, 105, 106, 132

Green, Henry, 72

Green Lake, 103
Greenland, 52, 53, 54, 56, 57, 70, 71, 154, 158, 160
Greenland Inuit, 56, 154
Grey Nuns, 214
Grinnel Expedition, 161
Griper, 156
Gros Ventres Indians, 211
Groseilliers, Médard Chouart, sieur des, 59, 63
Group of Seven, 167
Grove, Frederick Philip, 268
Guide Through the District of the Lakes in the North of England (Wordsworth), 150
guides, 104, 196, 198, 199, 202, 277-79, 281, 288, 291
Guilloux, Father Nicholas, 278, 286
Gulf of Mexico, 23, 256
Gulf of St. Lawrence, 13, 18
gunpowder, 59; *see also* ammunition

Haghe, Charles, 160
Haida Indians, 224
Hakluyt, 156
half-breed, 8, 196, 202, 205, 206, 214, 215, 240, 277, 280; *see also* Métis
Halfway Island, 287
Hall, Charles Francis, 71, 72
Hall, Gordon, 277; H. Herbert, 277, 281, 282; R.H., 277, 282
Hall, James, 53, 56
Hall, Sidney, 44
Hall, Fort, 282, 291
Hamilton, James, 151, 161
Hand Hills, 200
Hannah Bay, 64
hardship, 121, 132, 137, 140, 263
Harmon, Daniel, 113, 114, 121
Harper, J. Russell, 169, 171, 175
Harriott, C.F. Edward, 197
Harris, Cecil "Husky," 291
Harris, John, 156, 157
Harris, Lawren, 155, 161, 163, 169
Harvard University, 275, 276, 284
Hatchet Lake Band Chipewyan, 279
Hawkes Summit, 292
Hayes River, 21, 101, 102, 284
health, 217, 219, 259; *see also* disease

Hearne, Samuel, 4, 22, 26, 27, 46, 61, 62, 64-66, 81, 82, 84, 99, 133, 135, 137-39, 141, 151, 153, 165, 177, 186, 223, 281
Hearne, Thomas, 166
Hearne Bay, 292
heathen, 8, 215, 217, 218, 223
Hector, James, 28, 197-202, 205-206, 210, 211
height of land, 23, 152, 165, 166
hemiramas, 160, 173
Henday, Anthony, 22
Henderson, James, 260
Hendry, Charles, 221
Henley House, 66, 77
Henry, Alexander the Elder, 113, 115
Henry, Alexander the Younger, 113
Hepburn, John, 102
Hickey, Clifford G., 59
hides, 133, 137, 283
Hill, David Octavius, 230
Hime, Humphrey Lloyd, 229-31, 233, 235, 238-40
Hind, Henry Youle, 3, 16, 27, 49, 204, 229, 230
H.M.S. Assistance and Pioneer in Winter Quarters (Wm. May), 159, 178, 184
Historia-Norvegiae (Ari), 52
Hobbema, Meindert, 148
Hobbema Band, 222
Hodgson, John, 26
homesteading, 259, 260, 263, 264, 265, 266, 268
Hood, Robert, 104, 167, 169, 175, 178, 188
Hooker, William, 197, 210
Hope, James, 215
Hope, John, 215
Horden, John, 216
Horetzky, Charles, 232, 233, 235, 246, 247
hostility, 10, 205, 254
housing, 137, 259
Howse Pass, 198
Hudson, Henry, 13, 15, 18, 19, 51, 58, 60, 72, 213
Hudson Bay Mining & Smelting, 288
Hudson Strait, 13, 14, 26
Hudson's Bay Company: records,

22, 57, 132, 135; posts, 23, 26, 61, 132, 139, 149, 196, 275, 278, 279, 288, 291; mapping, 13-14, 15, 19, 20, 22-23, 26-27, 84, 279, 281
Hudson's Bay Record Society, 108
hunger, 64, 65, 97, 119, 120, 121, 134, 208, 286
hunters, 104, 105, 136, 139, 140, 202, 206, 208
hunting, 62, 63, 118, 133, 134, 135, 136, 139, 140, 142, 195, 196, 197, 198, 199, 206, 208, 254
Huron Indians, 61
Huronia, 60, 61, 74
Husky Post, 282
Hussey, Christopher, 164

Icebergs, Davis Strait (Harris), 161
Iceland, 53
Idthen, 136, 287; *see also* caribou
Idthen-Eldeli, 290; *see also* Caribou Eater Chipewyan
Île-à-la-Crosse, 102, 103, 108
Illustrated London News, 160
Illustri Viro, Domino Philippo Sidnaeo Michael Lok Civis Londinensis Hanc Chartram Dedicabat, 39
immigration, 7, 10, 156-60, 262-68
immigration propaganda, 10, 256-60, 261-65, 267, 268
infanticide, 140
$i^n ko^n ze^n$, 136, 138
inland waterway, 3, 23-26, 81, 203
Interior view of Carlton House, 1871, 247
International Boundary Commission, 201, 231, 237
interpreters, 55, 56, 67, 72, 154
Inuit, 3, 51-55, 57, 59-61, 64, 65, 67-68, 70, 74, 76, 108, 157, 216, 223-25, 232, 244, 275, 276, 281-85, 288, 291
Inuk at Little Whale River, 1865-75, 244
Inuktitut, 67, 216, 283
Investigator, 59, 159, 160
Ireland, 195
Iroquois Indians, 61
Irricana, Alberta, 199

Isabella, 154
Isham, James, 151
Island Lake, 281; *see also* Nueltin Lake
isolation, 10, 118, 119, 140, 168, 169, 203, 222, 257, 260, 262, 268, 276, 279, 285

Jackson, A.Y., 169
Jackson, William Henry, 229
Jaillot, Alexis-Hubert, 21
James, Edwin, 156
James, Thomas, 13, 19, 59, 70, 156, 157
James Bay, 14, 18, 21, 51, 58, 60, 61, 74, 232
James Bay Group, 232, 233, 235
Janey Canuck in the West (Murphy), 261
Jarvis, Edward, 45
Jasper House, 232
Jefferson, Thomas, 4, 79-81, 83, 84, 86-90, 92-94, 96
Jefferys, C.W., 260, 261
Jeffreys, Thomas, 26
Jérémie, Nicolas, 56, 59, 73, 74, 131, 132
Jesuit Relations and Allied Documents, 95
journal: Prentice Downes, 285ff.; George Nelson, 113ff., 132; Ernest Oberholtzer, 276ff.; David Thompson, 255
journals, 5-6, 10-11, 132, 156, 166, 167, 214, 254
A Journey from Prince of Wales's Fort in Hudson's Bay, to the Northern Ocean, 1769-1772 (Hearne), 99, 137, 165, 281

kabloonas, 55
Kakabeka Falls, 153
Kananaskis Pass, 208, 210
Kane, Elisha Kent, 161
Kaministikwia, 23
Kane, Paul, 151
Kara Sea, 195
Kasimir, Kasmere, Kasmir: *see* Casmir
Kasmere Lake, 282, 283, 284, 291

Kazan River, 10, 275, 276, 280, 281, 285, 288, 290, 291
Keewatin District, 134
Keith, George, 106
Kelsey, Henry, 20, 65, 66, 75, 76, 254
Kendall, Edward, 168
Kenderdine, Augustus, 260
Kicking Horse Pass, 199, 206, 208
King, Nicholas, 85, 86, 87, 89, 90, 91, 96
Knee Lake, 21
Knight, James, 64, 132, 139, 141
Knight, John, 53, 56
Knight, Richard Payne, 164, 166
Kootenay Indians, 202
Kootenay Lake, 200, 208
Kootenay River, 200, 203, 208
Kristinaux, *see* Cree Indians

La Bezette, 125
La France. Joseph, 26
La Nlle France (Franquelin), 41
La Roche Perée, 198
La Vérendrye family, 22, 23, 24, 25
Labrador, 14, 18, 26, 57, 284
Lacamamiouen, Lac, 24
Lac Alemipigon, 22
Lac des Assinibouels, 22
Lac des Christinaux, 22
Lac des Poux, 21
Lac du Bois, 24
Lac du Brochet, 286
Lac du Brochet, 278-80
Lachine, 199
Lacombe, Albert, 214
Lady Franklin, *see* Franklin, Jane
Laetita Bird, a Cree Halfbreed, Red River Settlement, 1858, 240
Lake Abitibi, 21
Lake Athabasca, 32, 102-104, 106, 142, 279
Lake Conibas, 18
Lake of the Woods, 24, 214, 233
Lancaster Sound, 97, 153, 158
Land of Cortereal, 17
Land of the Unipeds, 71
Land Magnetic Observations, 281
landscape, 1, 7, 9, 11, 117-19, 147-55, 161-64, 166-67, 169, 207, 229-31, 256, 260

"last best West," 256, 259, 262
Laurentian Shield, *see* Canadian Shield
Laurier, Wilfrid, 257
Leacock, Stephen, 262
Leopold Island, 161
Leslie, Hugh, 142
Lewis, Meriwether, 4, 7, 80-81, 85, 87-96
Lewis and Clark expedition, 4, 7, 80-81, 85, 87-96
Liber Studiorum (Turner), 168
lithography, 158-60, 166
Little Ice Age, 54
Little Seal River, 280
Little Whale River, 232, 244
Lofthouse, Joseph, 281
Lok, Michael, 17
Long, Stephen H., 256
Long Dog, Chief, 252
Lopez, Barry, 157
Lord, John Keast, 231
Lorraine, Claude, 148
Loucheux Indians, 62
Louisiana Territory, 87, 96
Lower Canada, 118, 121, 124, 125, 195, 213
Lubicon Band, 224
Lyell Island, British Columbia, 224
Lynn, Washington, 260

Machray, Robert, 218
Mackenzie, Alexander, 4, 7, 15, 79, 80, 83-85, 89, 93, 99, 100, 102, 115, 166, 169, 222, 254, 255
Mackenzie District, 98, 104
Mackenzie River, 16, 97, 214, 216, 224, 255
Macoun, John, 232, 233
Magee, Billy, 275-84, 287, 289, 290-92
magnetism, 197, 198, 281
Magnus, Olaus, 52, 70
Maguse River, 288
Main Street looking south, Winnipeg, Manitoba, 1879, 251
Mair, Charles, 259, 267
Mallet, Thierry, 285
Malloch, William, 232
Mandan villages, 24, 84-86, 88, 89,

91, 92

Manitoba, 25, 27, 218, 226, 258, 264, 265

Manitoba, Lake, 24

Manitoba lakes, 22, 23, 25

Manitonamingan Lake, 122

maps, 3, 13-50, 159, 199, 201, 276, 281, 285, 290, 291, 292; furtrade information, 21, 22, 24-25, 26, 27, 32, 44, 281; native information, 21, 23-24, 281. *See also* Hudson's Bay Company: mapping.

Margary, Mr., 208

Marias River, 90, 91, 92

Marshall, Messrs, 154, 155, 157

Martens, Frederick, 156, 157

Martin, Calvin, 138

Martin, Chester, 266

Martin, John, 151, 164

Matonabbee, 66, 137, 141

Mattagami River, 60

May, Walter William, 159, 176, 177, 182, 183

McClintock, Francis, 173

McClung, Nellie, 260

McClure, Robert, 149

McDougall, George, 216

McDougall, John, 216

McGillivray, Simon, 98, 107, 110

McIlwraith, J., 174

McIvor, Robert, 142

McLean, John, 219

McKay, Donald, 45

McKay, James, 198, 202, 209

McTavish, George Simpson, 232, 244

McTavish, John George, 100

McVicar, Robert, 104, 106, 108

Melville, Lord, 110

Mer Glaciale, 19

Mercator, Gerard, 18

Methodist Church, 202, 214, 216, 218, 223

Methye Portage, 2, 166, 168

Métis, 8, 26, 67, 198, 205-207, 214, 215, 220, 225, 240, 280

Metropolitan of Rupert's Land, 218

Michaux, Andre, 94

Michipicoten, 23

Micmac Indians, 70

Midewiwin Indians, 124

migration of caribou, 6, 11, 132, 133, 134, 142, 290

Milk River, 88, 90; *see also* Missouri River

Milles Lacs, 22

mining, 11, 202, 285, 288

Minnesota, 22, 201, 275

mission, 214-16, 220, 221, 253, 279

missionaries, 1, 2, 8-9, 21, 25, 131, 205, 213-26, 278, 280, 281, 285, 286, 287, 292

Mississippi River, 22, 23, 80-84, 86, 87, 96, 255, 256

Missouri Coteau, 198, 201

Missouri River, 4, 23, 24, 82-92, 95, 96, 195, 196, 200, 202

Mistassini, Lake, 20

Mistaya Valley, 197

Misty Lake, 289

Moberly, Frank, 232

Montagnais Indians, 60

Montreal, 115, 198, 199, 234, 254, 255

moose, 136, 204

Moose Deer Island, 105

Moose Factory, *see* Moose Fort

Moose Fort, 65, 67, 99, 162, 232

Moose Mountain, 24, 25, 198, 204

Moose River, 67

Moosonee, 216

morality, 6, 121, 131, 132, 134, 135, 142

Morris, Edmund, 223

Morton, A.S., 264

Morton, W.L., 268

Mountain, Chief, 199

Mountain Stoney Indians, 202, 208, 211

multicultural society, 68-69

Munk, Jens, 13, 59

Murchison, Roderick, 197

Murphy, Emily, 10, 260, 261

Murray, John, 168

muskoxen, 136

"My Four Years Experienced in the North West of America: Roughing It in the Far West," 263

myth, 10, 124, 259, 260; *see also* native legends

Naberkistagon River, 82

narrative, 5, 6, 113, 159, 213, 260, 281

Narrative of a Second Expedition to the Shores of the Polar Sea, 1825-27 (Franklin), 155, 167, 168

Narrative of a Second Voyage in Search of a North-West Passage ... during the years 1829, 1830, 1831, 1832, 1833 (Ross), 157

Narrative of the Arctic Land Expedition to the Mouth of the Great Fish River, 1833-35 (Back), 168

Narrative of the Discoveries of the North Coast of America (Simpson), 254

Naskapi Indians, 60

native: beliefs, 6, 134, 135, 138, 222, 223, 230, 285, 286, 287; customs, 4, 57, 123, 124, 136, 206, 207, 220, 221, 222, 223, 224, 284, 285, 286, 287; economy, 1, 6-7, 59, 66, 135, 140, 142, 205, 285; families, 122, 124, 128, 133, 139, 140, 220; languages, 67, 123, 131, 205, 207, 211, 216, 223, 280, 287 (*see also* Cree Indians; language *and* Chipewyan Indians; language); legends, 6, 124, 131, 132, 134, 138, 141, 284, 285, 287; social structure, 6, 58, 60, 61, 66, 125, 134, 135, 136, 138-40, 142, 206, 284; spirituality, 6, 8, 62, 124, 132, 134, 138, 217, 284, 285, 286; values, 8, 11, 123, 125, 126, 132, 135, 136, 221, 222, 224, 284, 286

nature, 117, 118, 131, 138, 141, 147, 150, 164, 227

Nēglē, Louis, 290

Nelson, George, 5, 113-30

Nelson, Jane, 115

Nelson, Mary-Anne, 124

Nelson, Robert, 125

Nelson, William, 115

Nelson, Wolfred, 125

Nelson River, 21, 22, 82, 215, 255

Netsilik Inuit, 3, 51

New France, 18, 21, 23, 61, 63, 214

New York, 197, 198, 199

Newfoundland, 16, 52, 53

Niagara Falls, 157, 197

Nimrod (Palliser's Mountain Stoney hunter), 208

Nipigon Post, 23

Nipigon, Lake, 21

Nipissing, Lake, 21

Nixon, John, 63, 64, 68

Noon in Mid-Winter at Port Leopold (Browne), 178, 186

Norse, 3, 51ff., 58

North Dakota, 85

North Kananaskis Pass, 199

North Kootenay Pass, 199, 200

North Pole, 154, 156, 159

North Pole Expedition (Seccetti), 155

North West Company, 5, 27, 82, 85, 93, 97-100, 102, 104, 106, 107, 113, 114, 116, 118, 121, 123, 125, 126, 137, 196, 254, 255

North West Mounted Police, 201, 234, 252, 257, 285, 286

Northern Indians, 131, 137; *see* Chipewyan Indians

Northwest Passage, 3, 13, 16, 17, 20, 25, 26, 27, 57, 61, 70, 97, 141, 148, 149, 153, 154, 157, 159, 213

Norton, Richard, 20

Norway House, 255, 284

Notman Photographic Archives, 159

Nottaway River, 60

Nova Francia, alio nomine dicta Terra nova (Claesz-Planicus), 37

Nueltin Lake, 10, 11, 280, 281, 283, 284, 288, 289-92

Nueltin Narrows, 291

Nell-get Josay, 283

Nunn, Allan, 280, 281

Nu-thel-tin-tu-eh, 281; *see also* Nueltin Lake

Oberholtzer, Ernest, 10-11, 275-84, 286ff.

Oblates of Mary Immaculate, 214, 215, 278-81, 286

Ojibway Indians, 60, 129, 134, 138, 275, 276, 278

Old Bow Fort, 196

Old Crow, 219

Old Swan, 199

Ontario, Lake, 18
opportunity, land of, 258
Oregon Question, 93
Orcgon River, 82, 83
Oregon Territory, 254
Orkney Islands, 100
ornithology, 198
Ortelius, Abraham, 18
Osoyoos, Lake, 201
Ostenso, Martha, 268
Oswalt, Wendell H., 56
Ottawa River, 21, 60
Ouinipigon, Lac, 24
outboard motor, 11, 285, 286
Owram, Douglas, 266
Oxford Lake, 21

Padlei, 288
pagan, *see* heathen
Palliser, Frederick, 196, 209
Palliser, John, 3, 7-8, 16, 27, 28, 50,
  195-211, 256
Palliser, Wray, 195, 196
Palliser's map of 1865, 8, 201
Palliser's Triangle, 8, 204, 256
Palmer, R.E., 201
Palmer, Samuel, 164
panorama, 7, 152-155, 157, 159-61,
  163, 166, 169
Panorama Royal, Leicester Square,
  160
*Panoramic View 8 Miles from Fort
  Franklin* (Back), 179, 192-93
*The Papers of the Palliser Expedi-
  tion*, 209
Parlby, Irene, 217
Parry, William Edward, 97, 149, 154,
  156, 163
The Pas, Manitoba, 275, 276, 279
Passage through the Ice (Ross),
  155, 177, 182
Passage to India, 23, 81, 83, 92
"pastoral" West, 260, 261
Pays d'en Haut, 23, 25
Peace River, 83, 220, 221
Peace River Pass, 232
Peck, James, 216
Pegwys, Chief, 215
Peigan Indians, 202
Peigan Post, 196

Pelican Narrows, 277, 278, 284, 286,
  291, 292
Pembina, 197
Pembina Mountain, 198, 201
pemmican, *see* food
Pentecostal Church, 216
Phipps, Constantine, 158
*Photographers Camp, North Ameri-
  can Boundary Commission, 1873*,
  237
photographic document, 9, 227,
  230-35, 259, 278
photography, 2, 9, 10, 11, 227-51,
  278, 279, 283
physical environment, 15, 233
pictorial, 147, 148, 158-60, 163, 232
picturesque, 7, 9, 118, 119, 147,
  149-52, 163-67, 169, 231, 233, 261
Pigeon River, 120
"pigmies," 52
Pike, Zebulon, 256
Pile of Bones Creek, 198
Pitt, Fort, 198
Plancius, Petrus, 37
Planinshek, Charlie, 290
Point Turnagain, 157
Pointe aux Lièvres, 118
Pond, Peter, 82, 84, 95
Pope Gregory, 221
Porcupine Hills, 201
Port Leopold, 160
Port Nelson, 21, 59
portage, the conceptual short, 83,
  84, 87, 89, 90, 92
Portage La Loche, *see* Methye Por-
  tage
Portage la Prairie, 220
Portuguese, 16, 55
Postes du Nord, 23
prairies, 1, 7-8, 9, 20, 22, 23, 24, 27,
  49, 66, 118, 133, 149, 152, 163,
  196, 197, 199-204, 207, 208, 214,
  216, 223, 227, 230, 232-34, 239,
  254-56, 258, 262, 265, 266
*The Prairies, Looking West near
  Red River Settlement,
  September-October 1858*, 239
prairie levels, 8, 28, 198, 201
The Prairies Looking West, 230
preconceptions, 1, 5-7, 9, 11, 126,
  152, 153, 164, 207, 227, 254-56

Pre-Dorset, 52
Pre-Raphaelites, 164
Presbyterian Church, 214, 215, 223
Price, Uvedale, 164
Primate of the Anglican Church of
  Canada, 218
primitivism, 222
Prince Albert, Saskatchewan, 158,
  161, 219, 287
Prince of Wales, 100
Prince of Wales Fort, *see* Churchill,
  Fort
Prince Regent Inlet, 157, 158, 160
Prince Rupert, 2, 13, 147
*Principal Navigations, Voyages,
  Traffiques and Discoveries of the
  English Nations* (Hakluyt and
  Purchas), 156
prisoners, 55-57, 98, 139
Pritchard, John, 99
*Promise of Eden: The Canadian
  Expansionist Movement and the
  Idea of the West 1856-1900*
  (Owram), 266
Providence, Fort, 104-106
prospectors, 285, 286, 288
prosperity, 10, 256, 257, 258, 261
Protococcus nivalis, 155
Provencer, Bishop Norbert, 214
Public School system, 218, 219
Purcell, Edward, 197
Purcell Mountains, 203
Purchas, Samuel, 156
Putahow Lake, 281, 283, 290
Putahow River, 289, 290, 291
pyramidal height of land, 4, 82-85,
  87

Qu'Appelle, Fort, 265
Qu'Appelle Valley, 153, 198, 260
Quebec, 23, 24, 60, 61, 117, 226
Quebec-Labrador peninsula, 60
Queen Elizabeth's Land, 17
Queen Victoria, 148
Quetico Provincial Forest Reserve,
  275

Radisson, Pierre Esprit, 63
Rae, John, 162
railway, 194, 201, 232-34, 246

*Railway Survey camp at the Elbow
  of the North Saskatchewan
  River, 1871*, 246
Rainy Lake, 24, 275, 276, 292
realism, 10, 268
Rebellion of 1837, 137
Red Deer River, 200, 202
Red Head, 282
Red Knife Indians, *see* Copper
  Indians
Red River, 7, 23, 24, 118, 196, 197,
  199-202, 205, 214, 215, 218, 253
Red River Settlement, 99, 118, 197,
  199, 201, 209, 213, 214-16, 229-31,
  234, 239, 240, 253, 254
Regent's Bay Inuit, 154
Regina, 198, 206
Regina Leader, 257
Regina Plains, 204
reincarnation, 134, 135
Reindeer Lake, 142, 276, 279, 282,
  284-87
Reindeer River, 278
religion, 207, 213-26
reminiscences, 6, 116, 119, 124, 126,
  264, 275, 288, 292
reservations, 222, 257
residential schools, *see* schools
Resolute, 160
Resolution, Fort, 98
Revillon Frères, 276-78, 285, 286,
  288, 291
Richardson, John, 27, 104, 165
Richmond Gulf, 22, 26, 232
Riding Mountain, 24, 25
Riel, Louis, 198, 215
The Rime of the Ancient Mariner
  (Coleridge), 157
Rindisbacher, Peter, 151
River Dauphine, 118, 119
River of the West, 3, 23, 24, 25; *see
  also* Oregon River
Robinson, Crabb, 160
Robson, Joseph, 65
Rock Depot, 101, 102, 105
Rocky Mountain House, 196, 197
Rocky Mountains, 4, 7, 30, 81-90,
  92, 155, 196, 199, 200, 201, 203,
  206, 232, 256
Rogers, Robert, 82

romantic, 117, 148, 166, 168, 171, 231, 233, 235, 259-63, 285, 286
Romanticism, 149, 156
romanticized view, 9, 10, 125, 228
Roper, Edward, 260
Rosa, Salvator, 148
Ross, Bernard Rogan, 232, 243, 245
Ross, Eric, 68
Ross, James Clark, 160
Ross, John, 97, 153-58, 168, 172, 177, 181, 182
Rousseau, Jean-Jacques, 6, 125
Royal Arctic Theatre, 160
Royal Academy, 151
Royal Botanical Garden, 197, 202
Royal Charter, 1, 2, 13, 14, 38, 147, 205, 214, 225, 279
Royal Engineers, 231, 233, 235, 237, 241, 242, 248-50
Royal Geographical Society, 148, 149, 157, 166, 196, 197
Royal Naval College, Greenwich, 197
Royal Naval College, Portsmouth, 164
Rundle, Robert, 216
Rundle Mountain, 216
Rupert House, 74, 232, 243
Rupert River, 60, 245
Rupert's House, Salt Store and Forge, 1865-68, 243
Rupert's River; Shooting a White Bear, 1865-68, 245
Russia, 8, 73, 74, 156, 196
Ruysdael, Jacob, 148

Saccheuse, John, 154, 177, 180
Sackhouse, *see* Saccheuse, John
Sabine, Edward, 197
Saguenay, 17
Saguenay River, 60, 61
St. Andrews on the Red, 220
St. Augustine, 221
Saint Boniface, 214
St. Joe's, 198
St. John's Church, 216, 218
St. John's College, 216, 218
St. John's Schools, 216
St. Lawrence River, 13, 18, 20, 23, 57, 60, 82, 203

St. Louis, 88, 96
St. Maurice, 60
St. Paul, 199
Ste Anne, Lac, 198, 202, 205
Sand Hills, 200
Sandby, Paul, 164, 165
Sandby, Thomas, 164
Sanson, Nicholas, 19
Sarcee Indians, 202, 211
Saskatchewan, 20, 50, 166, 200, 219, 265
Saskatchewan River, 8, 22, 23, 74, 81-84, 86, 102, 103, 196-98, 200-202, 229
Saskatoon, Saskatchewan, 219, 265
Sault Ste Marie, 197
Saulteaux Indians, 116, 123, 220
savagery, 57, 124
savages ("salvages"), 56, 57, 58, 63, 68, 125, 213, 217, 223, 231, 234
schools, 8, 214, 215, 217-20, 286
scientists, 3, 7, 27, 28, 131, 193, 194, 195
Scoresby, William, 149
Scotland, 205, 206, 214, 218, 230
Scott, Robert Falcon, 109
scurvy, 71
Sea of China, 13
The Sea of Ice (Friedrich), 155
Sea of the West, 3, 23, 25
Sea of Verrazzano, 17
Seal River, 131
Sealhole Lake, 284
search expeditions, 158-61, 168, 173, 174
Secchetti, Antonio, 155
self-determination, 222, 224
self-government, 4, 69
Selkirk Colony, *see* Red River Settlement
Selkirk, Lord, 214, 215, 216, 253
Selkirk Mountains, 203
Settle, Dionise, 213
settlement, 1, 2, 8, 9-10, 28, 51, 70, 118, 202-205, 213, 215, 216, 230, 231, 253-68, 276, 279
Settlers of the Marsh (Grove), 268
Shaftesbury, Alberta, 220
Sharp, H.S., 135, 139, 140
Shaw, Angus, 100

Shelley, Mary, 156
Shepherd, Fort, 200, 201, 208
shipwrecks, 59
The Shows of London (Altick), 160
Shuswap Indians, 202
Siberia, 119, 196
Sifton, Clifford, 257, 258
Silumiut, 53
Simons, Del, 285, 288
Simpson, George, 103, 106-108, 111, 142, 146, 149, 153, 197, 199, 202, 207, 254
Simpson, Thomas, 254
Sinclair, James, 202
Sioux Chief Long Dog and George Wells (NWMP), Fort Walsh, 1879, 252
Sioux Indians, 118, 138, 200, 252, 277
Sipiwesk Lake, 21
Skeena River, 25
skraelings, 52, 53, 58, 70
The Sky Pilot (Connor), 261
Slave River, 59
Slave Woman, *see* Thanadelther
sledges, sleds, 102, 103, 139, 160, 280, 281, 287
Sleeping Island (Downes), 288, 291
Sleeping Island Lake, 281; *see also* Nueltin Lake
Small Boy, Chief Robert, 222
Smith, Edward, 104, 106, 107
Smyth, William, 158
Smollett, Tobias, 113
Snow, William Parker, 161
snowshoes, 103, 287
Snuff the Blanket (Esquawino), 65, 77
solitude, *see* isolation
Sorel, Lower Canada, 114, 122
Souris River, 198, 202
South End, 278, 286
South Henik Lake, 281
South Kootenay Pass, 199
Southern Indian Lake, 21
Southern Indians, 131; *see* Cree Indians
Spain, 17, 66, 80, 85, 118
Spaniards, 66, 80, 118
Spanish River, 60

Spence, Thomas, 259
Spitzbergen, 154, 195
Split Lake, 21, 22
Spokane Indians, 231, 241
Spokane Indians at Fort Colville, Washington Territory, 1860-61, 241
sport, 195, 196, 199, 207, 208
Stanfield, Clarkson, 161, 164
starvation, *see* hunger
Staunton, Richard, 67
Stead, Robert, 10, 260, 268
Stefansson, Vilhjalmur, 109, 111, 157, 163
steppe, *see* prairie levels
Sterne, Laurence, 113
Stewart, C.C., 281
Stewart, William, 20, 132, 139, 141
Stoney Indians, 206, 216
"Stony Mountains," 84; *see* Rocky Mountains
Strait of Anian, 17
Strait of Belle Isle, 57
Stromness, 100
Sturgeon River, 74
Sturgeon-Weir River, 277
sublime, 7, 119, 149, 150, 151, 161-63, 165
subsistence, 66, 133, 142, 205, 256, 259
Sullivan, John W., 197, 199-201, 208, 210
Summer in the Valley (Henderson), 260
Superior, Lake, 23, 24, 25, 60, 75, 122, 196
supernatural, 135, 136, 138
superstition, 124, 230, 279, 283
supplies, 5, 104-109, 228
S.W. Silver & Co.'s Handbook to Canada, 149
Surrealist, 155
Swampy Cree, 123
Swanston, Chief Factor, 195
syllabic script, 216, 280
symmetrical geography, 4, 81, 85, 86

Tadoussac, 60, 61
taiga-tundra ecotone, 131, 142
Tartars, 54, 71, 73

Telemachus, 115, 158
Temiskaming River, 60
*Ten Coloured Views taken during
the Arctic Expedition of ...
"Enterprise" and "Inves-
tigator"*(Browne), 161
Tennyson, Alfred, 162
Terra de Labrador, 13
Terrae Incognitae, 18, 24, 254, 281
Terror, 158
Tète au Brochet, 118
Thackeray, William Makepeace,
159, 163, 173
Tha-anne River, 281
Thanadelther, 132, 139
Thanout Lake, 282
Theitaga Lake, 283
thematic mapping, 3, 16, 27
Theosophists, 155
Thevet, André, 18
thievery, 54, 64, 66, 205, 208
Thlewiaza River, 283, 284
tθ-en, 134, 136
Thomas, Lewis G., 267
Thompson, David, 4, 15, 26, 66, 77,
83, 85, 95, 118, 128, 145, 255,
270, 279
Thorfinnr Karlsefni Thordarson, 52
Thorgills, Orrabeinsfostri, 52
Thorton, Samuel, 20
Thule Inuit, 52, 53, 70
Thunder Capes, 153
Thwaites, Louis, 278, 286
tobacco, 61, 100, 101, 104, 105, 280,
283, 289, 290
Tobacco Plains, 199, 200
topography, 3, 14, 15, 19, 26, 27, 28,
147, 152, 159, 161, 163, 166, 167,
169, 207, 228, 232, 234
trade, 1, 4, 5, 6, 15, 22, 23, 26, 53,
58, 60-63, 65-68, 72, 80, 123, 126,
137, 147, 148, 204, 257
trading bands, 137
transcontinental water route, 88, 89
trapping, 7, 62, 63, 67, 139, 140, 142,
285, 286, 291
travel, 1, 2, 10-11, 25, 147, 150-52,
195, 196, 207, 208, 227-30, 232-34,
255, 260, 275-92
*Travels and Adventures in the
Indian Country* (Henry), 113

Travels through France and Italy
(Smollett), 113
treaties, 63, 224
Trent, 154
Trois-Rivières, 60
*Trout Fall and Portage on the Trout
River* (Hood), 178, 188
tundra, 1, 6, 16, 132, 133, 137, 138,
142, 150, 165, 276
Turner, J.M.W., 161, 164, 166, 168
Turnor, Philip, 15, 26, 34, 35
Turquetil, Father Arsène, 280
Turtle Mountain, 198, 201, 204
Tyrell, J.B., 275, 279, 281-84

Ultima Thule, 155
Ungava Bay, 26
Unicorn, 59
United Church, *see* Methodist
Church
United Empire Loyalist, 115
United States, 4, 8, 79, 80, 84, 87,
93, 115, 161, 195, 196, 200, 201,
203, 228, 229, 234, 254, 255, 262,
263, 266, 275, 278, 284, 289
*The U.S. Grinnell Expedition ...
1850-51*, 161
Unity, Saskatchewan, 207
University of Emmanuel College,
219
University of Manitoba, 216, 218
University of Saskatchewan, 219,
264
Upper Canada, 197, 213
Upper Country, *see* Pays d'en Haut
utopia, 257, 258, 260, 261, 262, 268

Vale of the Clearwater River, 153,
166, 175
*Vale of the Clearwater River from
the Methye Portage* (Back), 179,
192
van Wytfliet, Cornelis, 18
Vancouver, George, 15, 26, 27
Varley, F.H., 169
Vaux, W.S.W., 207, 211
Vauxhall Gardens, 160
Vermilion Pass, 199
Vermilion River, 202
Verrazzano, Giovanni da, 17
Vicariate Apostolic of the North-

west, 214

Victorian period, 9, 147, 148, 164, 227, 228, 230, 231

The View from Portage la Loche (Back), 179, 189

View from the Ridge of Portage la Loche, including the Clearwater River, and the Valley (Back), 179, 190

View of the Continent of Boothia (Burford), 157

Voltaire, 148

Voyage of Discovery (Ross), 153ff.

Voyages from Montreal (Mackenzie), 79, 80, 83, 85, 89, 93, 166, 255

voyageurs, 105, 121, 197, 202, 208

Waldseemüller, Martin, 16

Walhalla, N. Dakota, 198

Walsh, Fort, 252

Walton, Robert, 156, 157

warble fly, 133

Ward, James, 164

Warkentin, Germaine, 114

Warre, Henry, 254

wasteland, 9, 149, 202, 207, 234, 254-56, 268

Waterford Artillery Militia, 195

Watson, Wreford, 255

Waymouth, George, 13

Webber, John, 159

Weekes, Mr., 106, 107

Wells, George, 252

Wentzel, Ferdinand, 104, 105

West, John, 213, 215, 216, 218

western Canadian disillusionment, 10, 266-68

Western Woods Cree, 138

wet-plate process, 228, 229

whaling, 18, 51, 57, 68, 69, 73, 149

White, John, 157

white civilization, 124, 125, 217-19, 221-24, 227, 234, 286, 291

white men, 11, 51, 58, 68, 123, 132, 140, 215, 217-19, 222, 231, 254, 257, 281, 283, 285, 286, 287, 289, 291

wihtiko, see windigo

Wild Geese (Ostenso), 268

Williams, Governor William, 100, 101, 104

Wilson, Richard, 164

windigo, 134

Windy River post, 290, 291

Winnipeg, 10, 194, 214, 216, 251, 265, 266, 288

Winnipeg, Lake, 21, 22, 24, 27, 113, 114, 116-19, 121-24, 201, 284

winter, 119, 137, 159, 264, 282, 288

Winter Lake, 105

Winter Quarters (Wm. May), 177, 183

Winter Sojourn of the North Pole Expedition (Enslen), 155

A Winter View in the Athapuscow Lake (Hearne), 165, 178, 187

Wissler, Clark, 133

wives, Indian, 124, 128, 130, 140, 206, 215

Wollaston Lake, 135, 289

Wolseley, Colonel, 234

women, 124, 124, 128, 130, 131, 135, 136, 138, 139, 140, 205, 206, 215, 217, 265, 280, 283

Woolwich Military School, 164

Wordsworth, William, 150

World Council of Churches, 224

World War I, 285, 291

The Wreck of the "Hope," 155

Wreck in the Polar Sea (Friedrich), 157

XY Company, 113, 115, 121

Xeric and Mesic Mixed Grass Prairie, 204

Yathkyed Lake, 275

Yellowhead Pass, 232

Yellowknife River, 105

Yellowknives, *see* Copper Indians

Yellowstone River, 88, 90; *see also* Missouri River

York boat, 10, 276-79, 286, 292

York Factory, 23, 66, 73, 99, 100, 104, 105, 131, 132, 139, 141, 197, 198, 201, 214, 215, 254, 255, 284

York Fort, *see* York Factory

Yukon River, 16

Yukon Territory, 62, 288

Also published by Wilfrid Laurier University Press
for The Calgary Institute for the Humanities

RELIGION AND ETHNICITY
Edited by Harold Coward and Leslie Kawamura
Essays by: Harold Barclay, Harold Coward, Frank Epp, David Goa, Yvonne Yazbeck Haddad, Gordon Hirabayashi, Roger Hutchinson, Leslie Kawamura, Grant Maxwell, Cyril Williams

1978 / pp. x + 181 / ISBN 0-88920-064-5

THE NEW LAND
Studies in a Literary Theme
Edited by Richard Chadbourne and Hallvard Dahlie
Essays by: Richard Chadbourne, Hallvard Dahlie, Naïm Kattan, Roger Motut, Peter Stevens, Ronald Sutherland, Richard Switzer, Clara Thomas, Jack Warwick, Rudy Wiebe

1978 / pp. viii + 160 / ISBN 0-88920-065-3

SCIENCE, PSEUDO-SCIENCE AND SOCIETY
Edited by Marsha P. Hanen, Margaret J. Osler, and Robert G. Weyant
Essays by: Paul Thagard, Adolf Grünbaum, Antony Flew, Robert G. Weyant, Marsha P. Hanen, Richard S. Westfall, Trevor H. Levere, A. B. McKillop, James R. Jacob, Roger Cooter, Margaret J. Osler, Marx W. Wartofsky

1980 / pp. x + 303 / ISBN 0-88920-100-5

CRIME AND CRIMINAL JUSTICE IN
EUROPE AND CANADA
Edited by Louis A. Knafla
Essays by: J. H. Baker, Alfred Soman, Douglas Hay, T. C. Curtis and F. M. Hale, J. M. Beattie, Terry Chapman, André Lachance, Simon N. Verdun-Jones, T. Thorner and N. Watson, W. G. Morrow, Herman Diederiks, W. A. Calder, Pieter Spierenburg, Byron Henderson

1985, Revised Edition / pp. xxx + 344 / ISBN 0-88920-181-1

DOCTORS, PATIENTS, AND SOCIETY
Power and Authority in Medical Care
Edited by Martin S. Staum and Donald E. Larsen
Essays by: David J. Roy, John C. Moskop, Ellen Picard, Robert E. Hatfield, Harvey Mitchell, Toby Gelfand, Hazel Weidman, Anthony K. S. Lam, Carol Herbert, Josephine Flaherty, Benjamin Freedman, Lionel E. McLeod, Janice P. Dickin McGinnis, Anne Crichton, Malcolm C. Brown, Thomas McKeown, Cathy Charles

1981 / pp. xiv + 290 / ISBN 0-88920-111-0

IDEOLOGY, PHILOSOPHY AND POLITICS
Edited by Anthony Parel
Essays by: Frederick C. Copleston, Charles Taylor, John Plamenatz, Hugo Meynell, Barry Cooper, Willard A. Mullins, Kai Nielsen, Joseph Owens, Kenneth Minogue, Lynda Lange, Lyman Tower Sargent, Andre Liebich

1983 / pp. x + 246 / ISBN 0-88920-129-3

DRIVING HOME
A Dialogue Between Writers and Readers
Edited by Barbara Belyea and Estelle Dansereau
Essays by: E. D. Blodgett, Christopher Wiseman, D. G. Jones, Myrna Kostash, Richard Giguère, Aritha van Herk, Peter Stevens, Jacques Brault

1984 / pp. xiv + 98 / ISBN 0-88920-148-X

ANCIENT COINS OF THE GRAECO-ROMAN WORLD
The Nickle Numismatic Papers
Edited by Waldemar Heckel and Richard Sullivan

Essays by: C. M. Kraay, M. B. Wallace, Nancy Moore, Stanley M. Burstein, Frank Holt, Otto Mørkholm, Bluma Trell, Richard Sullivan, Duncan Fishwick, B. Levy, Richard Weigel, Frances Van Keuren, P. Visonà, Alexander G. McKay, Robert L. Hohlfelder.

1984 / pp. xii + 310 / ISBN 0-88920-130-7

FRANZ KAFKA (1883-1983)
His Craft and Thought
Edited by Roman Struc and J. C. Yardley

Essays by: Charles Bernheimer, James Rolleston, Patrick O'Neill, Egon Schwarz, Ernst Loeb, Mark Harman, Ruth Gross, W. G. Kudszus.

1986 / pp. viii + 160 / ISBN 0-88920-1887-0

GENDER BIAS IN SCHOLARSHIP
The Pervasive Prejudice
Edited by Winnifred Tomm and Gordon Hamilton

Essays by: Marlene Mackie, Carolyn C. Larsen, Estelle Dansereau, Gisele Thibault, Alice Mansell, Eliane Leslau Silverman, Yvonne Lefebvre, Petra von Morstein, Naomi Black

1988 / pp. xx + 206 / ISBN 0-88920-963-4

BIOMEDICAL ETHICS AND FETAL THERAPY
Edited by Carl Nimrod and Glenn Griener

Essays by: Carl Nimrod, Alan Cameron, Dawn Davies, Joyce Harder and Stuart Nicholson, Ruth Milner, Sydney Segal, David Hoar, David J. Roy, David Manchester, William Clewell, Michael Manco-Johnson, Dolores Pretorius and Paul Meier, Edward W. Keyserlingk, William Ruddick

1988 / pp. xii + 122 / ISBN 0-88920-962-6

THINKING THE UNTHINKABLE
Civilization and Rapid Climate Change
Lydia Dotto

Based on the Conference
Civilization and Rapid Climate Change
University of Calgary, August 22-24, 1987

1988 / pp. viii + 73 / ISBN 0-88920-968-5

RUPERT'S LAND
A Cultural Tapestry
Edited by Richard C. Davis

Essays by: Richard I. Ruggles, Olive P. Dickason, John L. Allen, Clive Holland, Sylvia Van Kirk, James G. E. Smith, Robert Stacey, Irene Spry, Fred Crabb, Edward Cavell, R. Douglas Francis, Robert H. Cockburn

1988 / pp. xii + 323 / ISBN 0-88920-976-6